THE

THEOLOGICAL EDUCATOR.

Edited by the
REV. W. ROBERTSON NICOLL, M.A., LL.D.,
Editor of "The Expositor."

REV. WILLIAM HENRY SIMCOX'S
THE WRITERS OF THE NEW TESTAMENT.

Other books available:

Dr. John Gerstner *A Predestination Primer*

George Smeaton *The Doctrine of the Atonement According to Christ*

Adolf Deissmann *Bible Studies*

George Smeaton *The Doctrine of the Atonement According to the Apostles*

David Baron *Rays of Messiah's Glory*

David Baron *The Ancient Scriptures for the Modern Jew*

Patrick Fairbairn *The Revelation of Law in Scripture*

J. B. Lightfoot *Notes on the Epistles of St. Paul* (Covers 1 & 2 Thes., Rom. 1-7, 1 Cor. 1-7, & Eph. 1:1-14)

H. A. W. Meyer *New Testament Commentary* (Available yearly only. Write for new publication schedule.) 11 vols.

W. H. Simcox *The Writers of the New Testament*

W. H. Simcox *The Language of the New Testament*

Franz Delitzsch *Old Testament History of Redemption*

S. R. Driver *Hebrew Tenses*

S. R. Driver *Notes on the Hebrew Text of the Books of Samuel*

S. R. Driver *The Life and Times of Isaiah*

F. W. Farrar *The Lives and Times of the Minor Prophets*

Dr. John Gerstner *A Reconciliation Primer*

Dr. John Gerstner *A Bible Inerrancy Primer*

H. B. Hackett *Commentary on Acts*

G. B. Winer *Grammar of the Idioms of New Testament Greek*

THE

WRITERS OF THE NEW TESTAMENT.

Their Style and Characteristics.

BY THE LATE REV.

WILLIAM HENRY SIMCOX, M.A.,

Rector of Harlaxton.

THE SECOND PART OF THE
LANGUAGE OF THE NEW TESTAMENT.

Eugene, Oregon

Wipf and Stock Publishers
199 West 8th Avenue, Suite 3
Eugene, Oregon 97401

The Writers of the New Testament
Their Style and Characteristics
By Simcox, William H.
ISBN: 1-59244-608-6
Publication date 3/17/2004
Previously published by Hodder and Stoughton, 1890

PREFACE.

THE "Language of the New Testament" was an attempt to describe what was common to its writers; what marked them off as a body, both from pagan writers, Attic and Hellenist, and from Jewish Hellenists, like Philo and Josepus. But though all New Testament writers approach more or less to a common type, and diverge more or less from the established style of their contemporaries and predecessors, each of them has not only a style and a manner, but almost a language, of his own,—each, at least, has his own compromise or compromises between the Hebraistic elements of his thought and the Hellenic or Hellenistic elements of his language. Then, too, each has, to some extent, a vocabulary of his own; and the vocabularies of the New Testament writers suggest groupings which do not always coincide with the groupings suggested by style. In the text of the present work, my brother has given a description in outline of the style and language of each of the writers of the New Testament. The first of the Appendices is intended to bring out

PREFACE.

something of the affinities of vocabulary between different groups of writers. Perhaps the most important point which they illustrate is that in vocabulary, though not in style, St. Luke stands closely related to the disputed or disputable works of St. Paul on one side and to the so-called catholic epistles of St. Peter, St. James, and St. Jude on the other. The second of the Appendices is intended to illustrate with something of detail the contrasts between the Greek of the New Testament and other Greek, which have been described in the "language" and in the "writers" of the New Testament. I have only to add that the book is printed from my brother's MSS., which he left ready for press, and that Mr. Thompson renewed his kindness in reading the proofs of the text.

G. A. SIMCOX.

CONTENTS.

	PAGE
PREFACE	v
INDIVIDUAL CHARACTERISTICS OF THE NEW TESTAMENT WRITERS.	1
CHAP. I. THE SYNOPTIC GOSPELS .	3
,, II. ST. LUKE	16
,, III. ST. PAUL'S EPISTLES	25
,, IV. THE EPISTLE TO THE HEBREWS (WITH ITS RELATIONS TO SS. PAUL AND LUKE) .	39
,, V. THE CATHOLIC EPISTLES	60
,, VI. THE FOURTH GOSPEL AND JOANNINE EPISTLES .	70
,, VII. THE APOCALYPSE .	80
APPENDIX I. TABLES ILLUSTRATING AFFINITIES IN VOCABULARY BETWEEN—	
(i.) SS. LUKE AND JOHN	90
(ii.) SS. PAUL, PETER, LUKE, AND HEBREWS	92
(iii.) ST. LUKE, HEBREWS; PASTORAL AND CATHOLIC EPISTLES	116

	PAGE
APPENDIX II. SPECIMENS OF HELLENIC AND HELLENISTIC GREEK—	. 155
(i.) TRANSLATIONS AND PARAPHRASES FROM THE OLD TESTAMENT	. 158
(ii.) ORIGINAL NARRATIVES AND DESCRIPTIONS .	. 162
NOTES .	. 168
(iii.) THEOLOGICAL AND PHILOSOPHICAL PASSAGES .	. 178
NOTES .	. 182

INDIVIDUAL CHARACTERISTICS OF THE
WRITERS OF THE NEW TESTAMENT.

SINCE the language of the N. T. is a kind of
compromise between the requirements of Greek
idiom and of Hebraic modes of thought, it is natural
that, in different parts of it, now one and now the
other of these elements should predominate. Thus
we are not surprised to find that the description we
have given of N. T. grammar applies in different
degrees to the different writers—eight at least in
number—whose works are included in this portion
of "the Divine Library."

For our present purpose, some of the N. T.
writings may be grouped together, though certainly
by different authors, while others must be described
separately, though possibly or probably by the same.
Even if we think it possible that the Epistle to the
Hebrews is the work of St. Paul, its literary form
—we may almost say its dialect, as well as its
style—is quite different from that of the Epistles
bearing his name. The difference between the
Apocalypse and the other writings of St. John is
even greater, and extends further into the region
of pure grammar. On the other hand, we have no
reason to notice doubts, even if we felt any, as to
the authenticity of the two shorter Epistles of St.
John,—hardly as to that of the Pastoral Epistles of

2 LANGUAGE OF THE NEW TESTAMENT.

St. Paul. Even if not written by the authors to whom they are ascribed, they have a style imitated from or influenced by theirs, to a degree that makes it necessary to examine them together, though it may be necessary also to note that they have peculiarities of their own.

We may thus arrange the twenty-seven books of the N. T. in seven groups—two of them, however, containing only a single member, though one of these has affinities to works outside the N. T. canon. The order in which it will be convenient to examine these is (1) SS. Matthew and Mark ; (2) St. Luke ; (3) St. Paul ; (4) the Epistle to the Hebrews, in connexion with the two books ; (5) SS. Peter, James, and Jude ; (6) St. John's Gospel and Epistles ; (7) the Revelation.

CHAPTER I.

THE SYNOPTIC GOSPELS.

IN style and language, as in substance, the features common to the first three Gospels are both more obvious and more important than the individual characteristics of each. No doubt, careful study will show such individual characteristics, both in the form and in the substance of each Gospel, and it is our business so to study them; only we must not overrate the importance of what we learn by careful study, in comparison with what forced itself on our attention at the outset. There are Hebraisms in St. Matthew, there are Latin words in St. Mark, and there is a tendency to classical idiom in St. Luke; but these are no more the chief characteristic of each, than it is the object of St. Matthew's Gospel to forbid, and of St. Luke's to promote, the admission of the Gentiles into the Church.

We thus find ourselves obliged to glance at a question which it is impossible for us to discuss, and for which we cannot indicate any answer as certainly or finally satisfactory. It is perhaps the hardest problem in the higher criticism of the N. T., and the one which has made least progress towards solution—what was the nature of the *Protevangelium*, the narrative forming the basis of at least three

4 LANGUAGE OF THE NEW TESTAMENT.

of the Canonical Gospels ? and how are we to correlate the fact, proved by internal evidence, of the existence of this common basis, with the traditional accounts of the origin and authorship of the Gospels as we have them ?

But though we cannot point to any answer to the first of these questions as commanding general assent, we may say there is at least a tendency to general agreement in this—that St. Mark's Gospel affords the nearest approach we have to an exact reproduction of the common basis of the three. And though we cannot enter on the discussion of the second question, we may have the satisfaction of feeling that what we learn from our present study will, in some modest measure, contribute to the exact statement, and perhaps at length to the solution, of the problem.

Now one characteristic of St. Mark's as compared with the other Gospels is a certain roughness of style, a broken and uneven method in narrative, which is almost sure to have been characteristic of the most primitive form of the Gospel story, as it would be far likelier to be softened than to be intensified in the hands of successive reporters or redactors. Such imperfections (tried by a European standard) in the style are natural enough, on any view that we may take of the nature of the Protevangelium :—whether it were an Aramaic document actually used by our Evangelists ; a document originally Aramaic, but used by them in a Greek translation ; a document originally written in Greek, but by a man whose acquaintance with Greek was lately acquired and imperfect ; or lastly, a tradition * never reduced to

---

* The suggested parallel with the Mishna (See Abbott & Rushbrooke's *Common Tradition of the Synoptic Gospels*,

THE SYNOPTIC GOSPELS. 5

writing before the date of our present Gospels, but
which had from the first been orally transmitted in
a nearly fixed form, which it assumed in the mouths
of Aramaic-speaking disciples. But, as it was natural,
humanly speaking, so it was in harmony with the
purposes of Providence, that this non-Greek character
of the Gospel story should disappear, as the Church
in which the Gospel was received came to be, in every
sense, more Greek than Jewish.

At all events, whatever theories may be adopted
or suggested as to the origin of the Gospels, there is
no doubt that all of them have a common Hebraistic character, more marked than in any other book
of the N. T. except the Apocalypse. Perhaps this
shows itself most, not in the body of any of the
episodes related either in individual Gospels or in
their common source, but in the way that the narratives are linked on to each other. All the Evangelists
use more or less frequently the Hebraistic formula
Καὶ ἐγένετο . . . representing the וַיְהִי of the
historical portions of the O. T.; but each of the three
has individual peculiarities in the way of using it.*
It is rarest in St. Mark, most frequent in St. Luke;
but once or twice in the former, and oftener in the
latter, it is attempted to harmonise the Hebraic
phrase with the requirements of Greek idiom. The

Introd., p. xi. etc.) is at least worthy of consideration. Our
Lord's words may have been preserved in memory by His
disciples, as those of contemporary and even earlier Rabbis
were by theirs; whether we accept or not the further suggestion, that the Evangelical sayings were originally preserved in
a form as crude and elliptical as the Talmudic.

* The correlative predictive phrase καὶ ἔσται c. fut. indic.
occurs only in quotations from the O. T.—Acts ii. 17, 21,
Rom. ix. 26. In Acts iii. 20 (where the quotation, though
founded on the LXX., is very loose) we have ἔσται δέ with the
same constr. answering to the Lucan ἐγένετο δέ.

6 LANGUAGE OF THE NEW TESTAMENT.

commonest constr. in all three Gospels is that of Matt. vii. 28, καὶ ἐγένετο ὅτε ἐτέλεσεν ὁ 'IC. τοὺς λόγους τούτους, ἐξεπλήσσοντο οἱ ὄχλοι—a constr. found in Hebrew (*e.g.* Gen. xl. 1), and more frequently in the LXX. But more characteristic of Biblical Hebrew, and often exactly reproduced in the LXX., is the fuller constr. with a second καὶ or its equivalent, after the defining note of time ; this we have probably once in St. Matthew (ix. 10), and possibly once in St. Mark (ii. 15); but nine or ten times in St. Luke (v. 12, 17, viii. 1, 22, ix. 51, xiv. 1, xvii. 11, xix. 15, xxiv. 4, 15 ?). On the other hand, once or twice (ii. 23, and prob. ii. 15) St. Mark writes καὶ γίνεται κατακεῖσθαι, αὐτόν, or καὶ ἐγένετο αὐτὸν ἐν τοῖς σάββασιν διαπορεύεσθαι—a constr. unknown to the LXX., and not really native to classical Greek, but defensible as an extension of that found in Theogn. 699 or in Xen. Hell. V. iii. 10 ; * or as analogous to the use of ἦν (2 Mac. iii. 16) which itself was an extension of the use of ἔστιν " it is possible." In the Acts, this half Hellenised form of the constr. is the only one used by St. Luke ; but in the Gospel we have it only five times (iii. 21, vi. 1, 6, 12, xvi. 22), compared with thirty-five where the phrase is followed by past indic., either with or without καί. But St. Luke, and he only, varies and to some extent Hellenises the phrase, by using ἐγένετο δέ nearly as often as καὶ ἐγένετο (accurately, seventeen times to twenty-one, the reading being twice doubtful).

Further, while there is always (except in Luke xvi. 22, where the inf. follows) a note of time

---

* Plat. Phaedr., c. xx. init. (p. 242, 6) is wrongly adduced as an example ; there γίγνεσθαι surely depends on εἰωθός, not on ἐγένετο.

accompanying this constr., the mode of marking this note of time varies a good deal. St. Matthew has almost always καὶ ἐγένετο ὅτε (vii. 28, xi. 1, xiii. 53, xix. 1, xxvi. 1), once only (ix. 10) a gen. abs., the Hebraistic constr. ἐν τῷ c. *inf.* not at all; but St. Mark has this last constr. once or possibly twice (ii. 15 ?, iv. 4), and ἐν ἐκείναις ταῖς ἡμέραις or the like twice (i. 9, ii. 23). One or other of these constructions is the rule in St. Luke; but in this respect as in the former, while generally preserving the more Hebraistic form he introduces a measure of Hellenic variety. We have ἐν τῷ c. inf. in i. 8, ii. 6, iii. 21, v. 1, 12, viii. 40, ix. 18 (29 is not really an instance of this constr.), 51, x. 38, xi. 1, 27, xiv. 1, xvii. 11, 14, xviii. 35, xix. 15, xxiv. 4, 15, 30, 51. We have ἐν or some other prep. with a subst. in i. 59, ii. 1, 6, 46, v. 17, vi. 1, 6, 12, vii. 11, viii. 1, 22, ix. 28, 37, xx. 1. We never find St. Matthew's καὶ ἐγ. ὅτε at all; but we have the equivalent καὶ ἐγ. (or ἐγ. δὲ) ὡς in i. 23, 41, ii. 15, xix. 29, and the gen. abs. in xi. 14, and perhaps in ix. 57.

Another Hebraistic formula of transition or connexion is καὶ ἰδού: this is never found in St. Mark at all (not even in v. 22, true text), but twenty-seven times in St. Matthew, perhaps * as often in St. Luke's longer Gospel,† and eight times (not counting x. 17) in the Acts. St. Matthew moreover has ἰδού 10 times (i. 20, ii. 1, 13, 19, ix. 18, 32, xii. 46, xvii. 5, xxvi. 47, xxviii. 11) without καὶ, but preceded by a gen. abs.

* In xiii. 30, xxiii. 14 it may be said that ἰδού has a distinctive force, and is more than a formula of transition—like καὶ ἴδε in John vii. 26. St. John never has καὶ ἰδού in the Gospel —eleven (or twelve) times in the Revelation.

† Including cases where it forms the apodosis (so to call it) to καὶ ἐγένετο.

8 LANGUAGE OF THE NEW TESTAMENT.

And, besides these formulæ of transition common to all the Evangelists each has one or more favourite ones of his own. St. Matthew constantly uses the simple τότε : he has it sixty-three times, counting only the use with historical tense, though that with futures and imperatives in cc. xxiv.-v. is the same in principle. Constantly, too, he introduces a new narrative or discourse by introducing a new person with προσῆλθεν or προσελθών. St. Mark is fond of καὶ εὐθύς (so, not εὐθέως, the best texts always) even when, as in i. 29, it is hard to see that the adv. has its distinctive force. This, we must note, is by no means confined to the introduction of fresh narratives ; it serves quite as often (*e.g.* i. 42, 43) to emphasise the conclusion of one. Then, from what we have seen, we may reckon καὶ ἐγένετο ἐν τῷ ... καί ... as characteristic of St. Luke ; ἐγένετο δέ, at any rate, is peculiar to him. Moreover, while in St. Matthew the formula καὶ ἰδού is always (except in ix. 10) grammatical if not idiomatic by a Hellenic standard, in St. Luke καί with or without ἰδού, often with the pron. αὐτός, used seemingly (see *Language of the New Testament*, pp. 84, 85) in their nom. in a sense no more emphatic than that of the oblique cases, serves to introduce the apodosis to a relative sentence, or itself takes the place of a relative clause, or in some form shows its Hebraistic meaning ; see ii. 21, v. 35, vii. 37, xix. 43 (simple καί) ; vii. 12 (καὶ ἰδού) ; ii. 28, xix. 2, καὶ αὐτός ; besides many instances of each where the break in the constr. is less marked.

But, when we pass from the consideration of the common characteristics of the three Gospels to that of the individual ones, we are obliged to postpone the case of the third, because we have in the N. T. collection another work of the same author. Com-

THE SYNOPTIC GOSPELS. 9

paring then the first Gospel with the second, we feel it to be, if not more elegant or more Hellenic, at least a great deal smoother and easier reading—contrary to what we might have expected in what is described as a translation from the Hebrew. An ellipsis like that in the probable text of Mark ii. 22 is, it may fairly be said, rather vigorous than harsh; but can we say the same of the absence of a verb in vii. 2 (true text), or of the way that the comment (for so we should doubtless read and interpret it) καθαρίζων πάντα τὰ βρώματα is introduced in vii. 19 ? See also viii. 2, 19-21, ix. 12, xi. 31-2, xii. 38-40, xiii. 14, 33-4, for sentences either incomplete or irregular in constr.; also the use of τί for ὅ τι in xiv. 36 is rather an extreme instance of what is, no doubt, a general tendency in Hellenistic Greek. And the general impression of roughness of style is more than proportioned to the number of quotable instances of harsh construction or strained use of words.

But most of the individual features of St. Mark's style which can be adequately illustrated by single quotations are referable to the one principle—that he is more careful of clearness and emphasis in expressing his meaning than of elegance in language. Thus it is that he so often repeats a subst. where the use of a pron.* might seem more natural—*e.g.* the repetition of the name, Σίμωνος after Σίμωνα in i. 16, of τὰ δαιμόνια in ver. 34: of τῶν ἁμαρτωλῶν

---

* The pronoun ἐκεῖνος has, we may almost say, this for its idiomatic object—to give, without actual repetition of a noun, the emphasis that repetition would give: often (as in John v. 35, or xiii. 6, *si vera l.*) the best translation is to repeat the noun, especially in the case of proper names; as the A. V. does in the latter place. Now St. Mark never has ἐκεῖνος otherwise than in agreement never in apposition with a subst. or substantival phrase—except in the last twelve verses, where it occurs three times.

10 *LANGUAGE OF THE NEW TESTAMENT.*

καὶ τελωνῶν in ii. 16 after πολλοὶ τελῶναι καὶ ἁμαρτωλοὶ in ver. 15, and the like. So we have repetitions, in similar or in varied terms, of what has already been said in another form; as in the passage last cited, ἦσαν γὰρ πολλοί after the πολλοὶ τελῶναι; or compare i. 42 ἀπῆλθεν ἀπ' αὐτοῦ ἡ λέπρα—καὶ ἐκαθαρίσθη with the parallels, Matt. viii. 3 which fuses the two expressions, and Luke v. 13, which omits the second. So we get adverbs —the frequent εὐθύς or others—coupled with almost equivalent phrases; *e.g.* ii. 20, τότε—ἐν ἐκείνῃ τῇ ἡμέρᾳ; so v. 5, vi. 25, vii. 21, x. 30, xiii. 29, xiv. 30, 43. Double negatives, again, are perhaps more frequent than ordinary Greek idiom would make them.

There is not very much that is significant in St. Mark's vocabulary. Critics duly note that, instead of St. Matthew's συμβούλιον λαμβάνειν, he uses some other phrase—it is uncertain whether συμβ. ποιεῖν or something else—both in iii. 6 and xv. 1; but nothing is suggested or can be inferred from this. Nor must we give too much weight to his use of Latin words; he has only two or three that are not common to him with other N. T. writers. Δηνάριον evidently was a word current, like the coin itself, all over the empire; the same was the case, no doubt, with κοδράντης, though it happens to be found only in Matt. and Mark, and with the still more thoroughly disguised ξέστης, though found in Mark only. So too with the terms of Roman military or political organisation—λεγιών, κῆνσος, πραιτώριον, one may add φραγελλῶσαι; these all come in other N. T. writers, though it is worth noticing that St. Luke uses more Hellenic equivalents for some of them. There remain only, as really

THE SYNOPTIC GOSPELS. 11

characteristic of St. Mark, two words of this last class, σπεκουλάτωρ, and κεντυρίων instead of the usual ἑκατοντάρχης or -ος; these may possibly suggest that the Evangelist wrote at Rome, or at all events somewhere where the army had not suffered any assimilation to Greek-speaking provincials.* Another alleged peculiarity, the use of diminutives, is almost wholly fictitious: θυγάτριον and χαλκίον are the only ones that do not appear in parallel passages of at least one other Gospel; and the latter (like βιβλίον) is hardly a dim. in more than form.

Before leaving the subject of St. Mark's language, it may be proper to refer to the question how far its general characteristics are shared by the twelve disputed verses at the end of the Gospel. The answer must be, that they to some extent share in the roughness of style which we have noted as his general characteristic, but that in more individual points their peculiarities are quite different from his. It has been proved by Dean Burgon and Canon Cook, that the external evidence against the passage has been greatly overstated—that the documentary evidence would be weak, apart from that —not of the remote common ancestor, but of the immediate common editor—of Codd. ℵ and B; and that the patristic evidence resolves itself into that (perhaps ultimately of Origen, but immediately) of Eusebius, who *may*, quite possibly, have been himself the common editor of the two MSS. But when we come to internal evidence, we must acknowledge

* If the Evangelist, St. Peter's "son," be (as is rather assumed than proved) the same person as St. Barnabas' cousin, the Mark of the Acts and Pauline Epistles, we know from Col. iv. 10, 2 Tim. iv. 11, that he not only was twice at least at Rome, but visited St. Paul there while he was under military custody.

12 LANGUAGE OF THE NEW TESTAMENT.

that, whatever its worth, it tells against the passage. Not only are the end of ver. 8 and the beginning of ver. 9 abrupt and unconnected with each other; not only is Mary Magdalene introduced as though mentioned for the first time; not only is the Saviour designated as "the Lord," or at least called by that title with His name, as He never is in the narrative* of either St. Matthew or St. Mark; but there are merely verbal differences, for which one cannot account, as one may for these, by tracing in them some subtlety of meaning. First, we have the unique πρώτῃ σαββάτου, when in ver. 2 we had the common μιᾷ τῶν σαββάτων. Then, as already noted (p. 9, n), we have ἐκεῖνος used without a subst. three or four times (vv. 10, 11, 13 bis), as it never is in Matt. or Mark, but sometimes in Luke and oftener in John. Again, θεᾶσθαι and (what almost proves more because it means less) πορεύεσθαι† are never elsewhere used by St. Mark. Μορφή is, within the N. T., peculiar to this passage and St. Paul; ‡ βλάπτειν to this passage and St. Luke; ἀπιστεῖν to this and SS. Luke and Paul

* In Matt. xxi. 3, Mark xi. 3, opinions may differ whether it is assumed that *the disciples* will call Jesus "the Lord" (John xiii. 13), or whether the ass is claimed by a prophet for the service of the LORD God of Israel. Here, no doubt, it would be quite credible that St. Mark uses a title of the glorified Saviour which he had not applied to Him in the days of His flesh; cf. Matt. xxviii. 6 T. R., but note that the reading is doubtful.

† It is noted that St. Luke uses this word oftenest of the Evangelists, avoiding ὑπάγειν, which never occurs in (the true text of) his first nine chaps., and only four or five times at all. SS. Matt. and Mark use it generally in the imper.—St. John (in all his works) more freely in all forms.

‡ The argument is cumulative; else it shows how little weight a fact like this would have, if it stood by itself, that τρόμος is peculiar to St. Paul and the unquestioned ver. 8 of this chapter.

THE SYNOPTIC GOSPELS. 13

(the latter having it once in Rom., once in 2 Tim.);
παρακολουθεῖν to this, St. Luke, and the Pastoral
Epp.; ἐπακολ. to this, the Pastoral Epp., and St.
Peter. The full significance of these facts will
appear when they are correlated with others in the
tables in the Appendix; but by themselves they are
striking enough. It seems a smaller thing, that
θανάσιμος is found here only in the N. T., but when
we reflect, it is hardly likely that a word of classical
stamp like this should, if in ordinary Hellenistic use,
be found only in almost the least classical of Hellenistic writers. It is thus certain that these verses
have quite a different character of diction from the
rest of the Gospel—whether we account for the
fact by supposing that they are not St. Mark's, or
that they *are* St. Mark's own words, while the rest
is given in St. Peter's,* or in some other way.

Whether we accept or no the traditional statement, that St. Matthew's Gospel as we have it is
not the original work of the Apostle, but a translation from the Hebrew, it is certain that it has less
marked individuality of style than either St. Mark
or St. Luke. Smoother than the one, it is more monotonous than the other, more mannered and less
varied; with fewer positive Hebraisms than St.
Luke, it is more constantly pervaded by the charac-

---

* So apparently Dr. Salmon, *Introd. to N. T.*, Lect. ix.,
and note at end. He says that the first fifteen verses of the
Gospel have the same character as the last twelve, but I fail
to see it. They seem to be of a piece with the rest of the
Gospel in their general style, in their relation to St. Matthew,
and in such points as the characteristic καὶ εὐθύς. Κύψας
indeed is peculiar to i. 7 and (*ps.*) John viii. 6, 8; but the
only other ἅπαξ λεγόμενα are σχιζομένους τοὺς οὐρανούς, which
(compared with St. Matthew's ἠνεῴχθησαν οἱ οὐρανοί) is only
an instance of St. Mark's picturesqueness, and πιστεύετε ἐν τῷ
εὐαγγ.

teristics of Hellenistic Greek, and might serve as the best sample of what Hellenistic narrative style is. We may add that, while from a purely literary point of view its style is inferior to that of the other Gospels, this very monotony is one of the features that enable it to be adequately represented by quotations of "texts," or by the reading of short pericopes: it is no mere accident that it has been, in the Western Churches at least, the favourite Gospel for ecclesiastical use.

The style being thus neutral or colourless, its individualisms of language lie mostly in the frequent repetition of certain phrases or formulæ. Every one must have noticed some of these—ἡ βασιλεία τῶν οὐρανῶν as a variant of the phrase common to all primitive Christians ἡ β. τοῦ Θεοῦ and ἵνα πληρωθῇ τὸ ῥηθὲν ὑπὸ Κυρίου διὰ τοῦ προφητοῦ (i. 22, cf. ii. 5), with variants according to context, or formed by mere omission (e.g. ii. 17, iv. 14). We notice the ὅπως instead of ἵνα in viii. 17, xiii. 35; which, with the τοῦτο δὲ ὅλον γέγονεν of i. 22, xxvi. 56, seems to show that the final sense of ἵνα may safely be pressed. Hardly less characteristic of this Evangelist is ὁ Πατήρ μου (ἡμῶν, ὑμῶν) ὁ ἐν [τοῖς] οὐρανοῖς or ὁ οὐράνιος; St. Mark has it only once (xi. 25, critics omit the next ver.), and St. Luke only once (xi. 13, not 2), and that with the variation ὁ ἐξ οὐρανοῦ. It is less a characteristic of language, and more of thought,* that here alone in the N. T. (iv. 5, xxvii. 53) Jerusalem is called ἡ ἁγία πόλις;

* We find it noted as parallel to this, that St. Matthew has the designation of Christ as "the Son of David" oftener than the other Gospels. This is so, and the occurrence of the phrase in xxi. 9, 15, and not in the parallels, is important; but the mere difference in degree of frequency is too slight to be of much significance.

but see τὴν π. τὴν ἁγίαν in Rev. xi. 2, and cf. *ibid.* xx. 9 : xxi. 2 etc., of the *new* Jerusalem, is of course a different case. Similarly we have τόπος ἅγιος in xxiv. 15, apparently of the Temple ; we have the same phrase, though with the art., in Acts vi. 13, xxi. 28, but only in the mouth of antichristian Jews. More purely verbal, but less exclusively peculiar is the use of ποιεῖν without an obj., but with an adv., esp. a *pronominal* adv., οὕτως, ὡς, ὥσπερ, etc., supplying the place of one. Not counting εὖ or καλῶς ποιεῖν (either in the sense "do good" or "do well") we have it eleven times in St. Matthew (i. 24, v. 47, vi. 2, vii. 12, xviii. 35, xx. 5, xxi. 6, 36, xxiv. 46, xxvi. 19, xxviii. 15); besides one or two adverbial phrases like that in xxiii. 3, and the use without any obj. at all, like xxv. 40, 45. In St. Luke's longer Gospel we have the same constr. only nine times, counting φρονίμως ἐποίησεν in xvi. 8, and once in Acts (xii. 8) ; in St. Mark only once (xv. 8), and in St. John not at all ; in St. Paul only two or three times (1 Cor. xvi. 1, 1 Thess. v. 11 ; perhaps we should count also Eph. iii. 20) ; once in St. James (ii. 12), who has so much in common with St. Matthew. One hardly knows whether it is a difference of substance or of language, that St. Matthew alone has the phrase κατ' ὄναρ (i. 20, ii. 12, 13, 19, 22, xxvii. 19), whereas in Acts (ix. 10, 12, x. 3) we have ἐν ὁράματι or (xviii. 9) δι' ὁράματος ; certainly St. Matthew himself uses ὅραμα (xvii. 9, of the Transfiguration).

CHAPTER II.

ST. LUKE.

WE have already noted some of the characteristic features of St. Luke's Gospel, and have seen that it shares, in at least equal measure, the Hebraistic tone of the other Synoptics. But it is no less true—it is perhaps more generally recognised—that St. Luke's Gospel has much in common with the Acts of the Apostles, so that internal evidence, as well as the statement of the prologue, supports the general belief that they are by the same author; and that the Acts is, of all the books included in the N. T., the nearest to contemporary if not to classical literary usage—the only one, except perhaps the Epistle to the Hebrews, where conformity to a standard of classical correctness is consciously aimed at.

The fact is, that St. Luke is the most versatile of the N. T. writers; his mind, if not the greatest among them, was the most many-sided. He, the companion of St. Paul, shows the strongest sympathy for Ebionism in its etymological sense—the poverty, partly but not wholly voluntary, of the primitive Church of Jerusalem; and in like manner, he writes in a Hebraistic or in a Hellenic style, according as he is describing events that took place in a Hebrew or in a Hellenic society.

ST. LUKE.

One literary quality, indeed, is still more prominent in St. Luke than his versatility—his picturesqueness. St. Mark, it is true, gives us oftener the little touches that mark a description as coming, at first hand or almost unaltered, from an eyewitness; but he does less than St. Luke to make us feel as if we were eyewitnesses ourselves. Late and historically worthless as is the story that makes St. Luke himself a painter, it has a certain ideal truth, for it is from him that Christian painters have mainly derived their inspiration; he is the father of Christian art, from the Good Shepherd wrought on chalices or in catacombs of the second and third centuries, through the Madonnas and Holy Families of the middle ages, down to Michel Angelo's Conversion of St. Paul, and Raphael's Deliverance of St. Peter.

It lies beyond our province, however, to illustrate this quality, which does not depend upon details of language. For illustrations of the author's versatility of style, we have not far to look. "Almost the only passage in the N. T. which reads like a Greek period of the time, is the first paragraph of the Gospel according to St. Luke, and the corresponding words of the Acts."* But in the Gospel we have a sudden transition from the literary style and periodic structure of the dedication to Theophilus, to the Hebraistic opening of the narrative itself, ’Εγένετο ἐν ταῖς ἡμέραις ‘Ηρῴδου κ.τ.λ. In the Acts, on the other hand, we can draw no such sharp line.

---

* Professor Jowett "On the Interpretation of Scripture," in *Essays and Reviews*, p. 396, original edition. It is an unfortunate consequence of the theological controversy which raged over that work, that attention was withdrawn from the excellent good sense of some of its non-controversial parts, such as most if not all of § 3 in the Essay cited.

18 LANGUAGE OF THE NEW TESTAMENT.

The opening words referring to "the former treatise" are in the Hellenising literary style; but they do not form a separate paragraph—hardly a complete sentence; they lead up to the record of the last discourse of the Lord with His disciples, which is written in much the same language as had been used in the Gospel to describe their earlier intercourse.

In general, we can see what considerations determine the predominance of one or the other element in St. Luke's style. Jewish affairs, or Christian religious conceptions for which the only appropriate language was derived from the Jewish Scriptures, are dealt with in Hellenistic language; mere narratives, especially those of which the scene lies in the Hellenic world, are told more or less Hellenically. But we could not have told beforehand which style would be used in individual passages—sometimes [*] we can hardly say what determined it, though we may be sure that the writer's judgment was sound; on such subjects good taste is almost a spiritual gift, or at least depends on spiritual qualities. Sometimes we are inclined to ask whether a Hebraising passage (*e.g.* the first two cc. of the Gospel) may not be an actual translation or compilation from the Aramaic; or again, what was the native language of the Evangelist himself. It was usually inferred from Col. iv. 11, 14, that he was not a Jew, though Acts xx. 5, 6 would suggest that he was; but if we give any weight to the tradition that he was a

[*] One of the most Hellenic passages in the Gospel (though introduced with a καὶ ἰδού) is the last portion of c. vii. It has been suggested that St. Luke was led to dwell on such stories by what he had seen of the effect of the Gospel in profligate cities like Antioch, Ephesus, Corinth, and Rome: are we to suppose that he told them in such language as would be current there?

native of Antioch, he may have been a bilingual Syrian, as much at home among "Hebrews" as among Hellenists or Hellenes.

However, our business is to record the facts about St. Luke's language, not to speculate as to their causes. We have seen already, that he is even more given than the other Evangelists to connect his narratives together by more or less Hebraistic formulæ— "It came to pass that . . . .," "In those days . . . .," "and behold! . . .," and the like. And yet even in his use of these formulæ we see the free spirit of liberal Hellenic culture at work. As he often retains more of Hebraistic form than the other Evangelists, so he often tones down the Hebraism into a constr. for which there are parallels and perhaps precedents in literary Greek. We have seen an instance of this in the transition from a sentence like Καὶ ἐγένετο ἐν μιᾷ τῶν ἡμερῶν καὶ αὐτὸς ἦν διδάσκων (v. 17), or Ἐγένετο δὲ ἐν τῷ ἱερατεύειν αὐτὸν . . . ἔλαχε τοῦ θυμιᾶσαι (i. 8, 9), through such as Ἐγένετο δὲ ἐν σαββάτῳ διαπορεύεσθαι αὐτόν (vi. 1), till we come to one in which we scarcely see a Hebraism, even if the idiom is not exactly classical, such as ἐγένετο δὲ ἐπὶ τὴν αὔριον συναχθῆναι αὐτῶν τοὺς ἄρχοντας (Acts iv. 5). Here the parallel is much closer to the classical use of συνέβη (which itself is used in Acts xxi. 35) than to the Hebrew phrase; or if any traces of Hebraism remain, they are further disguised by changes of order or other modifications, in Acts ix. 3, ἐν δὲ τῷ πορεύεσθαι ἐγένετο αὐτὸν ἐγγίζειν, till we come to x. 25, ὡς δὲ ἐγένετο τοῦ εἰσελθεῖν τὸν Πέτρον. Here, or in xxi. 1, 5, it would be simply impossible to substitute the Hebraic constr. so common in the Gospel.

20 LANGUAGE OF THE NEW TESTAMENT.

So it is with most of the other Hebraisms in St. Luke—the ἐν τῷ c. inf., the καί *in apodosi* (often coupled with αὐτός or ἰδού) that commonly accompanies it, or such phrases as καὶ ἐν ταῖς ἡμέραις ἐκείναις. They are more frequent in St. Luke than in St. Mark—some of them more than in St. Matthew; but they do not prevent our feeling the style to be more Hellenic than theirs, because it is harder to draw the line between cases where they are felt to be Hebraisms, and those where they have a distinctive sense that would justify their use in any Greek. *E.g.* the line is not easy to draw between the use of καὶ αὐτός in xix. 9 and that in *ib.* 2.* Similarly in iv. 2 ἐν ταῖς ἡμέραις ἐκείναις refers to the "forty days" mentioned just before; in vi. 12 the pronoun is varied; and in xii. 1, though the ἐν in a note of time connects the phrase with these, the constr. is free and semi-Hellenic. So with the use of ἦν with a present or perfect ptcp. as a periphrasis for the impf. or plupf. tense: this is an idiom characteristic of Aramaic and late Hebrew, and comes often in the Gospel (*e.g.* Matt. xix. 22 = Mark x. 22, but *not* in the parallel Luke xviii. 23), oftenest in St. Luke, in places where we may be sure it would not have been used in classical Greek, But the line is hard to draw between what was and what was not admissible in such Greek : see the examples of this constr. and remarks on them in *Language of the New Testament*, Part I., c. v. E.

Thus we are not surprised to find that this particular Hebraism, as on the whole we may call it, lasts on further into the Acts than others, though

* Note that in xxiii. 51 the best texts omit καὶ αὐτός; which, however, makes good sense, and is found in both the parables, Matt. xxvii. 57, Mark xv. 43.

the general character of that book is far more Hellenic than that of the Gospel. Even in the earlier chapters there is, at least in the narratives, a much less Hebraic tone; but in the earlier speeches —especially the sermons in cc. ii. and xiii. and St. Stephen's defence in c. vii.—the biblical element is so large that the character is not very different from that of the Gospel. In these speeches, indeed, we have such separable and easily avoidable Hebraisms as $\pi\alpha\rho\alpha\gamma\gamma\epsilon\lambda\iota\alpha$ $\pi\alpha\rho\eta\gamma\gamma\epsilon\iota\lambda\alpha\mu\epsilon\nu$ in v. 28 *
—in iv. 17 it is agreed that $\dot{\alpha}\pi\epsilon\iota\lambda\hat{\eta}$ $\dot{\alpha}\pi\epsilon\iota\lambda\eta\sigma\dot{\omega}\mu\epsilon\theta\alpha$ is not the original text, but if not, it proves almost more decidedly what was the idiom familiar to those who edited St. Luke or carried on his tradition.

But as we go on after c. xiii. in the Acts, the Hellenic element in the language becomes more and more predominant. We see this, not only in passages like the letter of Lysias and the speech of Tertullus, but even in the Epistle of the Church of Jerusalem in c. xv., and the defence of St. Paul before Agrippa, compared with the earlier speeches just referred to.

Nor is it only in such respects as these that he is more Hellenic than the other N. T. writers; he has a nearer approach to a sound instinctive knowledge, if not a complete mastery, of the shades of construction that make a writer's language idiomatic and elegant. He alone in the N. T. has the use of the opt. in indirect questions— Ev. i. 29, iii. 15, viii. 9 (xv. 26, xviii. 36, in these two places there is more or less authority for the insertion of $\ddot{\alpha}\nu$), xxii. 23, Acts xvii. 11, xxi. 33, xxv. 20. Peculiar to him,

* $\ ^{\prime}A\nu\alpha\theta\epsilon\mu\alpha\tau\iota$ $\dot{\alpha}\nu\alpha\theta\epsilon\mu\alpha\tau\iota\sigma\alpha\mu\epsilon\nu$ in xxiii. 14 is put into the mouth of Jews, apparently of Jerusalem, and so is a parallel case, though so much further on in the book.

22 LANGUAGE OF THE NEW TESTAMENT.

also, is the constr. of more doubtful correctness, where the opt. is accompanied by ἄν, and the indirect question often introduced by the art.—i. 62, vi. 11, ix. 46 (xv. 26, xviii. 36 ?), Acts v. 24, x. 17 (ii. 12, xvii. 20, xxi. 33 ?—cf. xvii. 18). For another similar idiomatic use of the opt. see *Language of the New Testament*, p. 110.

Still the language never ceases to be Hellenistic; however marked or however successful the effort at classical style may be, we usually see that it *is* an effort. Perhaps it may even be said, that he sometimes gets out of his depth when the effort is long continued, and in trying to be elegant ceases to be correct. Certainly, in Acts we have a good many anacolutha, esp. in the latter cc.: viii. 7 is at best a mixture of two constructions, unless it can be explained (cf. Mark v. 10, 11) as showing the interfusion of the personalities of the demons and the possessed. The redundant ὅτι in xxvii. 10 is occasionally found in classical Greek; in xxiii. 23-4 the transition from *or. rect.* to *obl.*, though rare and rather awkward, is not more essentially irregular than the reverse transition so common in St. Luke. The broken sentence in xxiv. 19 is quite natural in a speech; still we feel that the irregularities come rather thick. And in xvii. 2 the leaving the subject to be inferred from an oblique case is pronounced to be hardly Greek. At any rate, even when he is most Hellenic, we always feel the influence of biblical if not of Hebraic language; we feel it more, perhaps, than in the less deliberately classicalised style of St. Paul or St. James. For there is one thing, at least, that prevents St. Luke from breaking with Hebraic traditions—he never so far Hellenises" as to set Hellenic religion on a level with his own, or to disguise scriptural doctrines because scriptural language might sound uncouth.

We have dwelt on this point at special length, because the effort at literary elegance is the point which, in the Acts at least, differentiates St. Luke's style most from that of other N. T. writers, and because the student, especially if he be a classical scholar, is likely to overrate the importance of the Hellenic element in his language compared with the Hellenistic. Of his vocabulary we cannot at present speak, but must refer to C. IV. and the Tables in Appendix I. Of his characteristics of style not directly connected with the effort at classical elegance, or the faithful retention of semi-Hebraic formulæ, the most marked are in his modes of introducing speeches in the course of a narrative. Once at least (Ev. vii. 41) he leaves a change of speaker in a dialogue to be understood, without any word to mark it; oftener he introduces parenthetic breaks in the course of a speech, continuing it after them without fresh mention of the speaker: so Ev. vii. 29-31 (true text), xix. 25-6,* and in all probability Acts i. 18-20. Often (*how* often is a point in which texts vary) he omits the verb εἶπεν or φησίν where the speaker, and in general the person spoken to, are indicated (*e.g.* Acts v. 9, true text); often he slides from *oratio obliqua* into *recta* (as Acts i. 4, xiv. 22, xvii. 3; this again is a point as to which readings are often uncertain: see Westcott and Hort's Introduction, § 404): once (Acts xxiii. 23-4) he conversely slides from *recta* into *obliqua*.

* These are from passages peculiar to St. Luke, at least in their exact form. Referring however to v. 24 and its parallels (Matt. ix. 6, Mark ii. 11), and to Mark viii. 19-21, we ask if this was characteristic of the form in which our Evangelists received all their materials.

24 LANGUAGE OF THE NEW TESTAMENT.

And while he thus makes it difficult for a modern editor to mark speeches in his books by the usual modern device of inverted commas, he extends that use of the art. which is almost equivalent to inverted commas, so as to make it the introduction to an indirect question: see Ev. i. 62, ix. 46, xix. 48, xxii. 23, 24, Acts iv. 21, xxii. 30. (The only parallel cases in the N. T. are Rom. viii. 26, 1 Thess. iv. 1—even Mark ix. 23 is different.)

Other mannerisms, more or less referable to the effort at classical elegance, are the frequent use of the conj. τε, of the phrase οὐκ (or οὐχ) ὀλίγος (eight times in Acts), of cases of πᾶς (mostly after a prep.) followed by an attracted rel. (Ev. ii. 20, ix. 43, xxiv. 25, Acts i. 1, iii. 21, x. 39, xiii. 39, xxii. 10, xxvi. 2), and sometimes by another subst. or adj. in agreement (Ev. iii. 19, xix. 37). Perhaps we may class with these the greater frequency of πρός c. acc. after verbs of speaking, where the other Gospels usually have the dat. *Τοῦ* c. inf. in a final sense is relatively common in him—perhaps commoner in the received text than in a critical.

CHAPTER III.

ST. PAUL'S EPISTLES.

AS it was the personal action of the Apostle Paul that was the chief means of making the Gospel known to the Western world, so his writings give the most typical form of the language in which it reached them. If we want to see what shall be pure Hellenistic Greek—Greek that is composed in Greek, and not a version of something written, spoken, or at least thought out, in Hebrew or Aramaic; but which on the other hand is the unmistakeable composition of a Jew, to whom "Ἕλλην means "Gentile"—it is to St. Paul's writings that we shall turn,

In general, his language is grammatically correct; what irregularities he does admit are such as show freedom rather than inexperience in the use of a language, or else such slips as are almost inevitable in letters dictated, not written by the author himself. To this last cause we may ascribe the repetition of ἔτι which is strongly attested in Rom. v. 6,* the redundant ὅτε in 1 Cor. xii. 2—whether we suppose this to be a mere διττογραφία of the amanuensis, or a hesitation on the Apostle's own part as to the

---

* Westcott and Hort follow B (rather diffidently) in reading εἰ followed by some particle, and connecting the clause with what precedes.

26 *LANGUAGE OF THE NEW TESTAMENT.*

form the sentence should take : and also the more considerable anacolutha analysed below. The same cause may account for the unique solecism, εἴ τις σπλάγχνα in Phil. ii. 1 ; it is as natural that a man should have said εἴ τις before he decided on the next word, and not cared to correct himself when he decided that it should be a neuter, as it is incredible that a decently educated man should deliberately have *written* the words as they stand in the MSS.

Two points may be noted, one negative and one positive, as illustrative of St. Paul's command of pure Greek idiom. In the few passages (Gal. i. 13-ii. 14 is the longest) where he gives a consecutive narrative, we feel a contrast with the Hebraistic style of the Synoptic Gospels, and even of parts of the Acts. Instead of the constant καί, and frequent καὶ ἐγένετο, we have clauses and paragraphs introduced by varied and appropriate particles or asyndeta (Gal. i. 13 γάρ ; 15 δέ ; 18 ἔπειτα ; 20 δέ ; 21, ii. 1, ἔπειτα ; 3 ἀλλά ; 6, 11 δέ ; 14 ἀλλά). Again, a subtle test of Greek idiom is furnished by the use of the untranslatable particle μέν, in the exceptional cases where it is not balanced by a δέ, ἀλλά, ἔπειτα, or some equivalent word. Now St. Paul has nine or ten instances of this use (not counting the combination μὲν οὖν) : [*] nowhere is the particle meaningless, or felt to be unnatural ; and nowhere is it felt, as the rarer instances of its use in the Acts are, to be a conscious effort at classicalism.

And yet, though St. Paul writes Greek with freedom, and at the same time with grammatical

[*] Rom. i. 8, iii. 2, vi. 21 (v. l.), x. 1, xi. 13 (T. R.), 1 Cor. xi. 18, 2 Cor. xi. 4, xii. 12, Col. ii. 23, 1 Thess. ii. 18.

ST. PAUL'S EPISTLES.

and even idiomatic correctness, there is hardly a line in his writings which a non-Jewish author of his day would have written. The difference is greater in vocabulary than in grammar. Not only is there a new group of words, relating to specially Jewish or Christian religious conceptions; other conceptions, for which the classical language would have furnished some sort of expression, are rather expressed in terms of the new ecclesiastical dialect. And, while the language is enriched on the one side of its special purpose, it is impoverished on other sides. The vocabulary is less varied, not only than that of professed literary men, but than that of the few Christian writers whom we have to compare with the Apostle—men who deal with the same conceptions as he, with less native power, but with verbal instruments more flexible. Besides the writer of the Epistle to the Hebrews, St. Clement of Rome is more Greek than St. Paul: and this though his style is very largely influenced by St. Paul's own, as well as by the LXX. and other non-Hellenic influences that are common to both.

We may name, as characteristic instances of St. Paul's "new departure" in the formation of an ecclesiastical language, his uses of the words οἰκοδομεῖν and its cognates, and of πληροφορεῖσθαι, πληροφορία, and πλήρωμα. And yet we are forced to confess our ignorance, how far the coinage or appropriation of these words originated with St. Paul himself. The Wisdom of Solomon is a proof sufficient, though now almost solitary,* that Philo was not

---

* See Drummond's *Philo Judaeus*, Book II., c. v. for a discussion of this book; and Appendix 2 to the same Book on the fragments of Aristobulus, which might be coupled with it, if genuine, which is questioned.

28 LANGUAGE OF THE NEW TESTAMENT.

the only Jewish writer who, living at Alexandria or trained under Alexandrian influences, had acquired a knowledge of Greek literary style and assimilated the thoughts of Greek philosophy, while holding fast, more or less consistently, the monotheistic faith of a Jew. But the scanty remains which we have of that Alexandrian school should forbid us to be certain that there were not other schools, in which thoughts more purely Jewish found utterance in forms less purely Greek, but which were co-ordinate with the Alexandrian school in providing language for the Church of Jews and Gentiles. It is quite possible that among the disciples of Gamaliel and the opponents of St. Stephen, Saul of Tarsus found ready formed to his hand the language in which he preached his Gospel and wrote our memorials of it.

This possibility however is balanced by another. We must remember, that St. Paul had had a long Christian career before any of his extant Epp. were composed; so that the formed character of his vocabulary in these does not prove that it may not have been of his own formation. Without pretending to encourage speculation or to overvalue its results, we perhaps may incline to think that it was St. Paul himself who originated the metaphor of "edification." The ethical use may have been suggested to him, and to his precursors if he had any, by the metaphorical use, which however is really distinct, found in Ps. xxvii. (xxviii.) 5, and often in Jeremiah (i. 10, etc.); but St. Paul not only gives a new application to the metaphor, but uses it so often that the consciousness that it is a metaphor is lost, unless expressly revived as it is in 1 Cor. iii. 9 sqq., Eph. ii. 20 sqq.

On the other hand, the word $\pi\lambda\eta\rho o\phi o\rho\epsilon\hat{\iota}\nu$ seems to be of coinage internal to the Greek language, yet peculiarly Alexandrine if not Hellenistic Greek: and it received a special application in Christian usage. The alleged example of the use of πληροφορεῖν by Ctesias in the sense of "satisfying, assuring" a person, vanishes on examination: there is no evidence, express or internal, that Photius, in his summary of the history given in Ctesias' *Persica* (Bibl. Tom. 72, p. xli. v. 29), reproduces his author's language even in an abridged form. Thus the sole example of the word before St. Paul is in the LXX. of Eccles. viii. 11; for however late the composition of that book may be, there is no reason to doubt that both it and the Greek translation of it are pre-Christian. But it is not an accident, that Christians had occasion oftener than Pagans, or even Jews, to speak of "full assurance" or "confident conviction;" nor that the word, which in its solitary O. T. instance is used in a bad sense, in St. Paul and writers influenced by him (no others use it) has an exclusively good one.

On the growth of the theological sense of the word πλήρωμα, there is nothing to be added to Bp. Lightfoot's investigation, in an Excursus at the end of his edition of the Ep. to the Colossians. There is no difficulty in supposing that here we have materials for tracing the whole history of the word. In Rom. xv. 29 it is hardly differentiated from its secular meaning, yet from this the transition to the use in John i. 16 is not very hard.

It is of course impossible to give individual instances of a writer's style, in the sense that we can give instances of his vocabulary; but perhaps the difference between St. Paul and an ordinary Greek writer of his day may be best described by saying that he is more modern, and that he is less rhetorical. A lecturer on the Ep. to the Hebrews is reported to have said, that the three first words πολυμερῶς καὶ πολυτρόπως were enough to convince him that St. Paul did not write it. This is an exaggeration: assonances like φθόνου, φόνου; ἀσυνέτους, ἀσυνθέτους (Rom. i. 29, 30), assonances with an etymological basis (ἄστοργοι, ἄσπονδοι; προδόται, προπετεῖς, 2 Tim. iii. 3, 4), and words or clauses parallel in sense (1 Cor. xiii. *passim*) are quite in St. Paul's manner. Again, we have something like a rhetorical artifice in the use of different prepositions with the same noun in parallel or co-ordinate clauses—see Rom. iii. 22, 1 Cor. xii. 8, 9, 2 Cor. iii. 11, Gal. i. 1; and the passages which, when we recognise their rhetorical character, are seen to have less of the nature of the Aristotelian scholasticism (cf. *Language of the New Testament*, p. 141), of which perhaps they do contain the germs— Rom. xi. 36, Eph. iv. 6, Col. i. 16.* We may add as a kindred feature the accumulation of rhetorical questions—Rom. ii. 3, 4, 21-3, x. 14, 15, 1 Cor. ix. 1, etc.: and the many cases where a question is asked, only to be answered by μὴ γένοιτο. But if there are some words chosen for effect in St. Paul, some cases where their sound or order, not merely their sense, has been an object with him, it is far oftener remarkable how simple, often how modern, he is in these respects. It is in the sublimest passages, such as Rom. viii., 1 Cor. xiii., Phil. iii., that we perhaps feel this most—the words are glorious in themselves, but are not arranged

* It is worth while to refer to the striking parallel in M. Aurelius, Medit. IV. xxiii., ἐκ σοῦ πάντα, ἐν σοὶ πάντα, εἰς σὲ πάντα—addressed however to Nature, not to a personal God, though the following words, ὦ πόλι φίλη Διός may be held to make up what is wanting.

ST. PAUL'S EPISTLES.

for effect. In 1 Cor. xiii. 11 the Apostle, as it appears, wrote in the English order, with the identical member of the three balanced clauses last; his editors put the varied verbs last instead: compare the three clauses ending with αὐτοῦ in Phil. iii. 10. It is this absence of art, rather than any ignorance or positive awkwardness, that made him seem to Hellenic critics ἰδιώτης τῷ λόγῳ (2 Cor. xi. 6), and made him rather glory in than repudiate the criticism (1 Cor. i. 17, ii. 1, 4, where the repudiation of λόγος is more unqualified than that of σοφία : cf. 1 Thess. i. 5).

If St. Paul intentionally avoided the artifices of rhetoric, he did not, like the seer of the Apocalypse, intentionally strain the rules of grammar. But it is probable that he knew as little of formal rules in grammar as in rhetoric; that his general correctness is a matter of instinct rather than of care, and that accordingly instincts which led him to cast his thoughts in other than a strictly grammatical form were not rigorously repressed. St. Paul has been compared to Thucydides, as an author whose thoughts are so much more highly developed than his language, that the course of the latter is interrupted and its rules broken through by their expression. But the difference is at least as important and characteristic as the likeness. Thucydides is a rhetorical writer—his rhetoric is more developed than his grammar, and his grammar is as often sacrificed to his rhetoric as overpowered by his fulness of thought. St. Paul, on the contrary, uses a language of which the grammar is mature or declining ; and while he may be carried away by his subject, he never sacrifices simplicity or lucidity to ambition of style.

32 LANGUAGE OF THE NEW TESTAMENT.

Perhaps the parallel is least misleading, if we confine it to that work of St. Paul where the sentences are longest, and, for that and other reasons, anacolutha most frequent—the Epistle to the Ephesians, or rather its earlier, purely theological portion. If we may regard this Epistle as our best example of that σοφία which, according to 1 Cor. ii. 6, *was* to be found in St. Paul's teaching, we may see in its style something like a ὑπεροχὴ λόγου (*ib.* ver. 1), corresponding to the ὑπεροχὴ σοφίας. This Epistle is further, indeed, from being rhetorical than several passages in the earlier ones—especially that "spoken as it were foolishly" in 2 Cor. xi. But it would be less inappropriate than elsewhere to call the language elaborate; and it is at the same time apt oftener than elsewhere to stray beyond the bounds of symmetry and regularity.

But though more frequent, and more connected with a cumbrous length of sentence, the anacolutha of this Epistle fall into the same classes as those of the others, and need not be separated from them in analysis. Sometimes the principal sentence is never finished; the thread of it is lost among the subordinate clauses, and it is left to be inferred from some of these what the conclusion should have been. So Rom. xv. 23 (true text); Gal. ii. 4, 5 (where the want of a conclusion leaves the meaning really obscure); Phil. i. 22; 1 Tim. i. 3, 4. Sometimes the sentence is finished, but with a constr. different from that with which it began; so Rom. ix. 10, 12; 2 Cor. v. 6, 8; Gal. ii. 6; Eph. i. 20-23 (where indic. aorists are made co-ordinate with participles); Col. i. 21, 22 (more or less according to the reading); *ib.* 26; 1 Thess. ii. 10, 11; in the two last, participles appear co-ordinate with finite

ST. PAUL'S EPISTLES. 33

verbs). We get an example of this sort even in a short but impassioned sentence like 1 Cor. ix. 15 (true text); in this and some other cases the line is hard to draw between anacoluthon and aposiopesis. And lastly, sometimes a fresh start is made, after the parenthetical or otherwise dependent clauses are complete; the sentence runs almost or quite as it was meant to run from the first, and the chief or only irregularity is, that it makes a fresh beginning before receiving the destined end. (Compare 1 Thess. iii. 1, 5, where this feature of style appears, but each of the repeated commencements of the sentence is grammatically completed.) So Rom. v. 12, 18; 1 Cor. viii. 1-4 (probably); Gal. ii. 6-9; Eph. ii. 1-5; 11-13; iii. 1-14; Col. ii. 13 (true text); 1 Thess. iv. 1 (true text: these two last instances are on another scale). Of the passages cited, Gal. ii. 6-9 and Eph. ii. 11-13 are really compound instances. In the former, the sentence that begins ἀπὸ τῶν δοκούντων is never finished, but in ver. 6 a fresh start is made with οἱ δοκοῦντες for subject, which was intended apparently to have two verbs. But after the parenthesis of ver. 8, the subject is repeated, defined and amplified (the three pr. nn. in apposition with οἱ δοκοῦντες στῦλοι εἶναι), and then only comes the verbal predicate that was expected after ἀλλὰ τοὐναντίον. In the other instance, the ὑμεῖς of ver. 11 has been kept so long waiting for its verb, that when it gets it in ver. 12 the ὅτι is repeated with it: then, when the sentence is completed by its second clause in ver. 13, the subject is repeated as though we had not had it already.

To the principle of one or other of these classes may be referred the use of single redundant words,

34 LANGUAGE OF THE NEW TESTAMENT.

not modifying the constr. of the sentence as a whole : *e.g.* the superfluous ᾧ in Rom. xvi. 27, like the superfluous αὐτῷ in Eph. iii. 21 ; the superfluous ὅτε in 1 Cor. xii. 2, if this be more than a pure accident ; the ὅς, if it be superfluous, as is not unlikely, in 2 Cor. iv. 6 ; the double ἔτι in Rom. v. 6, the double ἐμοί in vii. 21. We can hardly reckon as redundant the οὖν in Rom. ii. 21 ; it introduces the apodosis to the εἰ δὲ κ.τ.λ. cf. ver. 17 (true text). In Phil. i. 27, ii. 22, the sentence does not end exactly in the way the beginning had prepared us for, but the grammar hardly breaks down in the process of alteration.

There remain a few passages, where either the constr. is too thoroughly confused, or on the other hand the irregularity is too slight, for them to fall into any of the three groups described above. Rom. viii. 3 is hardly more than an extension of the use of the cognate acc. : "What was impossible to the Law, God [did : He,] by sending . . . condemned . . . ;" so 2 Cor. vi. 13 ; Phil. iv. 10 is even easier. In Col. ii. 2 (true text) συμβιβασθέντες may be called either a nom. abs. or a constr. κατὰ σύνεσιν. In Rom. xii. 6-19, it is a question where the participles begin to become irregular in constr. It is possible, though not very usual with commentators, to connect vv. 5, 6 closely, taking the clauses with ἐν as depending on and explaining ἔχοντες χαρίσματα. But if ἔχοντες may be regular, ἀποστυγοῦντες in ver. 9, and the other participles that follow, interspersed among infinitives and imperatives, cannot be so.

Yet this use of participles is proved to have come easily to a Hellenistic writer, by the influence of this passage on the constr. as well as the thought

ST. PAUL'S EPISTLES. 35

of 1 Pet. iii. 8 sqq., and perhaps Heb. xiii. init. We may illustrate from Phil. ii. 2-5, where the participles are very little more numerous than strict rule would allow; and these passages may in turn illustrate 2 Cor. viii. 24. In 2 Cor. viii. 4, 5 we may either take δεόμενοι as a predicate, or more probably (omitting, as we should, δέξασθαι ἡμᾶς) as loosely co-ordinate with οὐ καθὼς ἠλπίσαμεν: "To their power—beyond their power—unasked—earnestly asking us—surpassing our hopes—they gave," etc. In the same Epistle, in xii. 17 there seems to be a sort of attraction: ἀπέσταλκα is felt to want an acc., and gets one, though ὧν, its real object, is (according to rule) attracted into the gen.: cf. Phil. iii. 18. But in 2 Cor. ix. 13, 14 the constr. is too doubtful, and in any case too complicated, to be discussed in less than a commentary. We can only call attention to the comparative frequency of such irregularities in these few chapters of that Epistle; in these, as in Gal. ii. 6 sqq., the Apostle feels that he is dealing with delicate subjects, and is embarrassed by the consciousness.

Two other points, less strictly grammatical, may be noticed as characteristic of St. Paul's style. He very often gives long enumeration of cognate moral qualities or actions, *e.g.* Rom. i. 29-31; xii. 9-19; 1 Cor. i. 20, 26; xii. 28, 29-30; xiii. 4-7; 2 Cor. iv. 8, 9; vi. 4-10; vii. 2; xi. 22-3, 24-5, 26-7; xii. 10, 20; Gal. v. 19-21, 22-3; Phil. ii. 1; iii. 5, 6; iv. 8; Col. iii. 8; 11; 12; 16 (true text); 1 Thess. v. 14 sqq.; 1 Tim. i. 9, 10; iii. 2-4; 8; 16; iv. 2; v. 10; vi. 4, 5; 11; 2 Tim. ii. 22; iii. 2-5; 16; Tit. i. 7-9; ii. 2, 3; 4, 5; iii. 1, 2 (asyndeta). Rom. viii. 35; 38-9; 1 Cor. vi. 9, 10; Eph. iv. 11 (polysyndeta: 1 Cor. iv. 11-13 may be reckoned to

either class, and in xii. 8-11 the authorities vary as to the retention or omission of some of the conjunctions. And he has some habitual phrases which he repeatedly uses, in the composition of one or more of his works, for the introduction or expansion of important topics. Everyone has noticed the πιστὸς ὁ λόγος of the Pastoral Epp.; but quite as marked a case, and equally peculiar to one work, is the τί (or τί οὖν) ἐροῦμεν of Rom. iii. 5, vi. 1, vii. 7, ix. 14, 30—iv. 1 and perhaps viii. 31 are *slightly* different, other words being added; but both in form and sense they are nearer to the other instances than 1 Cor. x. 19, xi. 22. Hardly less striking is the οὐ θέλω (or θέλομεν) ὑμᾶς ἀγνοεῖν of Rom. i. 13, xi. 25, 1 Cor. x. 1, xii. 1, 2 Cor. i. 8, 1 Thess. iv. 13.*
We may add, though the form is more variable, the epexegetical τοῦτο δὲ λέγω, λέγω δὲ τοῦτο, τοῦτο δέ φημι of 1 Cor. i. 12, vii. 6, 29, xv. 50, Gal. iii. 17 : in 1 Cor. vii. 35, Col. ii. 4, the sense is hardly epexegetical, but the λέγω of Rom. x. 18, 19, xi. 1, xv. 8, 1 Cor. x. 29, Eph. v. 32, Phil. iv. 11 is worth comparing, though in itself it does not amount to a mannerism.

We have dealt, in the above remarks, with the characteristics common to all the works (except of

---

* It is remarkable that the 1st person pl., used in this phrase in 2 Cor. and Thess. is specially characteristic of these Epp. In Thess. there is doubtless a reason for this : at the early date when these Epp. were written, "Paul and Silvanus," if not Timotheus also, were more nearly on an equal footing than Paul and any of his companions later on. Notice esp. 1 Thess. ii. 18 ; even in iii. 1 the pl. is hardly merely rhetorical : the three " send " Timothy, as in Acts viii. 14 the Twelve send (though the word is different) Peter and John to Samaria. In 2 Cor. we note, though in a less degree, the prevalence of the pl., but are less able to account for it; it does not reappear in Phil. and Col., where also Timothy is associated in the superscription.

course confessed forgeries, like the Epp. to the Laodiceans and to Seneca) that bear St. Paul's name, hardly noticing the features that separate the Pastoral Epp., and in a less degree Eph. and Col., from the rest. The reason is, that while it is impossible within our limits to discuss the genuineness of these works, we honestly believe that they are by the same author as the rest; and so we have used them with the rest as illustrations of the same verbal, and indirectly mental, habits of that author. For a full statement of the peculiarities of these two groups we must refer to commentaries on the Epp. themselves. Many of them are not peculiarities of *language* at all; of those that are so, most are in vocabulary rather than in grammar, and can be traced, either in Prof. Thayer's Appendix to Grimm's Lexicon (List IV.), or in our own Table on pp. 92 sqq.*

But perhaps, as we cannot avoid mentioning the question of the genuineness of these works, it may be worth while to say that so far as regards the

* It is hard, however, to frame such lists on a plan that shall give the whole evidence. *E.g.* our own does not state that μαρτυρία, though a very common word in the N. T. generally, is among the Pauline Epp. peculiar to the Pastorals. One curious and minute point may be mentioned. Several times in the undoubted Epp. St. Paul has occasion to say "in everything;" and he almost always expresses it by ἐν παντί (1 Thess. v. 18, 1 Cor. i. 5, 2 Cor. iv. 8, vi. 4, vii. 5, 11, 16, viii. 7, ix. 8, 11, xi. 6, 9, Phil. iv. 6). Now in Eph. v. 24 we have ἐν παντί again, but in Col. iii. 20, 22, κατὰ πάντα twice, and in the Pastoral Epp. ἐν πᾶσιν six times (1 Tim. iii. 11, iv. 15, 2 Tim. ii. 7, iv. 5, Tit. ii. 9, 10). This looks like a discrepancy, and not the less so that in Heb. we have twice (ii. 17, iv. 15), κατὰ πάντα, and once at least ἐν πᾶσιν (xiii. 18: xiii. 4, *may* be taken as masc.: so 1 Tim. iv. 15, Tit. ii. 10, where notice v. 1.). But in Phil. iv. 12 we find the rather surprising phrase ἐν παντὶ καὶ ἐν πᾶσιν: and this makes us ask whether we ought not to recognise, instead of a discrepancy, a gradual *transition* from one habit of speech to the other.

Pastoral Epp., at least, it is one that should be investigated without prejudice. Ephesians, if not really St. Paul's, may be thought likely to have been forged in order to gain the authority of his name for theological speculations: but it is far likelier that the Pastoral Epp., if written not by the Apostle but (like the works which we compare with them, pp. 47 sqq.) by friends and disciples of his, were written without any fraudulent intent. To a writer of the period, it would appear as legitimate an artifice to compose a letter as to compose a speech in the name of a great man whose sentiments it was desired to reproduce and record : the question which seems so important to us, whether the words and even the sentiments are the great man's own or only his historian's, seems then hardly to have occurred either to writer or readers. Now the Pastoral Epp. are undoubtedly so ancient, and so like St. Paul, that their author may be presumed to have known well the events and the sentiments of the close of his life. If we have in them not the Apostle's own utterance, but only the record of a disciple, we need not doubt that that disciple was aided in recording them, after the fashion of his time, by the same divine Spirit that dwelt in the Apostle himself.

CHAPTER IV.

THE EPISTLE TO THE HEBREWS.

THE language as well as the thought of the Epistle to the Hebrews * has affinities on the one hand with the other books of the N. T., most of all, perhaps, with the two books ascribed to St. Luke ; on the other with the apocryphal Book of the Wisdom of Solomon, and with the voluminous works of Philo, the Jewish philosopher of Alexandria, who was an elder contemporary of the Apostles. Christian readers, who have taken the former affinity for granted, are liable when they discover the latter to exaggerate it. Ancient biblical critics suggested (perhaps as early as the supposed Greek original of the Muratorian fragment, certainly by the time of St. Augustine) that Philo might be the author of Wisdom. One of the modern critics (Dean Plumptre improving on Noack) has suggested that the author of Hebrews may have written Wis-

---

* It lies of course beyond the limits of our subject to discuss any of the doubtful questions as to the origin of this Epistle. But in using the common title we cannot help remembering that it *means* (be the theory meant right or wrong) that it is addressed to the Hebrew or Aramaic-speaking Jews (see Acts vi. 1) of Palestine and the further East. It is of course conceivable that an Apostle of the Gentiles (whether St. Paul or one of his colleagues) should have written to them ; just as St. James wrote from Jerusalem in Greek " to the Twelve Tribes in the Dispersion."

dom before his conversion or at least before his complete introduction to the Gospel. But the latter theory, if less absurd than the former, is almost more incredible. Philo is not indeed a writer to be treated merely with contempt. He was a sincerely religious man; his theological meditations are often dignified, sometimes even suggestive; in ethical philosophy he seems to have made a real step of progress, in bringing forward the question of the freedom of the will, in its relation both to the uniform order of nature and to the omnipotence of divine grace. He was also a learned man, well read in Greek philosophy, and wrote, for a Jew, very pure Greek. Dr. Hort says that he is hardly more to be called a Hellenistic writer than Polybius. But though his form is classical and his matter is not worthless, he is on the whole a tedious and stupid writer; and his method of treating Scripture is something worse than stupid. It is utterly incredible that he could ever have attained either to the spiritual insight or to the magnificent style (whether we call it eloquence or poetry) which characterise the Book of Wisdom.

In that book, the vocabulary is in general pure Greek, but very far from classical Attic; late words and forms on the one hand, and words and forms exclusively poetical, sometimes archaic, on the other are extensively used. And in the style the Jewish element is much larger than in the vocabulary. The book has a parallelistic structure, imitated from the poetical portions of the O. T. which is consistently maintained in the earlier part, and never entirely dropped; one may say that it is written in the form of Hebrew poetry with the diction of Greek. And the grammar, though not incorrect, has the monotony of the Hellenistic style—the order of words, in particular, being hardly ever varied. On the whole we may say that Philo, as he could not have written so good a book, so would not have consented to write in no better language.

Our Ep., in its turn, differs from Wisdom almost in the same way as that differs from Philo: it is more spiritual, and less classical—we may even say less literary. We must not understand this, indeed, as implying any weakness or defect in even the natural or intellectual gifts of the writer. No one could desire higher eloquence than the eleventh and twelfth chapters, or deeper pathos than the middle of the fifth. But the apostolic gravity with which these passages are earnestly and exclusively directed to their object is utterly different from the spirit, serious and even religious, yet primarily literary, in which the author of Wisdom accumulates magnificent imagery to illustrate the despair of the Egyptians at the Plague of Darkness, or of the ungodly at the approach of death and judgment. Nor is the difference merely such as might be found in one mind before and after the gift of the Spirit, or the human influence of "more perfect exposition of the Way of God." We feel as much that the natural gifts of the Jewish writer are, if not higher, different from those of the Christian as we do that the latter uses his in a more excellent way. And, without doubting that the author of Wisdom had, as truly as the historical Solomon, sought and obtained true wisdom from God, we may venture to say that he would have had something to unlearn as well as to learn, before he could enter the Church of Christ. The Cross would have been no stumbling-block to the author of the second chapter; but the calling of the Gentiles would have been to the author of the eleventh.

It is therefore only with considerable reserves, that the Epistle can be spoken of as a work of the school of Philo: perhaps (as already suggested) it bore the same relation to his school as the other Pauline Epistles to the school of Gamaliel. In one point, at least, the earnest religious purpose of our Epistle necessitates a considerable difference in its style from that of the works we have been comparing with it: it makes much more extensive use of the O. T., and so is more conformed to it, even in its most original parts The literary form of the Book of Wisdom made direct quotation impossible: even when there is as close imitation of it as in v. 18 (cf. Isa. lix. 17) it is not long sustained. Philo, on the contrary, has occasion to quote the O. T. largely: many of his works are commentaries on portions of it, and he cannot but cite the words of the text that he is commenting on, or other passages illustrative of it. But the proportion of text to comment is very small: the spirit of the comment is so little ruled by that of the text, that there is no likelihood that the style should be: and in fact, though it would be unjust to charge Philo with being ashamed of his Greek Bible, which it is the object of all his writings to hold up to reverence as a fountain of wisdom surpassing that of all Gentile philosophers, we may yet say that he so handles the words of the LXX. as to produce the *minimum* of incongruity with his own carefully classicised language. A very characteristic instance of the difference between the two writers is supplied by their commentaries on the same passage, Gen. ii. 2, 3 (*Philo de Legis Alleg.*, I. 3, Heb. iv. 4-10).

Philo labours to find some subtlety of meaning that shall justify the use of the transitive form κατέπαυσεν. The Apostle* knows perfectly well that the form is properly transitive,† and uses it so in ver. 8; but he takes the intransitive use in the text as it stands, and even uses the word in the same sense himself (ver. 10), where his sense can better be brought home to his readers by recalling the biblical expression.

Thus if Philo be not a Hellenistic writer, there is no doubt that our Apostle is. But of Hellenistic writers he is the freest from the monotony that is the chief fault of Hellenistic compared with literary Greek; his words do not follow each other in a mechanically necessary order, but are arranged so as to emphasize their relative importance, and to make the sentences effective as well as intelligible.‡ One may say that he deals with the biblical language (understanding by this the Hellenistic dialect founded on the LXX., not merely his actual quotations from it) neither as a rhetorician on the one hand nor as a mere commentator on the other, but rather as a preacher, whose first duty is to be faithful, but his second to be eloquent.

The affinities of this Ep. with the acknowledged ones of St. Paul are, as regards the greater part of it, theological or at most intellectual, rather than

* This seems an allowable form of designating the unknown author. Of persons with whom he has been identified, St. Barnabas certainly bears the title in Scripture; St. Clement of Rome by implication denies it to Apollos, but later (yet still early) Church usage would probably have extended it to him, as it did to St. Luke and St. Clement himself.

† There are, however, one or two examples of the intr. use even in pure Attic.

‡ xii. 11, with δικαιοσύνης at the end, is an extreme instance.

grammatical or literary. It is only in the last c. that we have traces readily perceptible of St. Paul's manner. The resemblance in form as well as matter of the earlier vv. to Rom xii. 9 sqq. cannot be accidental: note the adjectives τίμιος and ἀφιλάργυρος, and the ptcp. ἀρκούμενοι, constructed as predicates, and meant to be understood as imperatives. Quite in St. Paul's manner, too, is the interpretation of a theological postscript (vv. 8-16), connected with the subject of the body of the Ep., after ethical exhortation, and in conjunction with personal appeals (17-19). And the last few verses are, in thought and tone, so like St. Paul, that any one who thinks the Epistle was written in his name and under his direction would have no difficulty in supposing that these few words, at least, came from his own mouth or hand.

And yet if it were so, it would be strange that even these few verses contain three words or phrases never elsewhere used by St. Paul, while all are by St. Luke, two being peculiar to him (τὸν λόγον τῆς παρακλήσεως, ἐπέστειλα, ἀπολελυμένον). Here we become conscious of a caution necessary in comparing the language of two writings—that we must not be satisfied with an instinctive sense of their likeness or unlikeness in the general, intangible qualities of "style," nor again with a merely mechanical enumeration of words and phrases peculiar to each, common to both, or common to either with other works. Such mechanical study is required, but it is only as supplying material for a further process: literary instinct—sometimes an understanding of qualities that are more than literary—is needed if we are to judge whether common or individual expressions do or do not indicate common or individual peculiarities of thought.

For instance, the subst. ἁγιότης is found in Heb. xii. 10, and in the true text of 2 Cor. i. 12. But the language of our Ep. is not appreciably more like that of St. Paul than if we there read ἁπλότητι with the T. R.: nor is it the less like, that in three other places he uses the equivalent form ἁγιωσύνη. All that the facts prove is this: the N. T. writers (all except St. James*) have, naturally, frequent occasion to speak of being "holy:" but the use of the abstract subst. "holiness" was comparatively rare, and no uniform usage was arrived at, as to which of the possible terminations should be employed. On the other hand, it is surely more than a coincidence, that νενεκρωμένος is used in Rom. iv. 19, Heb. xi. 12, both times of Abraham; the argument is scarcely weakened by the fact that St. Paul elsewhere uses νεκροῦν (Col. iii. 5) and νέκρωσις (2 Cor. iv. 10) in a different sense, or at least a different context. Again, it would not be quite unimportant, that the word καταργεῖν in Heb. ii. 14 is elsewhere (except for Luke xiii. 7, where it has a quite different sense) exclusively Pauline; but this would not prove much. But something is proved by the coincidence both of language and thought, between this passage in Heb. on the one hand, and on the other 1 Cor. xv. 26, 2 Tim. i. 10: especially when we have the similar application of Ps. viii. 6 just preceding the passages both in 1 Cor. and in Heb.

A comparison which neither neglects the labour

---

* And of course this exception is purely accidental. St. James of all men must have been familiar with the sense of ἅγιος as describing the purity required of the people of God, both in a ritual and a moral sense. Read his speech in Acts

of minute verbal analysis, nor refuses to subordinate its results to common sense and feeling for style, will lead us to the conclusion that the language of this Ep. has some features in common with that of St. Paul, but that the resemblance not only is much less in language than in thought, but is almost entirely confined to that side of language where the line between it and thought is hardest to draw. In the instances just quoted, of νενεκρωμένος, καταργεῖν, perhaps ὑποτάσσειν, language as well as thought is akin; of resemblances purely verbal, perhaps the chief is the use of the comp. adv. περισσοτέρως in Heb. ii. 1, xiii. 19, ten times in St. Paul, and nowhere else in the N. T. (in Mark xv. 14 read περισσῶς). Next to this we may rank the use of νυνί or νῦν in the sense "as things actually are." We have νυνί in Heb. viii. 6, ix. 26 (best text : but in xi. 16 νῦν has overwhelming evidence): nowhere else in the N. T. except in St. Paul's Epp., and once or twice in his speeches in the Acts. νῦν seems to have the meaning named in Luke xix. 42 ; John viii. 40, ix. 41, xv. 22, 24 ; Acts x. 5, xxii. 1 (v. l. νυνί); James iv. 16 ; but constantly in St. Paul (*e.g.* Rom. iii. 21, 1 Cor. vii. 14, 2 Cor. vii. 9, Col. i. 24) and three times in this Ep. (ii. 8, xi. 16, xii. 26). Counting the two forms together (as there is often a doubt which should stand), we have this sense of "now" five times in Hebrews, some twenty times in St. Paul's Epistles, twice in his speeches, five times in St. John, and only three times in the rest of the N. T. Καθάπερ, instead of καθώς, is only found in the N. T. in St. Paul (eleven times) and in Heb.

xv., and compare with it Lev. xi. 44-5. We notice that he and St. Peter use the similar word ἁγνίζω in a moral sense, Acts only in a ritual, St. John in both.

THE EPISTLE TO THE HEBREWS. 47

iv. 2 (in v. 4 we should probably read the unusual καθώσπερ).

Again, in Heb. ii. 11 ἐξ ἑνὸς πάντες, vi. 12 μιμηταί (cf. xiii. 17), the expressions as well as the thoughts remind us of St. Paul; μιμηταί is, in fact, peculiar to him, for in 1 Pet. iii. 13 we should read ζηλωταί. We are inclined to say the same of καύχημα in Heb. iii. 6; but seeing that St. James has καυχᾶσθαι and καύχησις, it is hardly certain that this has any significance. The use of ὑπόστασις in Heb. iii. 14, perhaps in xi. 1, is the same as in 2 Cor. ix. 4, xi. 17: but we notice that St. Paul happens to use the word only in one of his writings, and that in Heb. it occurs once at least (i. 3) in quite a different sense. The quasi-adverbial τὰ πρὸς τὸν Θεόν "to God-ward" of Heb. ii. 17, v. 1, is just like Rom. xv. 17, in form as well as in context. But when we come to resemblances like those of Heb. vi. 9 to Rom. xv. 14, or vii. 18 to Rom. viii. 3, Gal. iv. 9, are we to count these as resemblances of language, or only of temper and doctrine? The same may be said of the similar use of O. T. texts in Heb. ii. 8 sqq., 1 Cor. xv. 27-8; Heb. x. 30, Rom. xii. 19. Certainly the likeness of Heb. iii. 13 to Rom. vii. 11, Eph. iv. 22 is of the latter kind.

One curious fact, perhaps a suggestive one, is that this Ep. has several words and phrases in common, not with St. Paul's writings generally, but with the isolated and peculiar group of the Pastoral Epistles.† If this stood alone, it might at most serve so far to narrow speculation as to the authorship of our Ep., as to suggest that it is by a man whose intercourse with St. Paul had been chiefly towards the close of the latter's life.

But we are led a step further, when we observe

48 LANGUAGE OF THE NEW TESTAMENT.

that a number of words and phrases are common to the Pastoral Epp. and Hebrews with St. Luke, or to Heb. and St. Luke only. Our first thought might be, that Origen was right—that St. Luke was the author of Heb. with or without suggestions from St. Paul, and that he may have been (in view of 2 Tim. iv. 11 no one else could be) the amanuensis, or something more, of the Pastoral Epp. But this view will not really bear serious examination. Marked as are the resemblances of phraseology between the three writers, they are resemblances of phraseology alone; they do not extend to those qualities of style in respect of which "the style is the man." Theologically, there is hardly a nearer approach to Heb. in the Pastoral than in the earlier Pauline Epp.; in St. Luke perhaps there may be, but St. Luke has a personality of his own, as difficult to identify with that of this author as St. Paul's. He was, no doubt, an eminently versatile writer. He could tell a story after the manner of the O. T. or after the manner of a classical historian, as suited best with its subject-matter; he could report a speech after the manner of a Hebrew Rabbi or of a Greek rhetorician; and it may be rash to say that he *could* not have written a hortatory work in the style of Hebrews. But when we compare Acts xiii. 38-41, xxviii. 17-28 with Heb. iii. 12-iv. 13, not to say with vi. 4-12, we see that St. Luke *did* not in fact write like Hebrews, even in hortatory passages.

And moreover we find that the group of N. T. writings marked by these verbal affinities is not confined to these three authors; it includes the two Epp. of St. Peter, perhaps to some extent others of the Catholic Epp., and the appendix or conclusion to

THE EPISTLE TO THE HEBREWS. 49

St. Mark's Gospel. It is of course impossible to ascribe all these works to one writer; but all (if both St. Peter's be genuine) must be ascribed to one time, approximately the years 64-8, and most of them are certainly or probably connected with one place, viz. Rome. In Appendix I., Table 3, is given a list of words and phrases peculiar, in the N. T., to this group of writings. Students must judge whether they are numerous enough and significant enough to support the suggestion, that as Hellenistic Greek has a special vocabulary of its own—as N. T. Greek has peculiarities of vocabulary specialised from other Hellenistic Greek—so this group of writings has a vocabulary specialised from other N. T. Greek, and marking it as the product of a group of writers in closer intercourse with each other than existed between all Christian brethren.

It may however be worth while here to mention some phrases where the affinity between the works under discussion is more than verbal—where it extends to common thoughts and common doctrine. Perhaps it would be rash to say that we have such an affinity to St. Luke in the solemn passage, Heb. v. 7-10; if only because of the doubtful state of the text in St. Luke's account of the Agony. But we have a real resemblance to St. Luke, and one only less marked to St. Peter, in the use in Heb. of πάσχειν without an object of "the Passion" of Christ. Not counting Luke ix. 22 (πολλὰ παθεῖν: this passage has two parallels in each of the other Synoptic Gospels), xxiv. 26 (ταῦτα . . . παθεῖν), nor Acts iii. 18, we have Luke xxii. 15, xxiv. 46 (but here with οὕτως, cf. Matt. xvii. 12), Acts i. 3, xvii. 3, to compare with Heb. ii. 18, (v. 8?), ix. 26, xiii. 12. St. Paul uses πάσχω absolutely three times,

4

(1 Cor. xii. 26, Phil. i. 29, 2 Thess. i. 5), but never of Christ; though he speaks twice at least (2 Cor. i. 5, 7, Phil. iii. 10) of His παθήματα. We have the absolute use of the verb eleven times in St. Peter's First Epistle: of these passages three (ii. 21, 23, iv. 1 a—in iii. 18 read ἀπέθανεν) refer to the sufferings of Christ, and six (ii. 19, 20, iii. 14, 17, iv. 19, v. 10) to those of Christians; one (iv. 1 b) indirectly to the former, and one (iv. 15) to the latter. We may think it no mere accident that, while the occasion and object of St. Peter's Epistle leads him oftenest to couple the sufferings of the Head and the members, St. Luke and Heb. coincide in taking up that side of his language which is wanting in St. Paul— wanting, that is, as regards form: but see Col. i. 24. But the importance and significance of points like these must be judged by "him that is spiritual," not by the mere grammarian, or even the mere literary critic.

Thrice at least in this Ep. (i. 1, 2, v. 5, xii. 25) divine revelations are described as "God speaking." The same phrase occurs twice in St. Luke's Gospel (i. 55, 70), four times in Acts, elsewhere only John ix. 29: the nearest approach anywhere else in the N. T. being Rom. iii. 19. If we extend our view to cases where λαλεῖν is used of such revelations, but "God" not directly named as the speaker, the proportionate usage of St. Luke and this Ep. will remain much the same; only we shall get many more passages from St. John to couple with ἐλάλησεν ἐν Υἱῷ of Heb. i. 2.

Ἀρχηγός is used twice in Acts, twice in our Ep., always of Christ; once (Acts v. 31) absolutely, but coupled with σωτῆρα, which makes the parallel to Heb. ii. 10 (τὸν ἀρχηγὸν τῆς σωτηρίας αὐτῶν) almost closer than if it had a gen. as elsewhere.

THE EPISTLE TO THE HEBREWS. 51

Λύτρωσις is found only in Heb. ix. 12; Luke i. 68, ii. 38. Both writers have ἀπολύτρωσις (Heb. ix. 15, xi. 35, Luke xxi. 28) in common with St. Paul; but it seems that in St. Luke, not in our Ep., the distinction of sense between the words holds good which is recognised by St. Chrysostom (*In Rom. Hom.* XIV. [XV.] ad viii. 23).

A well-known feature of the doctrine of both writers makes it natural that ἱερατεία, the common biblical word for "priesthood," is peculiar to them (Luke i. 9, Heb. vii. 5) in the N. T.; though St. Peter has the cognate (*exclusively* biblical) ἱεράτευμα. But Heb. prefers the more classical ἱερωσύνη (vii. 11, 12, 14, 24); which is also used, though less often than ἱερατεία, in the LXX.

On one view, there is a similar significance in the use of ἀνάμνησις, which in the N. T. is confined to Luke xxii. 19, the parallel 1 Cor. xi. 24-5, Heb. x. 3. But many would say that the two uses are quite distinct.

The words μετέχειν and μέτοχος in ii. 14, iii. 1, 14, v. 13, vi. 4, vii. 13, xii. 8, are certainly characteristic of this Ep. (i. 9, from LXX., is hardly an instance co-ordinate with these; though there are other instances where it seems that the writer repeats a word often, because it had been suggested to him by a text that he has quoted). The use of the verb is common to Heb. with St. Paul (five times, all in 1 Cor.; but the abstract μετοχή in 2 Cor. vi. 14); that of the subst. only with St. Luke (v. 7), in whom however it has not a theological sense. St. Paul (like other N. T. writers) has the nearly synonymous κοινωνός: it has been suggested that in Philem. 17 he plays on the spiritual and the secular meanings of the word.

52 LANGUAGE OF THE NEW TESTAMENT.

It might seem a mere accident that 'Ερυθρὰ Θάλασσα is only named in Heb. xi. 29, Acts vii. 36. But the fact is really one instance of that method of treating the O. T. history which perhaps ought to be called Stephanic rather than Pauline. Certainly this gives significance to the use of πατριάρχης in Heb. vii. 4 ; Acts ii. 29, vii. 8, 9.

We have ἡγούμενος substantivally in the sense of "ruler," almost always of *spiritual* office, in Heb. xiii. 7, 17, 24 ; Luke xxii. 26, Acts vii. 10, xiv. 12, perhaps xv. 22. But perhaps we ought not to say that the word is in the N. T. peculiar to these two writers ; for Matt. ii. 6, though a quotation, is not from the LXX.

More purely verbal points of resemblance are, in one sense, of more importance than these that have more religious interest. If teachers of the same Gospel use the same words to express the same doctrine, this does less to prove personal connexion than if they use the same words where doctrine is not involved. The purely verbal features common to St. Luke and Hebrews will be found in the Appendix. In estimating the importance of the facts there given, it would be absurd to pretend that all of them are significant. Common words like διαβαίνειν, words cognate with others in use (*e.g.* the table itself shows that writers who do not use παροικεῖν have πάροικος and παροικία), and words used by the LXX. like ἔντρομος, certainly formed part of the vocabulary of other N. T. writers than those in whom we find them. But though almost any one instance might be fortuitous, the effect of all is cumulative ; we see that St. Luke's language * has more in common

* It is worth noticing, that ἦχος is declined differently

THE EPISTLE TO THE HEBREWS. 53

with that of Hebrews than any other canonical writer, and that the Pastoral Epp. come next in affinity.

Leaving the features which our Ep. shares with one or another of the N. T. writings, we come to those peculiar to itself. Most of these are such as may be referred to its general character already noted, as being more literary, in a sense more rhetorical, than any of the rest. Here only in the N. T. (unless we count Acts xxvi. 14—not ix. 5, πρὸς κέντρα λακτίζειν) do we get classical semi-proverbial phrases, such as ἔμαθεν ἀφ' ὧν ἔπαθεν (v. 8), ὡς ἔπος εἰπεῖν (vii. 9).* With these we may couple idiomatic periphrases like ἔχειν στάσιν (ix. 8), perhaps ἔχειν κράτος (ii. 14), ἀρχὴν λαβεῖν (ii. 3), πεῖραν λαβεῖν (xi. 29, 36); the constr. of λανθάνειν in xiii. 2; the use of participles in a conditional sense (ii. 3); and of particles like δήπου (ii. 16), ἐάν περ (iii. 6 *si vera l.*, iii. 14, vi. 3; καί περ (v. 8, vii. 5, xii. 17, only twice besides in true text of N. T.), with their proper and distinctive meanings; we note καθώσπερ in v. 4, related to the common καθώς as καθάπερ to the more classical καθά, and may add the comparative frequency of the conjunction τε. The art. too is used idiomatically and on the whole correctly, in its varied positions. But the use in xii. 25 (true text) is perhaps questionable, as it seemed to transcribers; that in vi. 7 is just within the limits of what

in Luke xxi. 25 (iv. 37 and Acts ii. 2 prove nothing) and in Heb. xii. 19; and that the pl. θεμέλια is found in Acts xvi. 26, but θεμελίους in Heb. xi. 10.

* It may or may not be thought characteristic, that κατὰ νόμον in viii. 4 (true text), and perhaps in ix. 19, is as capable of being read in the classical sense as in the Judaic. But in x. 8 (true text) the latter only is admissible.

54 LANGUAGE OF THE NEW TESTAMENT.

is correct and significant. The position either of the art. or of the adj. serves to indicate a secondary predicate in vi. 20, and tertiary predicates in vi. 5, vii. 24, x. 23.* The neut. adj. is used with the art. in an abstract sense in vi. 17, vii. 3, 18 ; note the use of εἰς τὸ διηνεκές in x. 1, 12, 14, which seems to be an idiom rather of secular contemporary Greek than of the purest classical.

Of grammatical irregularities we get hardly any ; the hortative use of the ptcp. in xiii. 5 can hardly be called one, as the associated adjectives are perfectly regular. The *case* of ἀρκούμενοι in that place may be described as a *nominativus pendens ;* [σκιὰν ἔχων] ὁ νόμος in x. 1 rather as a nom. absol., for we should almost certainly read δύνανται just below. One hardly knows or cares whether κεφάλαιον in viii. 1 is to be called a nom. or an acc. : its constr., and the loose appositions of δικαιώματα in ix. 10 (true text), the double acc. (τὴν εἴσοδον . . . ἣν ἕνεκ. ὁδὸν) in x. 19, 20, if they do not fall under any distinct rule, are quite in the spirit of Greek grammar and idiom.

Once and once only, in vii. 1, the critical text presents a real anacoluthon. If we read ὃς συναντήσας there, ὅς stands as a subject without a verb. We must leave to the best critics—the best qualified in judgement as well as in technical learning—the question which is the likelier, that our highest authorities for the N. T. text have behind them such errors as OCCΤN for OCΤN, or that a very careful writer, in a very elaborate passage, once and once only lost his way in a crowd of secondary predicates, and never properly correlated them to the primary.

* ix. 1 is not included, as the constr. is doubtful : see p. 57, n.

THE EPISTLE TO THE HEBREWS. 55

One slight but noticeable characteristic of the style is a partiality for the perfect tense—perhaps especially for the participle passive. Deducting the twice-repeated γεγέννηκά σε of the quotation from Ps. ii., we have seventy-seven perfect tenses in this Ep.: in 1 Cor., which is longer in about the proportion of 4:3, we have only sixty-seven, including seven instances of the Pauline formula ὡς (or καθὼς) γέγραπται. Of passive participles only, the proportion is twenty-seven in Heb. to sixteen in Cor. As a rule, the perfects have the distinctive force of the tense: sometimes, as in x. 14 τετελείωκεν . . . τοὺς ἁγιαζομένους, its force is essential to the sense. But, while in the ptcp. the perf. and aor. naturally approximate in sense, it is hard to think that in the indic. the distinction is always consistently maintained. The εἴρηκέν ποτε of i. 13 might have been interchanged with the εἶπέν ποτε of ver. 5; still here there is a slight difference in the point of view, between "Has He ever said?" and "Did He ever say?" But it is hard to see even as much force as this in the tense of εἴρηκεν in iv. 3, 4. In vii. 13, 14 there is little doubt that the perfects are significant; the passage gains a great deal in vividness, when we notice how both the exclusiveness of the Levitical priesthood and the birth of the eternal Priest are regarded as matters of contemporary history. Even in vv. 6-9, just above, the proper force is not impossible. Melchizedek may be identified with his antitype, so that the argument will be, "Levi *hath* paid tithe to Christ." But in xi. 17, 28 it is hard to see how the tenses can be other than historical, or why they are introduced except to vary the long series of aorists. The sound principle in dealing with matters like this appears to be,

56 LANGUAGE OF THE NEW TESTAMENT.

never to miss noticing a grammatical refinement, but not always to insist on being able to find an exegetical refinement depending on it.

The vocabulary of the Ep., as is well known, differs from that of the rest of the N. T. at least as much as the style. And the difference is much of the same kind: it strikes us at once as more literary, more elaborate. On the other hand, being not only ἀνὴρ λόγιος, but δυνατὸς ὢν ἐν ταῖς γραφαῖς, he has several words found in the LXX., but which apparently, so far as the evidence of N. T. usage goes, did not form part of the ordinary vocabulary of even religious Hellenists. We proceed, not to give a list of the words peculiar to the Ep. (which may be found in the Appendix to Thayer's Grimm's Lexicon, or elsewhere), but to name such of them as illustrate one or other of the characteristics.

To the classicalising or Alexandrian side of his mind we may ascribe his fondness for sonorous, often significant compounds, such as μισθαποδότης and -σία, μετριοπαθεῖν, αἱματεκχυσία, συγκακουχεῖσθαι, συνδεδεμένοι, εὐπερίστατος.* One might add ὁρκωμοσία, which, though common in all Greek, does not occur elsewhere in the N. T., and only once in the LXX.: the rest of those named were probably coined in the Alexandrian school, if not by our writer himself. The same may be said of many of his negative epithets—ἀμετάθετος, ἀγενεαλόγητος, ἀκατάλυτος, ἀπαράβατος, (ἀναρίθμητος,) ἀλυσιτελής. Classical influences or tendencies show themselves in the use of words like νωθρός, ἄπειρος, ἕξις, αἰσθητήριον,

---

* The words in these lists are arranged in the order in which they occur in the Ep., unless they fall naturally into groups on some other principle (as *e.g.* μισθαποδότης of xi. 6 is coupled with μισθαποδοσία of ii. 2, x. 35)

ἀφομοιοῦσθαι, ἀκροθίνια, κατάδηλος (on πρόδηλος see note on p. 144), ἔγγυος, ἄθλησις, ἐνυβρίζειν, ἔλεγχος (really peculiar to this Ep. in the N. T.: in 2 Tim. iii. 16 read ἐλεγμόν), καρτερεῖν, εὐλαβεῖσθαι (in Acts xxiii. 10 read φοβηθεὶς), δημιουργὸς, ἐπιλείψει (ὁ χρόνος), νέφος, ὄγκος, ἀναλογίζεσθαι, ἀντικαταστῆναι, νόθος, ἀνταγωνίζεσθαι (καταγων. is late), μετέπειτα, φαντάζεσθαι, ὑπείκειν. The same may be said of the phrase φέρεσθαι ἐπί (vi. 1); of κεφάλαιον in the sense found in viii. 1; of ἀπολείπεται as used in iv. 6, 9, x. 20; of ἀναιρεῖν (x. 9) in the late classical sense of "do away with"; everywhere else in the N. T. it has a personal obj., and means "kill." Πρόδρομος (vi. 20) is also virtually a classical not a biblical word: in the LXX. it is only used of "first-ripe" fruit. Κοσμικόν in ix. 1 must have a different sense from that in Tit. ii. 12: *what sense is less certain.** Θεατρίζεσθαι (x. 33) has practically a N. T. parallel in the use of θέατρον in 1 Cor. iv. 9; but the word is unique, only paralleled by ἐκθεατρ. in Polyb. XI. viii. 7, etc. (*Id.* III. xci. 10 is an avowed simile, showing the use of the word to be new.)

Ἀσπάζεσθαι in xi. 13 has a sense that appears as early as Plato, and is common in late literary Greek but not in biblical. Πατέρες for "parents" (xi. 23) is late, but not distinctively Hellenistic. Κλίνω, "to put to flight" (xi. 34), is of course quite classical,

* Neither "a sanctuary of this world" opposed to a spiritual one, nor "one representing the material universe" seems a very relevant sense. It has been suggested that here, and in the very difficult passage *Doct. Apost.* xi. 11, κοσμικόν may be a subst., "ritual furniture," as κόσμος in Ecclus. l. 19 is used for "ritual." *If admissible*, this meaning would make the constr. of the biblical, and the sense of the ecclesiastical passage, much simpler.

58 LANGUAGE OF THE NEW TESTAMENT.

and perhaps was felt by the writer and readers of our Ep. to have an archaic or poetical effect. Ἀφορᾶν (xii. 2) is late, but modelled on the classical ἀποβλέπω: cf. ἀφίδω in Phil. ii. 23. Κάμνω (xii. 3) is unique in the N. T. (its presence in Rev. ii. 3 is a mere blunder) in the sense "to be weary"; though it has the (equally classical) sense "to be sick" in James v. 15. Προσφέρεσθαι, "to deal with, behave towards" (xii. 7), is perhaps more exclusively classical. We can hardly say that τρόπος, "character," in xiii. 3 is unbiblical in more than a formal sense: besides that this meaning and the common one of "manner" shade into each other, this is implied in τροποφορεῖν, if that be the true reading in Acts xiii. 18. Ἀθέτησις (vii. 18, ix. 26) and μετάθεσις (vii. 12, xi. 5, xii. 27) would hardly deserve notice, the cognate verbs being common, except as exemplifying the frequency of abstract terms. Almost the same might be said of τελειωτής: it is characteristic of our author's thought that he uses the verb so often, and perhaps, but in a less degree, characteristic of his style that he, without any precedent that we know of, coined the verbal subst. Προβλεψαμένου in xi. 40 is unique in form, not in meaning; the word προβλέπειν is rare, and the middle forms in the aor. of the simple βλέπω only late. We should have thought it mere accident that ἐκβαίνειν (xi. 15) is unique, had not editors or transcribers substituted ἐξῆλθον, as though more familiar. Of biblical words it may suffice to notice ἐγκαινίζω (ix. 18), which seems to be called back in sense towards the classical καινίζω; and εὐαρεστεῖν, which in xi. 5, 6 is virtually a quotation from the LXX., but the pass. in xiii. 16 is an extension of its use, by a quasi-classical licence. It may serve as an instance of the way that the author, having had occasion to use a word in or from an O. T. passage, often goes on dwelling on it, though the word was not (so far as we know) in very common use in Christian circles. Ἐκδοχή (x. 27) seems to mean "expectation": the subst. never has that meaning elsewhere, but "to expect" is the only N. T. meaning (a rare but not unknown one in other Greek) of the verb ἐκδέχεσθαι.

CHAPTER V.

THE CATHOLIC EPISTLES.

"THE letter of that specially Jewish Apostle, St. James," says Dr. Salmon, "is perhaps the best Greek in the New Testament." (*Introduction to N. T.*, Lect. x., p. 139, 3rd ed.) Without any of the studied rhetoric of the Epistle to the Hebrews, or the studied classicalism of parts of the Acts, it expresses correctly and intelligibly what the writer has to say. The sentences have not much variety of structure or idiomatic liveliness, but they do not strike us, like those of St. John, as constrainedly simple, or as monotonous in their connexion. And as the matter and literary (as distinct from the grammatical) style of the author rises to a very high order of eloquence, so his vocabulary is quite adequate to it. It is in this feature, indeed, that he comes nearest to the more self-conscious rhetoric of Hebrews: negative adjectives or compound words such as ἀδιάκριτος, ἀκατάστατος, ἀνέλεος, ἀπείραστος, δίψυχος, εὐπειθής, θανατηφόρος, πολύσπλαγχνος, σητόβρωτος, χαλιναγωγεῖν, χρυσοδακτύλιος are just in the manner of that work, though no words of the class are common to both Epp. The same may be said of idiomatic words like ἄγε (iv. 13, v. 1), ἔοικα (i. 6, 23), λείπεσθαι (i. 4, 5, ii. 15): we may add ὁρμή (iii. 4), which has quite a different sense

THE CATHOLIC EPISTLES. 61

from that of Acts xiv. 5, and is not, like that, directly correlative to the not uncommon verb ὁρμᾶν.

So again we have the philosophical terms ἀποσκίασμα, παραλλαγή, τροπή (i. 17), ὕλη and perhaps τροχός (iii. 5, 6), φύσις in a half concrete sense (iii. 7), and picturesque or even poetical expressions like ἀνεμίζεσθαι, ἀποκύειν, ἐνάλιος, εὐπρέπεια, μαραίνεσθαι, ῥιπίζεσθαι, φρίσσειν. All these are, within the N. T., peculiar to St. James;* there is a smaller but not unimportant group of words which he has in common with St. Luke only—ἀνάπτειν, ἀτμίς, βραδύς, ἕλκειν, ἐπιστρέφειν (transitive), καταδυναστεύειν, κλύδων, ὁμοιοπαθής, περιπίπτειν, πορεία, ὑποδέχεσθαι. Fewer and less significant are the words common to St. James with St. Paul only†—κακοπαθεῖν, κατακαυχᾶσθαι, ὄφελος (or indeed the more distinctive phrase τί τὸ ὄφελος ;), παραλογίζεσθαι, σπαταλᾶν.

There is less to be said about the grammar than the vocabulary; it has no striking features either of elegance or of irregularity. The only serious difficulty which the Epistle presents is to trace the connexion of the thoughts and subjects; but each sentence is clear in itself, and the relations of successive sentences are regular, if they are connected

---

* So, besides some words of less distinctive character, is ἔμφυτος (i. 21). It seems rash to take the word in a different sense from what it has everywhere else, even in Wisdom xii. 10. "Receive what is innate in you" is no doubt an oxymoron; but does it not express the true relation between creation in the divine image, and regeneration after that image (Col. iii. 10)?

† At least, they throw less light on the character of St. James' language. As regards St. Paul's, they have some interest, as forbidding us to regard the words as individualisms either of the undoubted Paul or of the conceivably different authors of Colossians and the Pastoral Epistles.

at all; we have (in the true text) several marked asyndeta. There are really no anacolutha: ὥστε in i. 19 (true text) can hardly be called one, though we should expect it to have a more clearly expressed object; still less can the καί in apodosi in iii. ·3 (reading εἰ δέ at the beginning of the verse).

Correct however as the Greek is, vigorous, and even elegant, it is decidedly Hellenistic Greek; it never comes as near as Hebrews or Acts to throwing off that character. Downright Hebraisms are few, but they exist—the adjectival gen. in i. 25, and perhaps in ii. 1, 4, the instrumental ἐν in iii. 9. The use of the aorists in i. 11, 24 is not to be ascribed either to the classical idiom of the "frequentative aorist," or (at any rate exclusively) to the way that the LXX. in Isa. xl. 7 has used the tense to reproduce the so-called Hebrew preterite; in both passages the simile passes into a parable,* "the history of a blade of grass," and of the man that looked in the mirror. We have an exactly similar use of the aor. in John xv. 6, in the παροιμία of the Vine. But the unclassical feature of the language is negative —the uniformity of the structure and sequence of words and clauses, the use of possessive suffixes, and the like. St. James has the common Jewish and Christian vocative ἀδελφοί fifteen times, and μου is added in all cases but four; St. Paul has the word about sixty times without the added pronoun and only

* Those who heard our Lord's parables, and who could not fail to have been struck by their beauty, and by the force with which they brought to the mind the lessons they were meant to convey, never, as far as we know, used the same method of impressing any lessons of their own." (Salmon, *Intr. to N. T.*, Lect. viii., p. 114.) Noting the richness and frequency of St. James' metaphors and similes, the slightness of his "parables" makes him an exception that proves the rule.

THE CATHOLIC EPISTLES. 63

nine times with it. The possessive adjectives never occur at all; and the gen. always follows the noun, except ὑμῶν twice, in i. 3 and v. 12.

St. Jude's short Epistle has much the same general characteristics as his brother's: his language is picturesque, very vigorous, fairly correct Greek, but Jewish Greek all the same. His ἅπαξ λεγόμενα are of much the same character—ἄπταιστος, γογγυστής, ἐκχυθῆναι metaphorically, ἐπαφρίζω, πλανήτης, σπιλάς, ὑπέχειν δίκην, φθινοπωρινός all fall under one or other of the heads to which we referred the peculiar words of St. James. Like St. James, too, he has some words which otherwise are exclusively Pauline—ἀΐδιος, κυριότης, οἰκητήριον, προγράφειν: but the difference in the use of some of these is really more important than the identity of form.

Ἀντιλογία, μεγαλωσύνη, παραφέρεσθαι are peculiar to Jude and Hebrews, so is προκεῖσθαι except for one passage in St. Paul, and ζόφος except for the parallels to this Ep. in 2 Peter. We note the Hebraistic ὀπίσω in ver. 7; in ver. 18 the gen. τῶν ἀσεβειῶν might be thought to be merely adjectival, but for the trajection of order, which shows the feeling of the sentence to be semi-classical.

The two Epistles bearing the name of St. Peter are most conveniently examined in connexion with these. It is true, neither of them has much resemblance to them in style; but it is certain that St. Jude is used in the composition of the Second Epistle, and hardly less so that St. James is similarly used in the First. This supplies a sort of link between the two, besides their common ascription, and the real though limited common element which has been traced in their language. Another common feature is, that both give evidence (though in different ways) of the use of St. Paul's Epistles: and we have already intimated a fourth—the approximation of their vocabulary to the later Pauline or sub-Pauline works—the Pastorals, St. Luke, and Hebrews. We do not here offer any opinion as to the genuineness of the Second Ep. Every one knows that its external attestation is the weakest of any book that was finally received into the N. T. Canon; and that there are obvious internal difficulties in ascribing it to the same author as the First Ep. But this common affinity to three groups of writings—the Hierosolymitan, the Pauline, and the sub-Pauline—seems easier to account for if we ascribe both to a date so early, that there can have been no motive, and hardly an opportunity, for forging St. Peter's name: at any rate, we have to state the facts, however their significance may be estimated. It may at least be said, on the one hand that no one can pretend (except on *a priori* theological grounds) to be certain that the Second Ep. is genuine; on the other, that a superficial student is likelier than a thorough student to be certain that it is spurious.

For the full evidence supplied by the vocabulary of these Epp. we must refer to the Appendix, but it may help the student to use and appreciate the materials there given, if we examine in detail the first two or three sentences of the First Ep. It does not prove much, that the word ἐκλεκτός, though common to all N. T. writers, except SS. James and Jude, is used in epistolary salutations only here and in Titus, besides the peculiar case of 2 John. The thought, and the cognate verb or noun, come in the first paragraph of Eph. and

THE CATHOLIC EPISTLES. 65

1 Thess. But παρεπίδημος is peculiar to this Ep. (here and ii. 11) and Heb. (xi. 13); πρόγνωσις * to this passage and Luke (Acts ii. 23—a speech, by the way, ascribed to St. Peter); ῥαντισμός to this passage and Heb. (xii. 24). Ἁγιασμός is not rare in St. Paul: in 2 Thess. ii. 13 we have the identical phrase ἐν ἁγιασμῷ πνεύματος: still it is worth noticing that we get the word in 1 Tim. ii. 15, Heb. xii. 14, and here. Ὑπακοή too is peculiar to St. Paul, Hebrews, and this Ep.

The form of benediction, χάρις ὑμῖν καὶ εἰρήνη πληθυνθείη, being peculiar to the two Epp. of St. Peter, is, if the Second be not genuine, directly imitated in it from the First. We notice, however, not only that πληθυνθείη is similarly used by St. Jude, but that it is *predominantly* a Lucan word; coming, besides these three Epp., five times in Acts, once in Heb. (but in a quotation, so this proves nothing); otherwise only once in St. Paul (2 Cor. ix. 10), and once in St. Matthew.

The phrase ἀνάστασις ἐκ νεκρῶν is (one may be surprised to learn) peculiar to this place and St. Luke (Luke xx. 35, Acts iv. 2). The force of this is weakened, but hardly destroyed, by our finding the cognate verbal phrase ἀναστῆναι ἐκ ν. in Mark ix. 9, 10 (*not* in the true text of vi. 14, nor of Matt. xvii. 9), xii. 25 (the parallel to Luke *l. c.*), John xx. 9, Eph. v. 14; as well as three times (including ix. 22, best text) in Luke and twice in Acts. Ἀμίαντος is common to this Ep. with Heb. (vii. 26, xiii. 4) and James (i. 27); ἀμάραντος (and ἀμαράντινος further on), though peculiar to this, are comparable

---

* Προγινώσκω also comes once in Acts (xxvi. 5), twice in St. Paul (Rom. viii. 29, xi. 2), once in this Ep. (i. 20), and once in 2 Pet. (iii. 17).

with the long poetical epithets which we have noticed as characteristic of both those. Τετηρημένος εἰς is peculiar to the *two* Petrine Epp.; but τηρεῖν εἰς is found in John xii. 7, as well as Acts xxv. 21. Φρουρεῖν of the divine protection is peculiar to Peter and Paul (Phil. iv. 7, and perh. Gal. iii. 23). Ἕτοιμος never is joined with a simple inf. (ἐν ἑτοίμῳ ἔχοντες ἐκδικῆσαι in 2 Cor. x. 6 is hardly an instance) except in 1 Pet. i. 5, Luke xxii. 33 (cf. Acts xxiii. 15); with πρός, it comes only in 1 Pet. iii. 15, Tit. iii. 1. Ἑτοίμως ἔχω with inf. is found in Acts, Paul, and 1 Peter, once in each.

But whatever be the common or separate affinities of the two Petrine Epistles in vocabulary or in thought, in style each of them has marked features of its own, separating them both from each other and from any of the other works with which we have been comparing them. Perhaps the First Epistle is least unlike St. James', in purely formal and linguistic structure; but the unlikeness is not small. St. Peter's language is stronger where St. James is weak, and weaker where he is strong—it is more varied, more nearly classical, but less eloquent and of less literary power. We notice the accumulation of epithets on a single subst. (i. 4, 18, ii. 2), or of adjectives and participles as predicates (i. 19-20, ii. 5, ii. 18-iii. 1-7-8, iv. 8-11); the frequent and correct use of the various idioms by which the art. indicates the relation of words as secondary or tertiary predicates, according to its position. See *e.g.* i. 7—τοῦ . . . δοκιμαζομένου gives an instance, whatever we may think of the earlier words which, as they stand, come *verbatim* from St. James—9, 10, 11, 13, 14, 17; ii. 12, iii. 3, 7, v. 13, etc. In many of these passages, where a dependent word or clause

THE CATHOLIC EPISTLES. 67

is inserted between the art. and the subst., it would have been more natural in Hellenistic Greek, sometimes perhaps in classical, to postpone the word or clause, and repeat the art. with it. *E.g.* in iii. 3 it would have been more natural to St. Paul to write ὧν ὁ κόσμος ἔστω μὴ ὁ ἔξωθεν (ὁ) ἐν ἐμπλοκῇ κ.τ.λ., and perhaps it would have been clearer and more elegant to have written so; but in ver. 7 ὡς ἀσθενεστέρῳ σκεύει τῷ γυναικείῳ is certainly best as it stands, though only the most elegant of the N. T. writers would have put it so.

A strong test of the individuality of St. Peter's manner is this—that he works up texts, sometimes a whole series of texts, from the LXX. into sentences of his own, which sentences, though so largely composed of borrowed material, have the decided impress of his own style. It is thus that, while he almost indubitably uses both St. James' Ep. and some of St. Paul's, he has no very close likeness of style to either. Perhaps the participles in ii. 18, iii. 1 are influenced by the way that ὑποτασσόμενοι in Eph. v. 22 (true text) is carried on into the following clause; still more probably, those in iv. 8-10, and perhaps in iii. 8, 9, are more or less consciously imitated from Rom. xii. We hardly know whether, from a few hints in the Acts and in St. Paul's Epistles, we are entitled to say that St. Peter held a central and harmonising position between the schools of thought headed by St. Paul and St. James; but it is certain that in his Ep., as he makes use impartially of both St. Paul's and St. James' writings, so he holds a central position between the centripetal tendency of N. T. Greek—its approximation to its scriptural or Hebraistic basis —and the centrifugal force that tended to assimi-

68 *LANGUAGE OF THE NEW TESTAMENT.*

late it to such Greek as was written in the western world.

In the Second Ep. we see the same two tendencies in operation, and the fact that the Hebraising element is so unquestionable seems to forbid us, at any rate, to ascribe the work to a very late date. There are few definite Hebraisms, though we may count as such ἐν ἐμπαιγμονῇ ἐμπαῖκται (iii. 3), and perhaps κατάρας τέκνα (ii. 14), though for the Hebraism to be perfect we ought to have had the governing word before the gen. But the simple structure and unvaried order of the sentences marks the tone of the book as Hellenistic not Hellenic; and not the less so, because there are several signs of a special effort being made at classicalism. In truth, it seems that the writer* aimed at a more elegant and classical style than he could master—that he was too ambitious to be correct. We have sentences begun with participial construction that never get an apodosis (i. 3, 4 ; 17—the shortness of the latter sentence leaves

---

* If the most that can be said against these faults of style be admitted, nothing can be inferred either for or against the Petrine authorship. Tradition tells us that St. Peter employed more than one interpreter ; it is indeed hard not to think that we have the work of one in the First Ep. Is it credible that a Galilean fisherman who left out his H's (that, we are told, is what Matt. xxvi. 73, implies) should after middle life, and in the midst of absorbing occupation, have learnt to write scholarly Greek like this ? And if he employed more than one, one of them may have had weaknesses of taste, or even of character, that show themselves in the form of his writings, without making their matter less valuable ; or again such faults of judgment or of character are not surprising in the author of a pious fraud. The student may compare Dr. Abbott's criticisms on the style of the Ep. (*Expositor* for 1882, 2nd Series, vol. iii.) with Archdeacon Farrar's comments (*ibid.* pp. 401 sqq.), and with Dr. Salmon's reply in his *Introduction to the N. T.* The text above states what appears to myself to be the residuum of truth in Dr. Abbott's strictures.

less excuse for its incompleteness); or (what indeed proves less) participles introduced in the course of a sentence which either are very loosely constructed with it (iii. 3), or overload its construction, and confuse the principal verbs (ii. 12-16). So too with the choice of individual phrases, and the selection or even coinage of words. If ταρταροῦν had been a verb in ordinary Hellenic use, there was no reason why Jewish or Christian writers need shrink from using it, as they used the almost equally mythological word ᾅδης, to express the analogous doctrine of their own eschatology: but a Christian would hardly coin the word, except by a conscious effort at Hellenism. Then the senses in which we find καυσούμενα used in iii. 10, 12, and βλέμματι in ii. 8, seem to show both a fondness for uncommon words, and an imperfect knowledge of their idiomatic use. Ἀκατάπαυστος (ii. 14) is a peculiar and unobvious formation; παραφρονία (ii. 16) and ἐμπαιγμονή (iii. 3) seem to be formed on false analogies; ὄγδοον Νῶε (ii. 5) is at least doubtful Greek for Νῶε ὄγδοον αὐτόν; and phrases like μνήμην ποιεῖσθαι (i. 15), and perhaps εἰς μετάνοιαν χωρῆσαι (iii. 9) are studied rather than natural. Full weight must be given to the fact, that none of the Fathers who had an instinctive knowledge of Greek idiom remark on these faults of style (as Dionysius of Alexandria did on those of the Apocalypse) in discussing the genuineness of the writing. But it seems an uncalled-for diffidence in the power of modern scholarship, to refuse to say that we see in this Ep. compared with the First, at once less instinctive familiarity with Greek idiom and more conscious effort at elegant Greek composition.

CHAPTER VI.

THE FOURTH GOSPEL AND JOANNINE EPISTLES.

IN a passage which forms one of the most admirable, as well as the earliest, models of what biblical criticism ought to be,* Dionysius of Alexandria states the difficulties in the way of ascribing the Revelation of St. John to the same author as the other N. T. writings bearing his name. After enumerating the peculiarities of theological language characteristic of the latter, but absent in the former, he proceeds, "further, one may also argue from the difference of language of the Gospel and Epistle compared with the Revelation. For they are written, not only without error in the Greek language, but with the greatest literary skill in the words, the reasonings, the arrangements of the exposition; far from there being any barbarous word, ungrammatical phrase, or in fact vulgarism of any sort found there. For he had, as it seems, both forms of the Word, the Lord having granted him both, the word of knowledge and that of utterance.† But to this author [viz. of Rev.] I will not deny that he had seen a revelation, and received knowledge and prophecy; but I can see that his

* Ap. *Eus. H. E.*, VII. xxv.
† The writer probably has 1 Cor. i. 5 in his head, though he uses φράσις for St. Paul's λόγος.

ST. JOHN: GOSPEL AND EPISTLES. 71

dialect and language are not correct Greek, but that he uses barbaric constructions, sometimes ungrammatical. These," he adds, "it is not necessary now to recount: for I do not say this for ridicule—let no one suppose it, but only as defining the unlikeness of the writings."

A modern critic would hardly go as far as Dionysius in praise of the mere style of the Gospel and Epp.; we can see what he meant by it, and that he had real grounds to go upon, but his instinct in perceiving the difference between them and the Apocalypse was sounder than his analysis of the qualities in which they differ. That is the most Hebraistic of the N. T. books; these perhaps are the least so, if we judge of St. Luke's writings— even the Acts—as wholes, and not by selected passages. But if these are the least Hebraistic books, it does not follow that they are the most elegant or the most nearly classical. We may say of them the very reverse of what we said of 2 Peter; if there the style is too ambitious to be correct, here we feel it to be correct only on condition of being unambitious. No sentences are attempted but such as are short, simple, and straightforward in constr., so that the writer runs no risk of going astray in them. If he has, as he very often has, more to say on a subject than will go into one short and simple sentence, he does not amplify the sentence with subordinate clauses, but dwells on or recurs to its theme in fresh parallel sentences. We have rather extreme cases of this in Ep. I. i. 8, 10; ii. 7; 12-13, 14; but these are only extreme instances of a habit general throughout this Ep. and the next, and the speeches and reflexions in the Gospel—a habit of what at first sight we are disposed to call self-repetition, until we see that there is always something added by the second sentence to the first.

The method is not elegant, is not literary; but the result is always worth having: we are afraid to ascribe such self-repetition as this to the mere infirmities of old age. The simplicity of St. John's structure of sentences necessarily involves a general uniformity among them, so that we have few individual features to note in his grammar or style. There are indeed exceptions to his grammatical regularity, but so few and slight that almost all are disguised by the insensible corrections of popular texts. In i. 6, ὄνομα αὐτῷ Ἰωάνης hardly amounts to an anacoluthon. If more than an asyndeton, we might call it a Hebraism: it has been observed that the prologue is more Hebraistic than the main body of the Gospel. But in i. 15 the text which appears best attested gives a strangely broken sentence, such as has found favour neither with ancient nor with modern editors, between Origen and Westcott and Hort. In vi. 22, among the arguments that go to prove that St. John wrote εἶδον not ἰδών is the fact that it gives us two straightforward sentences, instead of a long and unmanageable parenthesis. In x. 12, the textual evidence points more decidedly to a reading which involves, not indeed an anacoluthon, but a rather harsh parenthesis. So in Ep. I. ii. 20 there is little doubt that we should read πάντες; and if that be adopted, it seems best to read and punctuate with Westcott and Hort, supposing an aposiopesis or anacoluthon, whichever we like to call it. In Ep. I. iii. 20, while there seems no doubt that the double ὅτι should be read, it is surely better to suppose the second to be redundant than, by making the first a pron., to destroy the symmetry with the next sentence.

Except in the prologue to the Gospel, and χαρι̂ χαίρει in iii. 29, we have hardly any downright Hebraism.* Instead of the frequent καί of Hellenistic narrative, we have habitual asyndeta—softened often, but less often in the primitive text than in the popular, by the particle οὖν, which apparently does not indicate much more than sequence, like St. Matthew's τότε. Still the Hebraic mode of thought, and the scriptural basis of theology, have their effect upon the language. We are reminded of St. Matthew again by the phrase ἵνα ἡ γραφὴ πληρωθῇ (xiii. 18, xvii. 12, xix. 24, 36: cf. xii. 38, xv. 25, also xviii. 9 and xix. 28, besides Mark xiv. 49) xix. 36 is just equivalent to St. Matthew's τοῦτο δὲ ὅλον γέγονεν ἵνα . . ., and like it compels us to dwell upon the final sense of the particle; and perhaps we ought to suspect that our own intelligence is more in fault than the writer's accuracy, if we fail to see the causal force of a γάρ like that in iv. 44. In xi. 6 the paradox of ὡς οὖν is certainly intentional.

While we feel that the style of these writings, far from being unworthy of their matter, is perfectly adapted to it, we may yet think that it is hardly such as to win admiration for its own sake, apart from that due to the matter. We may judge that Dionysius' λογιώτατα γέγραπται applies, not so much to what we should call *style* as to the choice of language on the one hand, and the composition—those elements of authorship where form and matter

---

* Υἱοὶ φωτός in xii. 36, and ὁ υἱὸς τῆς ἀπωλείας in xvii. 12, may be reckoned as distinctly religious conceptions, for which the Hebraistic terminology was the only one available.

are indistinguishable—on the other. We feel that, if St. John has an imperfect command of Greek idiom he has a quite adequate command of Greek vocabulary.* He frames his sentences as he can, but he chooses his words as he will.

We see this mastery of words if not of constr. in more ways than one. He has a full sense of the distinctive force of pronouns; and their use or non-use,—or even the use of an emphatic or an enclitic form,—where Greek idiom allows of either, has a larger proportionate importance with him than with other N. T. writers: † see *e.g.* v. 31-7. The emphatic personal pronoun ἐκεῖνος is much commoner with him than with any other, both in its absolute or substantival use, and where it follows a subst. in apposition.‡ We may say indeed that in the use of words in the Gospel, as in the use of constructions in the Apoc., there is more care to express the writer's sense than

---

* In this respect, as in some others, he has more in common with St. Luke than the other Evangelists. But, while in matter we feel that St. Luke stands between St. John and the other Synoptists, in language we rather feel that it is St. John who stands between the simpler writers and the man of letters. See Appendix I., Table I.

† In Rom. vii. 14-25, however, ἐγώ and its oblique cases have much significance: note esp. τῷ θέλοντι ἐμοί in ver. 21, almost as a modern psychologist might say, "to the I that wills." But one may take as an instance of the importance of St. John's pronouns οὗτοι in xviii. 21. On that one word depends the whole point of the passage, which the English reader is apt to miss. The Lord says in effect, "If I have spoken evil, your own officers (*vid.* vii. 32, 45-6) are competent witnesses to it:" one pick-thank among them resents the challenge, though he dares not accept it. We should remember, however, that a classical Greek writer would in this sense have used οἶδε not οὗτοι.

‡ We have specially important instances of these usages in iii. 28 and in xiv. 26, xvi. 13 respectively. In the first passage, ἐκείνου is not=αὐτοῦ ("Him" whom I have mentioned, viz. ὁ Χριστός) but="that Other," ὁ ὀπίσω μου ἐρχόμενος of

to conform to established usage. Thus it is hardly idiomatic—either according to Hellenic or Hellenistic idiom—where the unemphatic pron. of the 3rd person αὐτόν has a noun placed in appos. with it, as a sort of gloss, though of the writer's own; as in ix. 13; in ver. 18 perhaps αὐτοῦ before τοῦ ἀναβλέψαντος has the emphatic force, "the recovered man's *own* parents." But in most N. T. Greek this would have been expressed by τοὺς γ. τοὺς ἰδίους τοῦ ἀναβλ. St. John however, as he uses the adjectival possessive pronouns rather oftener (ἐμός a great deal oftener) than any other N. T. writer, so uses ἴδιος not infrequently as a mere reflexive possessive. It is hardly more frequent with him than with Luke, Paul, or Heb., less frequent relatively than in 2 Pet.; but he gets as it were more use out of it; see i. 11, v. 18, x. 12 etc.

Still more important, and still more characteristic of this Gospel, is the habit of contrasting, by suggestive juxtaposition, two (or more) nearly synonymous words. Thus we have ἦν and ἐγένετο in Ev. i. 1, 6, 8—cf. viii. 58; αἰτεῖν and ἐρωτᾶν in xvi. 23, 26; ἀγαπᾶν and φιλεῖν, βόσκειν and ποιμαίνειν, ἀρνία and προβατία or πρόβατα in xxi. 15-17; perhaps also θεᾶσθαι and ὁρᾶν in i. 32, 34, and even θεωρεῖν and ὁρᾶν in xvi. 16, for θεωρεῖν might well have been used in the fut., though ὄψομαι has no pres. of cognate form. We may add the less intelligible γνῶτε καὶ γινώσκητε of x. 38 (true text).

However, even in vocabulary, St. John's range is not wide: here also he effects more by reiteration

i. 15, 30. In the two others, esp. the latter (for the use of ὁ Παράκλητος just before softens the former), the use of the masc. pron. in apposition with the neut. subst. strains the grammar a little, and therefore is more certainly significant as to the theological teaching intended.

76 LANGUAGE OF THE NEW TESTAMENT.

than by variety. This too is noted by Dionysius, who enumerates as characteristic phrases and conceptions ζωή, φώς, σκότος (but in fact, St. John uses the form σκοτία much oftener), χαρά, "τὴν σάρκα καὶ τὸ αἷμα τοῦ Κυρίου," κρίσις, ἄφεσις τῶν ἁμαρτιῶν (but this phrase never occurs in St. John, and the cognate verb only once—xx. 23—in the Gospel, and twice in the Ep.—i. 9, ii. 12), ἀγάπη of God's love to us and our love to one another, φυλάσσειν τὰς ἐντολάς (in fact the verb is always τηρεῖν) : ὁ κόσμος, ὁ διάβολος, ὁ ἀντίχριστος as powers of evil, "the promise of the Holy Spirit, the adoption as sons of God, the demand for faith on our part, the Father and the Son everywhere."

Here however it is hard to draw the line between *phrases* which it is habitual with St. John to repeat, and theological *conceptions* which it is habitual with him to dwell on. The absence of verbal accuracy in many of them (besides those noted above, ἡ ἐπαγγελία τοῦ ΠΝC. is a Lucan phrase, υἱοθεσία a Pauline) shows that it was the conceptions rather than the expressions that Dionysius had in his mind; though if thus understood, the contrast which he seeks to establish with the Apoc. would be greatly weakened, since *e.g.* ὁ διάβολος and ὁ ἀντίχριστος are prominent figures there, but under other names. If we confine our attention to cases where the *phrase* is distinctive, we get the following results.

Ζωὴ αἰώνιος comes twenty-one times in the Gospel and Epistle—oftener than in the whole N. T. besides ; it is however relatively almost as frequent in the Pastoral Ep. Φῶς is used, directly and unquestionably, in an ethical or spiritual sense in eight or nine passages of St. John (Ev. i. 4-9 ; iii.

19-21; viii. 12; ix. 5; xi. 9, 10; xii. 35-6; 46; Ep. I. i. 5-7, ii. 8-10; perhaps we should add Ev. v. 35), and hardly oftener in the whole N. T. besides: if recurrences of the word were counted, instead of passages containing it, St. John's style would make its frequency with him still more preponderating. Σκοτία is similarly used in Ev. i. 5, viii. 12, xii. 35, 46, Ep. I. i. 5, ii. 8-11—six times—and nowhere else; but σκότος in Ev. iii. 19, and Ep. i. 6 only, compared with Luke i. 79, xxii. 53, Acts xxvi. 18, Rom. ii. 19, xiii. 12, 2 Cor. (iv. 6?) vi. 14, Eph. v. 8-11, vi. 12, Col. i. 13, 1 Thess. v. 4, 1 Pet. ii. 9: so that the antithesis may be traced seven times in St. John, at least as often in St. Paul, and four times elsewhere. Χαρά, though frequent in St. John, is not peculiar to him, being used by every N. T. writer except St. Jude and in the Apoc. (we may question if in SS. Mark and James it is exactly of *holy* joy). But the phrase χαρὰν πληροῦσθαι (Ev. iii. 29, xv. 11, xvi. 24, xvii. 13, Ep. I. i. 4, II. 12) is exclusively Joannine. Σὰρξ καὶ αἷμα are certainly named in a very different way in John vi. 51-56 from Matt. xvi. 17, 1 Cor. xv. 50, Gal. i. 16, Eph. vi. 12. But if we couple the use of the words in the Joannine passage with the use of σάρξ in Ev. i. 14, Ep. I. iv. 2, II. 7, and of αἷμα in xix. 34 compared with Ep. I. v. 6-8—in all of which the words are used of the Incarnation and the mystical extension of its benefits—we have to compare Luke xxiv. 39, Rom. i. 3, viii. 3, ix. 5, Eph. ii. 15, v. 29 [-30 ?], Col. i. 22, 1 Tim. iii. 16, Heb. ii. 14, v. 7, x. 20, 1 Pet. iii. 18, iv. 1, and again not only the Eucharistic texts, but the one in Acts xx. 28—(v. 28 of course is different), and the many in St. Paul, Heb., and Apoc., where, as in

78 *LANGUAGE OF THE NEW TESTAMENT.*

1 John i. 7, the blood of Christ is spoken of as redeeming and cleansing. Just as the doctrine of the Incarnation as a condition of the Atonement, though implicitly contained in the other apostolic writings, is most articulately stated by St. John, so the words "flesh and blood" in this relation are found in all of them, though not combined and accentuated as by him.

The case is much the same with the remaining points: as phrases, no less than as doctrines, they are emphasised by St. John, but nót peculiar to him. $T\eta\rho\epsilon\hat{\imath}\nu$ $\tau\grave{\alpha}\varsigma$ $\grave{\epsilon}\nu\tau o\lambda\acute{\alpha}\varsigma$, indeed, can hardly be called distinctively Joannine; it is only the repetition of the word in three passages (Ep. I. ii. 3-8, iii. 22-4, v. 2-3) that gives an exaggerated impression of its frequency. Similarly, the use of $\tau\acute{\epsilon}\kappa\nu\alpha$ $\Theta\epsilon o\hat{v}$ in Ep. I. iii. 1, 2 strikes the mind, and one forgets that, though we have the phrase also in Ev. i. 12, xi. 52, Ep. I. iii. 10, v. 2, we have the same phrase nearly as often in St. Paul (Rom. viii. 16-21, ix. 8, Phil. ii. 15), while the equivalent $vio\grave{\imath}$ $\Theta.$ is used by most of the N. T. writers, but nót by St. Jude.

But St. John is $\acute{o}$ $\theta\epsilon o\lambda\acute{o}\gamma o\varsigma$, and he is the Apostle of love; Ev. iii. 16, xiv. 21-23, xvi. 27, xvii. 23, Ep. I. iv. 10-11, 19, even without iv. 8, 16, are more emphatic, if hardly more numerous than Rom. viii. 37-9, 2 Cor. xiii. 11, Eph. ii. 4, Col. iii. 12, 1 Thess. i. 4, 2 Thess. ii. 13, 16; and Ev. xiii. 34-5, xv. 12, 17, Ep. I. ii. 10, iii. 10-14, 23, iv. 7, II. 5, more than Rom. xiii. 8-9, Gal. v. 13-14, Eph. iv. 2, v. 2, Col. i. 4, iii. 14, 1 Thess. iii. 12, iv. 9, 2 Thess. i. 3, Heb. x. 24, 1 Pet. iv. 8. It is of course in form not in spirit that these passages differ from 1 Cor. xiii., and many others of which the root is in the Sermon on the Mount and the saying about

ST. JOHN: GOSPEL AND EPISTLES. 79

the two great Commandments; but in form statements of God's love and the mutual love of Christians are relatively commonest in St. John. He has, however, the subst. ἀγάπη less often than St. Paul, and never uses φιλαδελφία, like him and St. Peter (in both Epp.), and the author of Heb.

Mention of the Holy Spirit under that name is actually less frequent in St. John than in SS. Paul and Luke; in the Gospel he uses the title four times (i. 33, vii. 39, xiv. 26, xx. 22), which is no more than St. Mark does in his shorter Gospel. What is really distinctive in St. John is his use of the personal title Παράκλητος, with masc. pronouns corresponding to it, and with perhaps more ascription than elsewhere of personal action to Him. Almost equally distinctive is the mention of "the Father and the Son everywhere," by those names used absolutely, without a dependent gen. We have ὁ Υἱός so named in thirteen passages in St. John's Gospel and Epp., ὁ Πατήρ at least as often in the first six cc. alone; while (excluding the voc. use such as Mark xiv. 36, Luke xxii. 42) we have neither name in more than four passages (or six, if we so reckon them) of the other Gospels (Matt. xi. 25-7 = Luke x. 21-2; Matt. xxiv. 36 = Mark xiii. 32; Matt. xxviii. 19; Luke ix. 26; ὁ Πατήρ thrice in Acts (i. 4, 7, ii. 33), and (excluding vocatives and apposition or juxtaposition with Θεός) twice or thrice in St. Paul (Rom. vi. 4, Eph. ii. 18, perh. Col. i. 12); ὁ Υἱός once in St. Paul (1 Cor. xv. 28), and once at least in Heb. (i. 8; see also i. 2, iii. 6, v. 8). If these passages are enough to show that St. John's doctrine was not confined to him, they are too few to make his language other than characteristic of him.

CHAPTER VII.

THE APOCALYPSE.

THE language of the Revelation of St. John is
Hebraistic Greek in a different sense from
that in which the term will apply to any other part
of the N. T., unless possibly to some elements in
the Synoptic Gospels. The other books are written
by men who habitually spoke and wrote Greek,
though not Greek of the purest kind; this seems
the work of a man whose knowledge of Greek was
imperfect, or at all events to whom Greek was a
foreign language.[*] If the Apocalypse and the
Gospel are to be ascribed to the same author, it
seems hard to find any way of accounting for the
difference between their language except this—that
the Gospel is the later work by many years, and
that in the meantime the author had, not matured
his Greek style, but had learnt the conditions
necessary to be observed if one was to write in
Greek, not in a language which is not Greek.

[*] One is loth to call up ludicrous or ignoble associations
with such a subject ; or one might illustrate the difference
by that between the language of Shakspere's Captain Mac-
morris, or of the ballad of Lilliburlero, and that of a modern
stage Irishman. In the seventeenth century, English was
not an Irishman's native language; now he speaks it, not as
an unfamiliar tongue, but with peculiarities of accent and
dialect.

THE APOCALYPSE. 81

It is however to be remembered that the eccentricities of language in the Apocalypse consist much oftener in disregard of the laws of Greek idiom than either in blank ignorance of those laws, or in disregard of the general laws of language; and that sometimes at least, when the laws of language are broken, it is because either the Greek language, or all human speech, is unaccustomed or inadequate to express what the Seer has to express. When he writes ὁ ὤν καὶ ὁ ἦν (i. 4, 8, iv. 8, xi. 17, xvi. 5), it is not because he does not know the difference between a participle and an indic., but because he does know the difference between εἶναι and γίνεσθαι—both between the ideas themselves, and the Greek words for them. And when, in the first place cited, he writes ἀπὸ ὁ ὤν καὶ ὁ ἦν καὶ ὁ ἐρχόμενος, it is not because he does not know that ἀπὸ governs the gen., but because he is determined to convey the thought of Absolute Being, and it will appear less absolute if the Name expressing it be allowed to be "governed" at all. It perhaps was only for fear of irreverence, that Dionysius rather hints than asserts that there are βάρβαροι φθόγγοι, σολοικισμοὶ, and ἰδιωτισμοὶ in the Apocalypse; but, though no one need fear to say with him διάλεκτον καὶ γλῶσσαν οὐκ ἀκριβῶς ἑλληνίζουσαν βλέπω, not only reverence, but the caution and accuracy that comes of thorough study, will make us hesitate to say more.

For we shall find that the Apocalypse has a grammar of its own, though different in its rules, and laxer in the application of some of them, than the grammar of ordinary Greek, even of Hellenistic Greek. It is probable that there are some uses of cases, and some false concords in gender, that are

82 LANGUAGE OF THE NEW TESTAMENT.

real blunders, to be ascribed to the writer's imperfect mastery of his language, not to his chosen method of using it; but the great majority of the irregularities of the book are irregularities οὐ φύσει ἀλλὰ νόμῳ, while in some of them (like the one already cited) the irregularity has a distinct and important meaning.

I. In Hebrew as in European languages, the verb subst. is constantly found as a copula. But it is not used as a *mere* copula, only where it has a certain emphasis; the normal mode of simple categorical statement is by the direct juxtaposition of subject and predicate. The same can be done in Greek—Aristotle gives ὁ ἵππος λευκός as an example of a simple proposition, and did not regard it as formally different from one like ὁ ἵππος τρέχει: still in Greek one feels that there is an ellipsis, while in Hebrew the sentence is complete and normal. Now in the Apocalypse the normal method of predication is the Hebrew one; iii. 17, where the copula is used, but where the art. is used with the predicate, shows how little Greek the idiom is, except by coincidence. Thus we have the copula omitted in iv. 1, 3, v. 2, vi. 8 (ὄνομα αὐτῷ ὁ Θάνατος), ix. 7, 10, 16, 17, x. 1, xi. 8, xix. 1, 12, xxi. 8, 13, 19; also xxii. 8, unless we punctuate with Dionysius, making μακάριος still the predicate: in that case the omission of the copula is quite natural Greek; but it is likely that Dion. misunderstood the passage, in consequence of an instinct to read it as if it *were* natural Greek.

In some of these cases the predicate is a ptcp. with or without the art. But we have not included cases where the pres. ptcp. is used, as it constantly is, as fully equivalent to a pres. indic.:

THE APOCALYPSE. 83

i. 16 (bis), vi. 2, 5, x. 2, xix. 12, xxi. 12. It will be noticed that in all of these (except the ἐκπορευομένη in i. 16) the ptcp. thus used is ἔχων or more rarely ἔχουσα, and it may be that the irregular forms of the past tenses of ἔχειν led the writer to avoid using them; but it is also possible that he is following the Hebrew usage, according to which what we call the participle is the nearest approach there is to a distinctive present tense.

Certain it is, that his use of participles, and his construction of them in relation to finite verbs, is different from that of ordinary Greek: see i. 5-6, 18, ii. 2, 20, iii. 9. We get however a constr. not unlike this once at least besides in the N. T.—Col. i. 26. We notice that these passages go smoothly into English, because we naturally resolve the ptcp. into a relative clause, with which the following verb is co-ordinate: this indicates the limits of the usage.

II. What are called the tenses in Hebrew and kindred languages have functions other than the simple indication of past, present, and future time. Now it seems as though the Seer either does not use the Greek tenses in their Greek, purely temporal, sense, or if he aims at this only, does not use them with perfect accuracy. In x. 7 the easiest way of understanding καὶ ἐτελέσθη is to suppose that, like the so-called Hebrew preterite or perfect with ׀, it is used of the future. There is indeed no parallel instance to this in the book; the way we pass from fut. tenses to past (in the former instance, through pres.) in xi. 7-11, xx. 7, 9 is a peculiarity in its literary, not in its grammatical character.* But

---

* However truly this book is a divine revelation, it is the record of a vision, and it is a work of genius. It therefore

84 *LANGUAGE OF THE NEW TESTAMENT.*

we get tenses used otherwise than is natural in Greek in ii. 5, 22, 24, iv. 10 (?), xii. 4. The *sequence* of tenses also is Hebrew, not Greek, in xi. 3 ; cf. xiv. 10, though that does not go further in the way of Hebraism than we might get in other Hellenistic Greek.

III. Another very frequent Hebraism (such we should no doubt consider it rather than a colloquialism) is the insertion in a relative clause (see *Language of the New Testament*, p. 59) of a redundant pronoun or pronominal adv. : iii. 8, vii. 2, 9, xii. 6, 14, xiii. 12, xvii. 9, xx. 8. The same, in principle, is the use of the redundant pron. in i. 6, ii. 7, 17.

We may probably regard as a Hebraism what, if it is to be explained in terms of Greek grammar at all, can only be called a harsh sort of apposition —the βασιλείαν ἱερεῖς of i. 6. We should say that the literal translation of מַמְלֶכֶת כֹּהֲנִים in Ex. xix. 6 was "a kingdom *of* priests;" but St. John has hardly realised the equivalence of the Hebrew constr. with the former noun inflected, and the Greek constr. with the latter ; and sets down "a kingdom, priests" side by side, leaving the mere juxtaposition of the two nouns to express the relation between them, as though both were indecl. Similar, probably, is the origin of the ὅμοιον υἱὸν of i. 13, xiv. 14 ; though that cannot be explained as a literal translation of Dan. vii. 13, which is ὡς υἱὸς ἀνθρώπου ἐρχόμενος ἦν. (So the common

may not be irrelevant to illustrate the change of the point of view in these passages, on the one hand by that in M. Morris's "Land East of the Sun and West of the Moon" (*Earthly Paradise*, vol. iii.), where the dreamer seems first to hear the story, then to tell it, and then to act it, and on the other to the similar experiences which most people, probably, have had in their own dreams,

version, ascribed to Theodotion; and the so-called LXX. only differs, in these words, by reading ἤρχετο.)

IV. When two nouns are in what we understand by apposition, the second is usually put in the nom., whatever be the case of the first. So i. 5, ii. 13,* 20, iii. 12, vii. 4, viii. 9, ix. 14, xiv. 12, 14, xvii. 3,† xx. 2. In xiv. 6 λέγων after πετόμενον and ἔχοντα is similar in principle; so perhaps in xxi. 12 ἔχουσα after ἔχουσαν at the beginning of the previous verse, but perhaps we should rather take this as a new independent predicate.

Connected with this idiom is the use of a nom. to indicate the *subject* of a sentence in the popular sense, when the subj. in the grammatical sense is different, so that the other comes in in an oblique case; here also we have the nom. and the oblique case in a sort of apposition. So ii. 26, iii. 12, 21, vi. 8. This however is by no means peculiar to this book—see *e.g.* Acts vii. 40. Similar to this use of the nom. before an oblique case is that of the acc. after a different oblique case in xi. 18; which seems to explain the reading περιβεβλημένους above in ver. 3. Περιβεβλημένοι would never have been altered; -μένοις, though irregular, would have been possible to this writer after δώσω; and the principle we are stating explains -μένους being substituted for the latter. This brings us far on the way to such strange attractions as iii. 9, x. 8, xvii. 3, xxi. 9; and these in turn throw light on such variations as i. 20, iv. 4, vii. 9, xviii. 12-13,

* Reading ἐν ἡμέραις 'Αντίπας, we must take 'Αντ. as virtually a gen., though indecl. But the passage is suspected to be corrupt; and if so, the T. R. is a plausible correction.

† The reading ἔχων indeed is not certain. But the presumption always is, in this book, that scribes have eliminated rather than introduced the anomalous constr.

xxii. 5. In comparison with these, the second λίθῳ in xxi. 11 seems almost regular, and ὀνόματα ἀνθρώπων χιλιάδες ἑπτά in xi. 13 quite so.

V. In Greek as in most if not all languages, while there are some rules naturally evolved from the essential structure of the language, there are others that are fixed by usage, if not without a determining reason, yet as it were arbitrarily, and that might have been otherwise had usage taken a different turn. In an inflected language like Greek, it was hardly likely that relative clauses or appositions should originally be expressed as they are in this book; still in the former case the fashion has come in, and it conceivably might have in the latter. Still more decidedly, it is usage not the nature of things that determines that διδάσκω shall take a double acc., not, like most other verbs capable of analogous use, a dat. of the person and an acc. of the thing. The constr. of ii. 14 of this book, therefore, might have been correct Greek, though it is not; and so with iii. 17, which is like *nil opus est*.

Again, there is an intelligible reason for the use in Greek of a sing. verb with a subject in the neut. pl. But the reason need not have prevailed to determine usage—in so closely similar and kindred a language as Latin it did not; and even in Greek the limits within which the rule is obligatory are not strictly fixed. The pl. verbs in iii. 4, iv. 5, xi. 13, 18, xviii. 3, xix. 21, xxi. 24 are all, on one ground or another, quite admissible as correct Greek; there is no reason why, if the pl. is used in these, the sing. should be in xix. 14, but in such cases classical usage would tolerate either. But while iv. 1, xxi. 12, etc. show that the rule is recognised, i. 19 violates it, esp. as the pl. is coupled with a sing. in the same sentence;

THE APOCALYPSE. 87

so xxi. 4. ix. 12 is irregular, because οὐαί is made fem. in the first clause (as in xi. 14); else treating it as a neut. would be natural enough.

VI. Intermediate between these cases, and those where irregularity can come from nothing but ignorance or inadvertence, are constructions κατὰ σύνεσιν; such as a man with a mastery of a language may indulge in safely but sparingly, while a man who has not mastered it will oftener feel unable to express himself without them, and will produce more of a sense of awkwardness by them. Many but not all of the false concords in gender, which appear to be frequent in this book, can be thus explained. Thus in vi. 10 there is hardly an irregularity; the subj. to ἔκραξαν may as easily be conceived to be οἱ ἐσφαγμένοι as αἱ ψυχαί. In iv. 7, 8, ix. 5, 6, ix. 5*, 7*, xi. 4, xiii. 14, 15*, xvii. 3, perhaps even xxii. 2*, and again vii. 9, xix. 14, we may say that though there no such formal defence of their accuracy is available, their sense justifies them on the same principle; fem. or neuter nouns indicating persons are constructed as if masc. (cf. John xiv. 26, xvi. 13, *Language of the New Testament*, p. 66), or nouns of multitude as if pl. There is however some inconsistency; there is no reason why in xiv. 1 the concord should be formally regular, and in vii. 4, 8 be constructed to the sense.

In iv. 1, v. 13, xi. 15 we have the same sort of principle carried a little further; the ptcp. agrees with the speaker whose existence is implied in the voice. And in xi. 1 the force is really the same, only here the subst. to be supplied is "the giver" from ἐδόθη, not, as *e.g.* in ver. 15, "the speakers"

* Assuming the readings which give irregularities to be the true ones.

from φωναί. But if we acknowledge that in the latter place λέγοντες agrees loosely with φωναί, it is hardly worth while to make believe in the former that λέγων has a Hellenic constr. by calling it a *nominativus pendens*, though it is more like that than anything else.

VII. There now remain only two of the anomalies of the book which we have not, in some sort, accounted for or at least classified. These are the *avowed* false concord, as we may call it, in xiv. 19, and what appears to be the best attested text in i. 15, though we may explain that partly by regarding χαλκολίβανος as fem. like לְבֹנָה though unlike λίβανος, not to say χαλκός. These too, and with them some or all of the changes of case noted near the end of § IV, must be allowed to form a *residuum* of errors due to imperfect knowledge or care in the writer. For the rest, he no doubt would have written differently had he known more Greek; if he be the Evangelist, we may say that he *did* write differently when he knew more. But it does not follow that his language as it is, is not better for its purpose than that of a better Greek scholar: the Seer's exact position towards Hellenism as it made him write *as* he did, so was one of his qualifications for writing *what* he did. We may conclude by noting one or two peculiarities of style which are hardly to be called irregularities. When a number of co-ordinate substantives have a common possessive gen. depending on them, it is usually repeated with each—*e.g.* vi. 11, ix. 21. Some even argue that in i. 6 τῷ Θεῷ καὶ Πατρὶ αὐτοῦ cannot be translated, " His God and Father," as it almost certainly should in St. Paul, for that in this sense the Seer would have written τῷ Θεῷ αὐτοῦ κ.τ.λ.

THE APOCALYPSE. 89

The vocabulary of the Apoc. is far less eccentric, far more perfectly under the writer's control, than its style and grammar. We note however κατήγωρ in xii. 10 as a Greek word used in the form in which it was borrowed in Rabbinical Hebrew: the enigmatic χαλκολίβανος or -νον (i. 15, ii. 18), possibly a hybrid Greek and Hebrew word: λιβανωτὸς (viii. 3, 5) used in a wrong sense, perhaps because λίβανος appeared (rightly) to be the same as the Semitic name, and it seemed that the derivative ought to mean something different. In ix. 16 it is a matter of choice whether we call δὶς μυριάδες or δισμυρ. a peculiarity of vocabulary or of constr.

APPENDIX I. TABLE I.

AFFINITIES IN VOCABULARY BETWEEN SS. LUKE AND JOHN.*

Word or Phrase.	St. Luke.	St. John.
ἀπόκρισις	Ev. ii. 47, xx. 26.	Ev. i. 22, xix. 9.
ἀρεστός	A. vi. 2, xii. 3.	Ev. viii. 29, Ep. I. iii. 22.
ἀριστᾶν (-ον Matt.)	Ev. xi. 37.	Ev. xxi. 12, 15.
βάπτειν	Ev. xvi. 24.	Ev. xiii. 26 bis, Ap. xix. 13.
γείτων	Ev. xiv. 12, xv. 6, 9.	Ev. ix. 8.
διαδιδόναι	Ev. xi. 22, xviii. 22, A. iv. 35.	
διατρίβειν	A. xii. 19, xiv. 3, 18 (?), 28, xv. 35, xvi. 12, xx. 6, xxv. 6, 14.	Ev. iii. 24, xi. 54 (?)
ἐκμάσσειν	Ev. vii. 38, 44.	Ev. xi. 2, xii. 3, xiii. 5.
ἑλκύειν	A. xvi. 19.	Ev. vi. 44, xii. 32, xviii. 10, xxi. 6, 11.
Ἑλληνιστί	A. xxi. 37.	Ev. xix. 20.
ἐνθάδε	Ev. xxiv. 41, A. x. 18, xvi. 23, xvii. 6, xxv. 17, 24.	Ev. iv. 15, 16.
ἐξηγεῖσθαι	Ev. xxiv. 35, A. x. 8, xv. 12, 14, xxi. 19.	Ev. i. 18.
ζωννύναι	A. xii. 8.	Ev. xxi. 18 bis.
καίτοιγε	A. xiv. 17 (?), xvii. 27.	Ev. iv. 2.
κῆπος	Ev. xiii. 19.	Ev. xviii. 1, 26, xix. 41 bis.
κόλπος	Ev. vi. 38, xvi. 22, 23, (A. xxvii. 39 = "gulf.")	Ev. i. 18, xiii. 23.
μονογενής	Ev. vii. 12, viii. 42, ix. 38. (Also Heb. xi. 17.)	Ev. i. 14, 18, iii. 16, 18, Ep. I. iv. 9.
νεύειν	A. xxiv. 10.	Ev. xiii. 24.
ὀθόνια	Ev. xxiv. 12.	Ev. xix. 40, xx. 5, 6, 7.
ὁμοῦ	A. ii. 1 (?), xx. 18 (?)	Ev. iv. 36, xx. 4, xxi.
πλευρά	A. xii. 7.	Ev. xix. 34, xx. 20, 25.

* Excluding words found nowhere in St. John but in the Apocalypse. Coincidence with St. Luke in such words are very few, and purely casual; but words common to the Gospel or Epp. and Apoc. are worth noting.

APPENDIX I. TABLE I.

Word or Phrase.	St. Luke.	St. John.
προδραμεῖν	Ev. xix. 4.	Ev. xx. 4.
προσαιτεῖν	Ev. xviii. 35 (?). †	Ev. ix. 8.
πώποτε	Ev. xix. 30.	Ev. i. 18, v. 37, vi. 35, viii. 33, Ep. I. iv. 12.
στόα	A. iii. 11, v. 12.	Ev. v. 2, x. 23.
συντίθεσθαι	Ev. xxii. 5, A. xxiii. 20, xxiv. 9 (?).	Ev. ix. 22.
σύρειν	A. viii. 3, xiv. 19, xvii. 6.	Ev. xxi. 8, Apoc. xii. 4.
σχοινίον	A. xxvii. 32.	Ev. ii. 15.
ὑπολαβαβάνειν	Ev. vii. 43, x. 30, A. i. 9, ii. 15.	Ep. III. 8 (?).
φρέαρ	Ev. xiv. 5.	Ev. iv. 11, 12, Apoc. ix. 1, 2 ter.

† Prob. we should read ἐπαιτῶν here, and προσαίτης (cf. St. John, l.c., true text) in Mark x. 46. Thus the verb will be peculiar to St. John.

APPENDIX I.

ILLUSTRATING AFFINITIES IN VOCABULARY

Word or Phrase.	St. Paul.	St. Luke.
ἀγνωσία	1 Cor. xv. 34.	
ἀγών	†Phil. i. 30, Col. ii. 1, 1 Thess. ii. 2, 1 Tim. vi. 12, 2 Tim. iv. 7.	
ἄδηλος (-ως, ότης)	1 Cor. xiv. 8, † (ib. ix. 26, 1 Tim. vi. 17).	Ev. xi. 44.
ἀδόκιμος	†Rom. i. 28, 1 Cor. ix. 27, 2 Cor. xiii. 5, 6, 7, 2 Tim. iii. 8, Tit. i. 16.	
αἱρεῖσθαι	Phil. i. 22, 2 Thess. ii. 13.	
αἰφνίδιος	1 Thess. v. 3.	Ev. xxi. 34.
αἰχμαλωτίζειν	†Rom. vii. 23, 2 Cor. x. 5, 2 Tim. iii. 6 (?).	Ev. xxi. 24.
ἄκακος	Rom. xvi. 18.	
ἄμεμπτος	Phil. ii. 15, iii. 6, 1 Thess. iii. 13.	Ev. i. 6.
ἀναγκαῖος	†1 Cor. xii. 22, 2 Cor. ix. 5, Phil. i. 24, ii. 25, Tit. iii. 14.	A. x. 24, xiii. 46.
ἀνάγνωσις	†2 Cor. iii. 14, 1 Tim. iv. 13.	A. xiii. 15.
ἀναλίσκειν	Gal. v. 15, 2 Thess. ii. 8 (?).	Ev. ix. 54.
ἀναλύειν	Phil. i. 23.	Ev. xii. 36.
ἀναπέμπειν	Philem. 11.	Ev. xxiii. 7, 11, 15, A. xxv. 21 (?)
ἀναστατοῦν	Gal. v. 12.	A. xvii. 6, xxi. 38.
ἀνατίθεσθαι	Gal. ii. 2.	A. xxv. 14.
ἄνεσις	2 Cor. ii. 13, vii. 5, viii. 13, 2 Thess. i. 7.	A. xxiv. 23.
ἀνιέναι	Eph. vi. 9.	A. xvi. 26, xxvii. 40.
ἀνόητος	†Rom. i. 14, Gal. iii. 1, 3, 1 Tim. vi. 9, Tit. iii. 3.	Ev. xxiv. 25.
ἀνταποδιδόναι	Rom. xi. 35 (quotn.), xii. 19 (from LXX.), 1 Thess. iii. 9, 2 Thess. i. 6.	Ev. xiv. 14 bis.
-δομα	Rom. xi. 9 (from LXX.).	Ev. xiv. 12.
ἀνταποκρίνεσθαι	Rom. ix. 20.	Ev. xiv. 6.
ἀντικεῖσθαι	†1 Cor. xvi. 9, Gal. v. 17, Phil. i. 28, 2 Thess. ii. 4, 1 Tim. i. 10, v. 14.	Ev. xiii. 17, xxi. 15.
ἀξιοῦν	†2 Thess. i. 11, 1 Tim. v. 17.	Ev. vii. 7, A. xv. 38, xxviii. 22.

* Excluding words found nowhere in St. Paul but in the Pastoral Epp.: for these see Table

TABLE II.

BETWEEN SS. PAUL,* PETER, LUKE, AND HEBREWS.

1 Peter.	2 Peter.	Hebrews.	Other N.T. Books.
ii. 15.	..	..	..
..	..	xii. 1.	..
..	..	..	..
..	..	vi. 8.	..
..	..	xi. 25.	..
..	..	..	..
..	..	..	..
..	..	vii. 26.	..
..	..	viii. 7.	..
..	..	viii. 3.	..
..	..	..	..
..	..	..	..
..	..	..	..
..	..	..	..
..	..	..	..
..	..	..	..
..	..	..	..
..	..	xiii. 5 (fr. LXX.).	..
..	..	..	..
..	..	x. 30 (quotn.).	..
..	..	..	..
..	..	..	..
..	..	..	..
..	..	..	..

{II. Words found in these, *as well as others*, are marked † for convenience of counting.

94 LANGUAGE OF THE NEW TESTAMENT.

Word or Phrase.	St. Paul.	St. Luke.
ἀόρατος	†Rom. i. 20, Col. i. 15, 16, 1 Tim. i. 17.	..
ἀπειθής	†Rom. i. 30, 2 Tim. iii. 2, Tit. i. 16, iii. 3.	Ev. i. 17, A. xxvi. 19.
-θεια	Rom. xi. 30, 32, Eph. ii. 2, v. 6, Col. iii. 6 (?).	..
ἀπιστεῖν	†Rom. iii. 3, 2 Tim. ii. 13.	Ev. xxiv. 11, 41, A. xxviii. 24.
ἀποδεικνύναι	1 Cor. iv. 9, 2 Thess. ii. 4.	A. ii. 22, xxv. 7.
ἀποκρύπτειν	1 Cor. ii. 7, Eph. iii. 9, Col. i. 26.	Ev. x. 21.
ἀπολογεῖσθαι	Rom. ii. 15, 2 Cor. xii. 19.	Ev. xii. 11, xxi. 14, A. xix. 33, xxiv. 10, xxv. 8, xxvi. 1, 2, 24.
-για	†1 Cor. ix. 3, 2 Cor. vii. 11, Phil. i. 7, 16, 2 Tim. iv. 16.	A. xxii. 1, xxv. 16.
ἀπολούεσθαι	1 Cor. vi. 11.	A. xxii. 16.
ἀπολύτρωσις	Rom. iii. 24, viii. 23, 1 Cor. i. 30, Eph. ι. 7, 14, iv. 30, Col. i. 14.	Ev. xxi. 28.
ἀπορεῖσθαι	2 Cor. iv. 8, Gal. iv. 20.	Ev. xxiv. 4, A. xxv. 20.
ἀποστολή	Rom. i. 5, 1 Cor. ix. 2, Gal. ii. 8.	A. i. 25.
ἀπρόσκοπος	1 Cor. x. 32, Phil. i. 10.	A. xxiv. 16.
ἀπωθεῖσθαι	†Rom. xi. 1, 2, 1 Tim. i. 19.	A. vii. 27, 39, xiii. 46.
ἆρα (or ἄρα interrog.)	Gal. ii. 17.	Ev. xviii. 8, A. viii. 30.
ἀροτριᾶν	1 Cor. ix. 10.	Ev. xvii. 7.
ἀσφαλής	Phil. iii. 1.	A. xxi. 34, xxii. 30, xxv. 26.
-λεια	1 Thess. v. 3.	Ev. i. 4, A. v. 23.
ἀτενίζω	2 Cor. iii. 7, 13.	Ev. iv. 20, xxii. 56, A. decies.
ἄφθαρτος	†Rom. i. 23, 1 Cor. ix. 25, xv. 52, 1 Tim. i. 17.	..
ἄφρων	Rom. ii. 20, 1 Cor. xv. 36, 2 Cor. xi. 16 bis, 19, xii. 6, 11, Eph. v. 17.	Ev. xi. 40, xii. 20.
βάρβαρος	Rom. i. 14, 1 Cor. xiv. 11 bis, Col. iii. 11.	A. xxviii. 2, 4.

APPENDIX I. TABLE II.

1 Peter.	2 Peter.	Hebrews.	Other N.T. Books.
..	..	xi. 27.	..
..	..	..	..
..	..	iv. 6, 11.	..
..	..	..	Mark xvi. 11, 16.
..	..	..	..
..	..	..	Matt. xi. 25 (?), xxv. 18 (?)
..	..	..	..
iii. 15.	..	..	..
..	..	ix. 15, xi. 35.	..
..	..	..	Joh. xiii. 22.
..	..	..	..
..	..	..	..
..	..	..	..
..	..	..	..
..	..	vi. 19.	..
..	..	..	..
..	..	..	..
..	..	..	..
..	..	..	..
i. 4, 23, iii. 4.	..	..	..
ii. 15.	..	..	..
..	..	..	..

96 LANGUAGE OF THE NEW TESTAMENT.

Word or Phrase.	St. Paul.	St. Luke.
βέβαιος . . .	Rom. iv. 16, 2 Cor. i. 7.	..
-οῦν	Rom. xv. 8, 1 Cor. i. 6, 8, 2 Cor. i. 21, Col. ii. 7.	..
-ωσις . .	Phil. i. 7.	..
βουλεύομαι .	2 Cor. i. 17 bis (terve?)	Ev. xiv. 31, A. v. 33 (?), xv. 37 (?), xxvii. 39 (?)
βούλημα . . .	Rom. ix. 19.	A. xxvii. 43.
γνωστός . . .	Rom. i. 19.	Ev. ii. 44, xxiii. 49,[1] A. decies alio sensu.
γράμμα, ματα . .	†Rom. ii. 27, 29, vii. 6, 2 Cor. iii, 6 bis, 7; Gal. vi. 11, 2 Tim. iii. 15.	Ev. xvi. 6, 7; xxiii. 38, A. xxvi. 24, xxviii. 21.
δηλοῦν . . .	1 Cor. i. 11, iii. 13, Col. i. 8.	..
διαγγέλλειν .	Rom. ix. 17 (from LXX.).	Ev. ix. 60, A. xxi. 26.
διάκρισις . .	Rom. xiv. 1, 1 Cor. xii. 10.	..
διαμαρτύρεσθαι .	†1 Thess. iv. 6, 1 Tim. v. 21, 2 Tim. ii. 14, iv. 1.	Ev. xvi. 28, A. novies.
διαμένειν .	Gal. ii. 5.	Ev. i. 22, xxii. 28.
διαπορεύεσθαι . .	Rom. xv. 24.	Ev. vi. 1, xiii. 22, xviii. 36.
διαταγή . . .	Rom. xiii. 2.	A. vii. 53.
διάφορος . . .	Rom. xii. 6.	
διερμηνεύειν . .	1 Cor. xii. 30, xiv. 5, 13, 27.	Ev. xxiv. 27, A. ix. 36.
δικαίως . . .	†1 Cor. xv. 34, 1 Thess. ii. 10, Tit. ii. 12.	Ev. xxiii. 41.
δουλεία . .	Rom. viii. 15, 21, Gal. iv. 24, v. 1.	..
-οῦν	†Rom. vi. 18, 22, 1 Cor. vii. 15, ix. 19, Gal. iv. 3, Tit. ii. 3	A. vii. 6 (from LXX.).
δωρεά . . .	Rom. v. 15, 17, 2 Cor. ix. 15, Eph. iii. 7, iv. 7.	A. ii. 38, viii. 20, x. 45, xi. 17.
ἐγκαλεῖν .	Rom. viii. 33.	A. xix. 38, 40, xxiii. 28, 29, xxvi. 2, 7.
ἐγκόπτειν . .	Rom. xv. 22, Gal. v. 7 (?), 1 Thess. ii. 18.	A. xxiv. 4.
ἐγκράτεια . .	Gal. v. 23.	A. xxiv. 25.
εἶδος . .	2 Cor. v. 7, 1 Thess. v. 22.	Ev. iii. 22, ix. 29
εἰδωλολατρεία . .	1 Cor. x. 14, Gal. v. 20, Col. iii. 5.	..

[1] In both passages of acquaintances.

APPENDIX I. TABLE II.

1 Peter.	2 Peter.	Hebrews.	Other N.T. Books.
..	i. 10, 19.	ii. 2, iii. 6, 14, vi. 19, ix. 17.	..
..	..	ii. 3, xiii. 9.	Mark xvi. 20.
..	..	vi. 16.	..
..	..	..	Joh. xi. 53 (?), xii. 10.
iv. 3.	..	..	..
..	..	..	Joh. xviii. 15, 16.
..	..	..	Joh. v. 47, vii. 15 (both pl.)
i. 11.	i. 14.	ix. 8, xii. 27.	..
..	..	..	..
..	..	v. 14.	..
..	..	ii. 6.	..
..	iii. 4.	i. 11 (fr. LXX.).	..
..	..	..	..
..	..	..	..
..	..	ix. 10.	..
..	..	..	..
ii. 23.	..	..	..
..	..	ii. 15.	..
..	ii. 19.	vi. 4.	Joh. iv 10.
..	..	..	..
..	..	..	..
iii. 7 (?)	..	..	..
..	i. 6 bis.	..	..
..	..	..	..
iv. 3.	..	..	Joh. v. 37.

98 LANGUAGE OF THE NEW TESTAMENT.

Word or Phrase.	St. Paul.	St. Luke.
εἰλικρινής	Phil. i. 10.	..
εἴσοδος	1 Thess. i. 9, ii. 1.	A. xiii. 24.
εἴτε	Saepissime.	..
ἔκβασις	1 Cor. x. 13.	..
ἐκδίκησις	Rom. xii. 19 (quotn.), 2 Cor. vii. 11, 2 Thess. i. 8.	Ev. xviii. 7, 8, xxi. 22, A. vii. 24.
ἐκκακεῖν (vel potius ἐγκ, sive ἐνκ)	2 Cor. iv. 1, 16, Gal. vi. 9, Eph. iii. 13, 2 Thess. iii. 13.	Ev. xviii. 1.
ἐκκλίνειν	Rom. iii. 12, xvi. 17.	..
ἐκλογή	Rom. ix. 11, xi. 5, 7, 28, 1 Thess. i. 4.	A. ix. 15.
ἐκφεύγειν	Rom. ii. 3, 2 Cor. xi. 33, 1 Thess. v. 3.	Ev. xxi. 36, A. xvi. 27, xix. 16.
Ἕλλην	Rom. i. 14, 16, ii. 9, 10, iii. 9, x. 12, 1 Cor. i. 22, 23 (?), Gal. ii. 3, iii. 28, Col. iii. 11.	A. novies ad minimum.
ἐμμένειν	Gal. iii. 10 (from LXX.).	A. xiv. 22.
ἐμπιμπλάναι	Rom. xv. 24.	Ev. i. 53, vi. 25, A. xiv. 17.
ἐνδείκνυσθαι	†Rom. ii. 15, ix. 17 (from LXX.), ix. 22, 2 Cor. viii. 24, Eph. ii. 7, 1 Tim. i. 16, 2 Tim. iv. 14, Tit. ii. 10, iii. 2.	..
ἔνδικος	Rom. iii. 8.	..
ἔνδοξος	1 Cor. iv. 10, Eph. v. 27.	Ev. vii. 25, xiii. 17.
ἐνδυναμοῦν, -μοῦσθαι	†Rom. iv. 20, Eph. vi. 10, Phil. iv. 13, 1 Tim. i. 12, 2 Tim. ii. 1, iv. 17.	A. ix. 22.
ἐνεργής	1 Cor. xvi. 9, Philem. 6.	..
ἐνίστασθαι,[1] ἐνεστηκέναι	†Rom. viii. 38,* 1 Cor. iii. 22,* vii. 26,* Gal. i. 4,* 2 Thess. ii. 2, 2 Tim. iii. 1.	..
ἔννομος	1 Cor. ix. 21.	A. xix. 39.
ἔντιμος	Phil. ii. 29.	Ev. vii. 2. xiv. 8.
ἐντυγχάνειν	Rom. viii. 27, 34, xi. 2.	A. xxv. 24.
ἐξαποστέλλω	Gal. iv. 4, 6.	Ev. i. 53, xx. 10, 11, A. septies.
ἐπαγγελία	†Saepius.	Ev. xxiv. 49, A. octies.
ἔπαινος	Rom. ii. 29, xiii. 3, 1 Cor. iv. 5, 2 Cor. viii. 18, Eph. i. 6, 12, 14, Phil. i. 11, iv. 8.	..

[1] The form of the participle differs in St. Paul and Hebrews.

APPENDIX I. TABLE II.

1 Peter.	2 Peter.	Hebrews.	Other N.T. Books.
	iii. 1.		
	i. 11.	x. 19.	
ii. 13, 14.		xiii. 7.	
		x. 30 (quotn.)	
ii. 14.			
iii. 11 (fr. LXX).			
	i. 10.		
		ii. 3, xii. 25 (?)	
			Joh. vii. 35 bi xii. 20.
		viii. 9 (fr. LXX.)	
			Joh. vi. 12.
		vi. 10, 11.	
		ii. 2.	
		xi. 34 (?)	
		iv. 12.	
		ix. 9.*	
ii. 4, 6 (fr. LXX.).			
		vii. 25.	
	iii. 4, 9.	Saepissime.	Joh. Ep. i. 5 ii. 25.
i. 7, ii. 14.			

100 *LANGUAGE OF THE NEW TESTAMENT.*

Word or Phrase.	St. Paul.	St. Luke.
ἐπαινεῖν . . .	Rom. xv. 11 (from LXX.), 1 Cor. xi. 2, 17, 22 bis.	Ev. xvi. 8.
ἐπαναπαύεσθαι .	Rom. ii. 17.	Ev. x. 6.
ἐπειδή . . .	1 Cor. i. 21, 22, xiv. 16, xv. 21, 2 Cor. v. 4 (?), Phil. ii. 26.	Ev. vii. 1, xi. 6, A. xiii. 46, xiv. 12, xv. 24.
ἐπιείκεια . .	2 Cor. x. 1.	A. xxiv. 4.
ἐπικεῖσθαι . .	1 Cor. ix. 16.	Ev. v. 1, xxiii. 23, A. xxvii. 20.
ἐπιμένειν . .	†Rom. vi. 1, xi. 22, 23, 1 Cor. xvi. 7, 8, Gal. i. 18, Phil. i. 24, Col. i. 23, 1 Tim. iv. 16.	A. x. 48, xii. 16, xiii. 43 (?), xv. 34, xxi. 4, 10, xxviii. 12, 14.
ἐπιστολή . .	Rom. xvi. 22, 1 Cor. v. 9, xvi. 3, 2 Cor. octies, Col. iv. 16, 1 Thess. v. 27, 2 Thess. ii. 2, 15, iii. 14, 18.	A. ix. 2, xv. 30, xxii. 5, xxiii. 25, 33.
ἐπισυναγωγή .	2 Thess. ii. 1.	
ἐπισύστασις vel potius ἐπίστασις .	2 Cor. xi. 28.	A. xxiv. 12.
ἐπιτελεῖν . .	Rom. xv. 28, 2 Cor. vii. 1, viii. 6, 11 bis, Gal. iii. 3, Phil. i. 6.	Ev. xiii. 32 (?).
ἐπιχορηγεῖν . .	2 Cor. ix. 10, Col. ii. 19.	
ἐργασία . . .	Eph. iv. 19.	Ev. xii. 58, A. xvi. 16, 19, xix. 24, 25.
εὐάρεστος . .	†Rom. xii. 1, 2, xiv. 18, 2 Cor. v. 9, Eph. v. 10, Phil. iv. 18, Col. iii. 20, Tit. ii. 9.	
εὐγενής . . .	1 Cor. i. 26.	Ev. xix. 12, A. xvii. 11.
εὐπρόσδεκτος .	Rom. xv. 16, 31, 2 Cor. vi. 2, viii. 12.	
εὔσπλαγχνος .	Eph. iv. 32.	
ἐφάπαξ . . .	Rom. vi. 10, 1 Cor. xv. 6.	
ἐφίστασθαι . .	†1 Thess. v. 3, 2 Tim. iv. 2, 6.	Ev. septies, A. undecies.
ζέων τῷ πνεύματι .	Rom. xii. 11.	A. xviii. 25.
ζηλωτής . . .	†1 Cor. xiv. 12, Gal. i. 14, Tit. ii. 14.	Ev. vi. 15, A. i. 13, xxi. 20, xxii. 3.
ζημία . . .	Phil. iii. 7, 8.	A. xxvii. 10, 21.

1 Peter.	2 Peter.	Hebrews.	Other N.T. Books.
..	..	..	..
...	..	..	
..	..	..	Matt. xxi. 46 (?).
..	..	ix. 10.	Joh. xi. 38, xxi. 9.
..	..	..	
..	..	..	(Ps.) Joh. viii. 7.
..	iii. 1, 16.	..	..
..	..	x. 25.	..
..	..	..	..
v. 9.	..	viii. 5, ix. 6.	..
..	i. 5, 11.	..	..
..	..	xiii. 21.	..
..	..	..	..
..	..	..	..
ii. 5.	..	..	..
iii. 8.	..	..	..
..	..	vii. 27, ix. 12, x. 10.	...
..	..	..	..
..	..	..	..
iii. 13 (?).	..	..	..
..	..	..	..

102 LANGUAGE OF THE NEW TESTAMENT.

Word or Phrase.	St. Paul.	St. Luke.
ζωοποιεῖν	Rom. iv. 17, viii. 11, 1 Cor. xv. 22, 36, 45, 2 Cor. iii. 6, Gal. iii. 21, 1 Tim. vi. 13 (?).	..
ἡττᾶσθαι	2 Cor. xii. 13 (?).	..
ἠχεῖν	1 Cor. xiii. 1.	Ev. xxi. 25 (?).
θαρρεῖ (sed θάρσει, -ειτε alibi)	2 Cor. v. 6, 8, vii. 16, x. 1, 2.	..
θέατρον	1 Cor. iv. 9 (metaph.).	A. xix. 29, 31 (lit.).
θεμέλιος, -ον	†1 Cor. iii. 10, 11, 12 (masc.), Eph. ii. 20, 1 Tim. vi. 19, 2 Tim. ii. 19 (-ος).	Ev. vi. 48, 49, xiv. 29, A. xvi. 26 (a).
θιγεῖν	Col. ii. 21.	A. xx. 9.
θυρίς	2 Cor. xi. 33.	..
ἴχνος	Rom. iv. 12, 2 Cor. xii. 18.	..
καθάπερ	Rom. iv. 6, xii. 4, 1 Cor. xii. 12, 2 Cor. quater., 1 Thess. quater.	..
καθήκειν	Rom. i. 28.	A. xxii. 22.
καταγγέλλειν	Rom. i. 8, 1 Cor. ii. 1, ix. 14, xi. 26, Phil. i. 16, 18, Col. i. 28.	A. undecies.
κατάγειν	Rom. x. 6.	Ev. v. 11, A. septies.
καταισχύνεσθαι	Rom. ix. 33 (from LXX.), x. 11 (do.), 2 Cor. vii. 14, ix. 4.	Ev. xiii. 17.
καταλαλιά	2 Cor. xii. 20 (-λος Rom. i. 30).	..
καταντᾶν	1 Cor. x. 11, xiv. 36, Eph. iv. 13, Phil. iii. 11.	A novies.
καταξιωθῆναι	2 Thess. i. 5.	Ev. xx. 35, xxi. 36 (?), A. v. 41.
καταργεῖν	†Saepius.	Ev. xiii. 7 (in different sense).
κατευθύνειν	1 Thess. iii. 11, 2 Thess. iii. 5.	Ev. i. 79.
κατέχειν	Saepius.	Ev. iv. 42, viii. 15, xiv. 9, A. xxvii. 40.
κινδονεύειν	1 Cor. xv. 30.	Ev. viii. 23, A. xix. 27, 40.
κλῆσις	†Rom. xi. 29, 1 Cor. i. 26, vii. 20, Eph. i. 18, iv. 1, 4, Phil. iii. 14, 2 Thess. i. 11, 2 Tim. i. 9.	..

1 Peter.	2 Peter.	Hebrews.	Other N.T. Books.
iii. 18.	..	..	..
..	ii. 19, 20.	..	..
..	..	..	..
..	..	xiii. 6.	..
..	..	vi. 1, xi. 10 (-ους).	Apoc. xxi. 14, 19 bis (masc.).
..	..		
..	..	xi. 28, xii. 20 (quotn.).	..
..	..	..	..
ii. 21.	..	..	..
..	..	iv. 2, v. 4 (?).	..
..	..	..	..
..	..	..	..
ii. 6 (fr. LXX.), iii. 16.	..	..	..
ii. 1 (-λέιν ii. 12, iii. 16, et. Jac. iv. 11, ter.).	..	..	..
..	..	..	..
..	..	..	..
..	..	ii. 14.	..
..	..	iii. 6, 14, x. 23.	Matt. xxi. 38 (?) ps. Joh. v. 4.
..	..	..	..
..	i. 10.	iii. 1.	..

104 LANGUAGE OF THE NEW TESTAMENT.

Word or Phrase.	St. Paul.	St. Luke.
κοινωνία	Saepe.	A. ii. 42.
κοίτη	Rom. ix. 10, xiii. 13.	Ev. xi. 7.
κραταιοῦσθαι	1 Cor. xvi. 13, Eph. iii. 16.	Ev. i. 80, ii. 40.
κρείσσων, -ττων	1 Cor. vii. 9, 38, xi. 17, xii. 31 (?), Phil. i. 23.	..
κυριεύειν	†Rom. vi. 9, 14, vii. 1, xiv. 9, 2 Cor. i. 24, 1 Tim. vi. 15.	Ev. xxii. 25.
λειτουργεῖν, -γία	Rom. xv. 27, 2 Cor. ix. 12, Phil. ii. 17, 30.	A. xiii. 2, Ev. i. 23.
-γὸs	Rom. xiii. 6, xv. 16, Phil. ii. 25.	..
λιθάζειν	2 Cor. xi. 25.	A. v. 26, xiv. 19.
λογικὸs	Rom. xii. 1.	..
λοιδορεῖν	1 Cor. iv. 12.	A. xxiii. 4.
μάλιστα	†Gal. vi. 10, Phil. iv. 22, Philem. 16, 1 Tim. iv. 10, v. 8, 17, 2 Tim. iv. 13, Tit. i. 10.	A. xx. 38, xxv. 26, xxvi. 3.
μαρτύρεσθαι	Gal. v. 3, Eph. iv. 17.	A. xx. 26.
ματαιότης	Rom. viii. 20, Eph. iv. 17.	..
μεθιστάναι vel -νειν	1 Cor. xiii. 2, Col. i. 13.	Ev. xvi. 4, A. xiii. 22, xix. 26.
μεθύειν, -σκεσθαι	Eph. v. 18, 1 Thess. v. 7.	Ev. xii. 45.
μὲν οὖν vel μενοῦνγε	Rom. ix. 20, x. 18, Phil. iii. 8.	Ev. xi. 28.
μέρις	2 Cor. vi. 15, Col. i. 12.	Ev. x. 42, A. viii. 21, xvi. 12.
μεσίτης	†Gal. iii. 19, 20, 1 Tim. ii. 5.	..
μεταδιδόναι	Rom. i. 11, xii. 8, Eph. iv. 28, 1 Thess. ii. 8.	Ev. iii. 11.
μιμητὴς	1 Cor. iv. 16, xi. 1, Eph. v. 1, 1 Thess. i. 6, ii. 14.	..
μόλις	Rom. v. 7.	A. xiv. 18, xxvii. 7, 8, 16.
νεκροῦν	Rom. iv. 19, Col. iii. 5.	..
νουθετεῖν	Rom. xv. 14, 1 Cor. iv. 14, Col. i. 28, iii. 16, 1 Thess. v. 12, 14, 2 Thess iii. 15.	A. ii. 31.

APPENDIX I. TABLE II.

1 Peter.	2 Peter.	Hebrews.	Other N.T. Books.
..	..	xiii. 16.	Joh. Ep. I. i. 3 bis, 6, 7.
..	..	xiii. 4.	..
iii. 17	ii. 21.	Saepius.	..
..	..	,,	..
..	..	x. 11, viii. 6, ix. 21.	..
..	..	i. 7 (fr. LXX.), viii. 2 (-γικὸς i. 14).	..
..	..	xi. 37.	Joh. viii. 5 (?), Joh. x. 31-33, xi. 8.
ii. 2.	..	..	..
ii. 23.	..	..	Joh. ix. 28.
..	ii. 10.	..	..
..	ii. 18.	,,	..
..	..	..	..
..	..	..	..
..	..	..	..
..	..	..	..
..	..	viii. 6, ix. 15, xii. 24 (-τεύειν vi. 17).	..
..	..	..	..
..	..	..	..
iii. 13 (?).	..	vi. 12.	..
iv. 18 (from LXX.).	..	..	..
..	..	xi. 12.	..
..	..	..	..

106 LANGUAGE OF THE NEW TESTAMENT.

Word or Phrase.	St. Paul.	St. Luke.
νοῦς	†Rom. sexies, 1 Cor. septies, alibi quater, 1 Tim. vi. 5, 2 Tim. iii. 8, Tit. i. 15.	Ev. xxiv. 45.
νυνί	Saepius	A. xxii. 1, xxiv. 13(?).
ξενία	Philem. 22.	A. xxviii. 23.
ξυρᾶσθαι	1 Cor. xi. 5, 6.	A. xxi. 24.
οἰκέτης	Rom. xiv. 4.	Ev. xvi. 13, A. x. 7.
οἰκονομία	†1 Cor. ix. 17, Eph. i. 10, iii. 2, 9 (?), 1 Tim. i. 4.	Ev. xvi. 2, 3, 4.
-μος	†Rom. xvi. 23, 1 Cor. iv. 1, 2, Gal. iv. 2, Tit. i. 7.	Ev. xii. 42, xvi. 1, 3, 8.
οἰκτιρμὸς	Rom. xii. 1, 2 Cor. i. 3, Phil. ii. 1, Col. iii. 12.	..
ὁμολογία	†2 Cor. ix. 13, 1 Tim. vi. 12, 13.	..
ὀνειδισμὸς	†Rom. xv. 3 (from LXX.), 1 Tim. iii. 7.	..
ὀνομάζειν	†Rom. xv. 20, 1 Cor. v. 1 (?), 11, Eph. i. 21, iii. 15, v. 3, 2 Tim. ii. 19 (quotn.).	Ev. vi. 13, 14, A. xix. 13.
ὀπτασία	2 Cor. xii. 1.	Ev. i. 22, xxiv. 23, A. xxvi. 19.
ὁρίζειν	Rom. i. 4.	Ev. xxii. 22, A. ii. 23, x. 42, xi. 29, xvii. 26, 31.
ὁσιότης	Eph. iv. 24.	Ev. i. 75.
οὐδέπω	1 Cor. viii. 2 (?).	Ev. xxiii. 53 (?), A. viii. 16 (?).
ὀψώνιον	Rom. vi. 23, 1 Cor. ix. 7, 2 Cor. xi. 8.	Ev. iii. 14.
παγὶς	†Rom. xi. 9 (from LXX.), 1 Tim. iii. 7, vi. 9, 2 Tim. ii. 26.	Ev. xxi. 35.
πάθημα	†Rom. vii. 5, viii. 18, 2 Cor. i. 5, 6, 7, Gal. v. 24, Phil. iii. 10, Col. i. 24, 2 Tim. iii. 11.	..
παιδεία, -ευτής	†Eph. vi. 4, 2 Tim. iii. 16.	..
πάντως	Rom. iii. 9, 1 Cor. v. 10, ix. 10, 22, xvi. 12.	Ev. iv. 23, A. xviii. 21 (?), xxi. 22, xxviii. 4.
παράβασις	†Rom. ii. 23, iv. 15, v. 14, Gal. iii. 19, 1 Tim. ii. 14.	..

APPENDIX I. TABLE II.

1 Peter.	2 Peter.	Hebrews.	Other N.T. Books.
..	..	..	Apoc. xiii. 18, xvii. 9.
..	..	viii. 6, xi. 16 (?).	..
..	..	..	..
..	..	..	..
ii. 18.	..	..	..
..	..	..	..
iv. 10.	..	..	..
..	..	x. 28.	..
..	..	iii. 1, iv. 14, x. 23.	..
..	..	x. 33, xi. 26, xiii. 13.	
..	..	..	..
..	..	..	..
..	..	iv. 7.	..
..	..	..	..
..	..	..	Joh. vii. 39 (?), xix. 41, xx. 9.
..	..	..	..
..	..	..	..
i. 11, iv. 13, v. 1, 9.	..	ii. 9, 10, x. 32.	..
..	..	xii. 5 (fr. LXX.), 7, 8, 11.	..
..	..	..	..
..	..	ii. 2, ix. 15.	..

108 LANGUAGE OF THE NEW TESTAMENT.

Word or Phrase.	St. Paul.	St. Luke.
παραγγελία	†1 Thess. iv. 2, 1 Tim. i. 5, 18.	A. v. 28, xvi. 24.
παράκλησις	†Rom. xii. 8, xv. 4, 5, 1 Cor. xiv. 3, 2 Cor. saepius, Phil. ii. 1, 1 Thess ii. 3, 2 Thess. ii. 16, Philem. 7, 1 Tim. iv. 13.	Ev. ii. 25, vi. 24, A. iv. 36, ix. 31, xiii. 15, xv. 31.
παρασκευάζειν	1 Cor. xiv. 8, 2 Cor. ix. 2, 3.	A. x. 10.
παραχειμάζειν	†1 Cor. xvi. 6, Tit. iii. 12.	A. xxvii. 12, xxviii. 11.
παροξύνεσθαι	1 Cor. xiii. 5.	A. xvii. 16 (-σμὸς xv. 39, et Heb. x. 24).
παρρησιάζεσθαι	Eph. vi. 20, 1 Thess. ii. 2.	A. ix. 27, 29, xiii. 46, xiv. 3, xviii. 26, xix. 8, xxvi. 26.
πατριά	Eph. iii. 15.	Ev. ii. 4, A. iii. 25 (quotn.).
παύεσθαι	1 Cor. xiii. 8, Eph. i. 16, Col. i. 9.	Ev. v. 4, viii. 24, xi. 1, A. v. 42, vi. 13, xiii. 10, xx. 1, 31, xxi. 32.
περιαιρεῖν	2 Cor. iii. 16.	A. xxvii. 20, 40.
πηλίκος	Gal. vi. 11.	
πικρία	Rom. iii. 14 (from LXX.), Eph. iv. 31.	A. viii. 23.
πλάκες	2 Cor. iii. 3 bis.	
πλεονάζειν	Rom. v. 20 bis, vi. 1, 2 Cor. iv. 15, viii. 15 (from LXX.), Phil. iv. 17, 1 Thess. iii. 12, 2 Thess. i. 3.	
πληροφορεῖν, -εῖσθαι	†2 Tim. iv. 5, Rom. iv. 21, xiv. 5, Col. iv. 12 (?), 2 Tim. iv. 17.	Ev. i. 1.
-ία	Col. ii. 2, 1 Thess. i. 5.	
πλουσίως	†Col. iii. 16, 1 Tim. vi. 17, Tit. iii. 6.	
πολιτεία, -τεύεσθαι	Eph. ii. 12, Phil. i. 27 (-ευμα iii. 20).	A. xxii. 28, xxiii. 1.
πορθεῖν	Gal. i. 13, 23.	A. ix. 21.
που (encl.)	Rom. iv. 19.	
πράσσειν	Rom. decies, alibi octies.	Ev. sexies, A. saepius.

APPENDIX I. TABLE II.

1 Peter.	2 Peter.	Hebrews.	Other N.T. Books.
.. ..	.. ..	vi. 18, xii. 5, xiii. 22.	.. ..
.. ..	.. ..	.. ..	.. ..
..	..	..	..
..	..	..	..
..	..	..	..
iv. 1 (iii. 10 $\pi a\theta\epsilon\iota\nu$, quotn.).	..	x. 2.	..
.. .. ..	.. .. ..	x. 11. vii. 4. xii. 15.	.. .. ..
.. ..	.. i. 8.	ix. 4. ..	.. ..
..	..	..	..
.. ..	.. i. 11.	vi. 11, x. 22. ..	.. ..
..	..	..	..
.. .. ..	.. .. ..	.. ii. 6, iv. 4. ..	.. .. Joh. iii. 20, v. 29.

LANGUAGE OF THE NEW TESTAMENT.

Word or Phrase.	St. Paul.	St. Luke.
πρεσβύτης	†Philem. 9, Tit. ii. 2.	Ev. i. 18.
προειπεῖν	Gal. v. 21, 1 Thess. iv. 6.	A. i. 16.
προθυμία	2 Cor. viii. 11, 12, 19, ix. 2.	A. xvii. 11.
προϊδεῖν	Gal. iii. 8.	A. ii. 31.
προκόπτειν	†Rom. xiii. 12, Gal. i. 14, 2 Tim. ii. 16, iii. 9, 13.	Ev. ii. 52.
πρόνοια	Rom. xiii. 14.	A. xxiv. 2.
προορίζειν	Rom. viii. 29, 30, 1 Cor. ii. 7, Eph. i. 5, 11.	A. iv. 28.
πρόσκομμα	Rom. ix. 32, 33 (quotn.), xiv. 13, 20, 1 Cor. viii. 9.	
προσφορά	Rom. xv. 16, Eph. v. 2.	A. xxi. 26, xxiv. 17.
πως (encl.)	Saepe.	xxvii. 12, 29 (?).
ῥαβδίζειν	2 Cor. xi. 25.	A. xvi. 22.
σαρκικός	Rom. vii. 14 (?), xv. 27, 1 Cor. iii. 1 (?), 3 bis, 4 (?), ix. 11, 2 Cor. i. 12, x. 4.	..
-νος	Rom. vii. 14 (?), 1 Cor. iii. 1 (?), 2 Cor. iii. 3.	..
σέβασμα	2 Thess. ii. 4.	A. xvii. 23.
σκληρύνειν	Rom. ix. 18.	A. xix. 9.
σκολιός	Phil. ii. 15.	Ev. iii. 5 (from LXX.), A. ii. 40.
σκοπεῖν	Rom. xvi. 17, 2 Cor. iv. 18, Gal. vi. 1, Phil. ii. 4, iii. 17.	Ev. xi. 35.
σπουδάζειν	†Gal. ii. 10, Eph. iv. 3, 1 Thess. ii. 17, 2 Tim. ii. 15, iv. 9, 21, Tit. iii. 12.	..
-αίως	†Phil. ii. 28, 2 Tim. i. 17, Tit. iii. 13.	Ev. vii. 4.
στεναγμός	Rom. viii. 26.	A. vii. 34 (quotn.).
στοιχεῖν	Rom. iv. 12, Gal. v. 25, vi. 16, Phil. iii. 16.	A. xxi. 24.
συγκαθίζειν	Eph. ii. 6.	Ev. xxii. 55 (?).
συγκεράννυμι	1 Cor. xii. 24.	..
συμβιβάζω	1 Cor. ii. 16, Eph. iv. 16, Col. ii. 2, 19.	A. ix. 22, xvi. 10, xix. 33 (?).
συναντιλαμβάνεσθαι	Rom. viii. 26.	Ev. x. 40.

APPENDIX I. TABLE II.

1 Peter.	2 Peter.	Hebrews.	Other N.T. Books.
..	..	..	..
..	..	..	..
..	..	..	..
..	..	..	..
..	..	..	..
..	..	..	..
..	..	..	..
ii. 8 (quotn.).	..	..	..
..	..	x. 5 (fr. LXX.), 8 (do.), 10, 14, 18.	..
..	..	..	..
..	..	..	..
ii. 11.	..	vii. 16 (?).	..
..	..	vii. 16 (?).	..
..	..	..	..
..	..	iii. 8 (fr. LXX.), 13, 15, iv. 7 (do.).	..
ii. 18.	..	..	..
..	..	..	..
..	i. 10, 15, iii. 14.	iv. 11.	..
..	..	..	..
..	..	..	..
..	..	..	..
..	..	..	..
..	..	iv. 2.	..
..	..	..	..
..	..	..	..

112 LANGUAGE OF THE NEW TESTAMENT.

Word or Phrase.	St. Paul.	St. Luke.
συναπάγεσθαι . .	Rom. xii. 16 (a different sense from the rest), Gal. ii. 13.	..
σύνδεσμος . .	Eph. iv. 3, Col. ii. 19, iii. 14.	A. viii. 23.
συνειδέναι . .	1 Cor. iv. 4.	A. v. 2, xii. 12, xiv. 6.
συνευδοκεῖν . .	Rom. i. 32, 1 Cor. vii. 12, 13.	Ev. xi. 48, A. viii. 1, xxii. 20.
συνοχή . . .	2 Cor. ii. 4.	Ev. xxi. 25.
συστέλλειν . .	1 Cor. vii. 29.	A. v. 6.
σωματικος, -κῶς .	†1 Tim. iv. 8, Col. ii. 9.	Ev. iii. 22.
σωτήριον . .	Eph. vi. 17.	Ev. ii. 30, iii. 6.
τάξις . . .	1 Cor. xiv. 40, Col. ii. 5.	Ev. i. 8.
ταπεινοφροσύνη .	Eph. iv. 2, Phil. ii. 3, Col. ii. 18, 23, iii. 12.	A. xx. 19.
ταχέως . . .	†1 Cor. iv. 19, Gal. i. 6, Phil. ii. 19, 24, 2 Thess. ii. 2, 1 Tim. v. 22, 2 Tim. iv. 9.	Ev. xiv. 21, xvi. 6.
τελειότης . .	Col. iii. 14.	..
* τετράποδα . .	Rom. i. 23.	A. x. 12, xi. 6.
τήρησις . . .	1 Cor. vii. 19.	A. iv. 3, v. 18.
τοιγαροῦν . .	1 Thess. iv. 8.	..
τοίνυν . . .	1 Cor. ix. 26.	Ev. xx. 25.
τοὐναντίον . .	2 Cor. ii. 7, Gal. ii. 7.	..
τυγχάνειν . .	†1 Cor. xiv. 10, xv. 37, xvi. 6, 2 Tim. ii. 10.	Ev. x. 30 (?), xx. 35, A. xix. 11, xxiv. 3, xxvi. 22, xxvii. 3, xxviii. 2.
ὕβρις . . .	2 Cor. xii. 10.	A. xxvii. 10, 21.
ὑπακοή . . .	Rom. septies, 2 Cor. vii. 15, x. 5, 6, Philem. 21.	..
-ήκοος . . .	2 Cor. ii. 7, Phil. ii. 8.	A. vii. 39.
ὑπεναντίος . .	Col. ii. 14.	..
ὑπεράνω . .	Eph. i. 21, iv. 10.	..
ὑπερέχειν . .	Rom. xiii. 1, Phil. ii. 3, iii. 8, iv. 7.	..
ὑπόστασις . .	2 Cor. ix. 4, xi. 17.	..
ὑποστέλλειν, -εσθαι .	Gal. ii. 12.	A. xx. 20, 27.
ὑποτάσσειν, -εσθαι .	†Saepissime.	Ev. ii. 51, x. 17, 20.
ὑποφέρειν . .	†1 Cor. x. 13, 2 Tim. iii. 11.	..
ὑστέρημα . .	1 Cor. xvi. 17, 2 Cor. viii. 13, 14, ix. 12, xi. 9, Phil. ii. 30, Col. i. 24, 1 Thess. iii. 10.	Ev. xxi. 4.

* It is not worth giving reference to a word like τετρακόσια.

APPENDIX I. TABLE II.

1 Peter.	2 Peter.	Hebrews.	Other N.T. Books.
..	iii. 17.	..	..
..	..	..	..
..	..	..	..
..	..	..	..
..	..	..	..
..	..	..	..
..	..	..	..
..	..	Septies ex LXX.	..
v. 5.	..	..	..
..	..	..	Joh. xi. 31.
..	..	vi. 1.	..
..	..	..	..
..	..	..	..
..	..	xii. 1.	..
..	..	xiii. 13.	Jac. ii. 24 (?).
iii. 9.	..	..	..
..	..	viii. 6, xi. 35.	..
i. 2, 14, 22.	..	v. 8.	..
..	..	..	..
..	..	x. 27.	..
..	..	ix. 5.	..
ii. 13.	..	..	..
..	..	i. 3, iii. 14, xi. 1.	..
..	..	x. 38 (fr. LXX.)	..
ii. 13, 18, iii. 1, 5, 22, v. 5.	..	ii. 5, 8 (fr. LXX.), xii. 9.	Jac. iv. 7.
ii. 19.	..	..	..
..	..	..	..

114 LANGUAGE OF THE NEW TESTAMENT.

Word or Phrase.	St. Paul.	St. Luke.
φάσκειν	Rom. i. 22.	A. xxiv. 9, xxv. 19.
φείδεσθαι	Rom. viii. 32, xi. 21 bis, 1 Cor. vii. 28, 2 Cor. i. 23, xii. 6, xiii. 2.	A. xx. 29.
φθαρτὸς	Rom. i. 23, 1 Cor. ix. 25, xv. 53, 54.	..
φιλαδελφία	Rom. xii. 10, 1 Thess. iv. 9.	..
φίλημα	Rom. xvi. 16, 1 Cor. xvi. 20, 2 Cor. xiii. 12, 1 Thess. v. 26.	Ev. vii. 45, xxii. 48.
φιλοξενία	Rom. xii. 13 (-ος 1 Tim. iii. 2, Tit. i. 8).	..
φόρος	Rom. xiii. 6, 7.	Ev. xx. 22, xxiii. 2.
φράττειν	Rom. iii. 19, 2 Cor. xi. 10.	..
φρόνησις	Eph. i. 8.	Ev. i. 17.
φρουρεῖν	2 Cor. xi. 32, Gal. iii. 23, Phil. iv. 7.	..
φυσικὸς	Rom. i. 26, 27.	..
χαρίζεσθαι	Saepius.	Ev. vii. 21, 42, 43, A. iii. 14, xxv. 11, 16, xxvii. 24.
-σμα	†Rom. sexies, 1 Cor. septies, 2 Cor. i. 11, 1 Tim. iv. 14, 2 Tim. i. 6.	..
χαριτοῦν	Eph. i. 6.	Ev. i. 28.
χειροτονεῖν	2 Cor. viii. 19.	A. xiv. 23.
χορηγεῖν	2 Cor. ix. 10.	..
χρῆσθαι	1 Cor. vii. 21, 31, ix. 12, 15, 2 Cor. i. 17, iii. 12, xiii. 10, 1 Tim. i. 8, v. 23.	A. xxvii. 3, 17.
χρίειν	2 Cor. i. 21.	Ev. iv. 18 (from LXX.), A. iv. 27, x. 38.
ψαλμὸς	1 Cor. xiv. 26, Eph. v. 19, Col. iii. 16.	Ev. xx. 42, xxiv. 44, A. i. 20, xiii. 33.
ψῦχος	2 Cor. xi. 27.	A. xxviii. 2.

APPENDIX I. TABLE II. 115

1 Peter.	2 Peter.	Hebrews.	Other N.T. Books.
.. ..	ii. 4, 5.	.. ..	F. L. Apoc. ii. 2. ..
i. 18, 23.	..	..	..
i. 22. v. 14.	i. 7 bis. ..	xiii. 1. ..	.. ..
(-ος iv. 9.)	..	xiii. 2.	..
.. .. .. i. 5.	.. ..	.. xi. 33.	.. ..
.. ..	ii. 12. ..	.. ..	-κῶς Jud. 10. ..
iv. 10.	..	..	..
.. .. iv. 11. ..	.. ..	.. ..	.. ..
..	..	i. 9 (fr. LXX.).	..
..	..	..	Joh. xviii. 18.
..	..	..	..

APPENDIX I.

ILLUSTRATING THE AFFINITIES OF ST. LUKE WITH

Word or Phrase.	SS. JAMES AND JUDE.	ST. PETER.	HEBREWS.
ἀγαθοποιεῖν, -ία, ός	..	I. ii. 15, 20; iii. 6, 17; iv. 19; ii. 14.	..
ἀγαθουργεῖν or -οεργεῖν	..	..	..
ἀγαλλίασις	Jud. 24.	..	i. 9 (LXX.).
ἁγιασμός	..	I. i. 2.	xii. 14.
ἄγκυρα	..	..	vi. 19.
ἁγνίζειν	Jac. iv. 8.	I. i. 22.	..
ἄγνοια	..	I. i. 14.	..
[ᾄδειν]	..	..	..
ἀθέμιτον	..	I. iv. 3.	..
ἀθλεῖν, -ησις	..	..	-ησις x. 32.
αἰδώς	..	..	xii. 28 T. R.
αἰσχροκερδής, -ῶς	..	-ῶς I. v. 2.	..
ἄκαρπος	Jud. 12.	II. i. 8.	..
ἄλογος	Jud. 10.	II. ii. 12.	..
ἀμελεῖν	..	II. i. 12 (T. R.)	ii. 3, viii. 9 (fr. LXX.).
ἀμίαντος	Jac. i. 27.	I. i. 4.	vii. 26, xiii. 4.
ἄμωμος	Jud. 24.	I. i. 19 (ἀμώμητος II. iii. 14.)	ix. 14.
ἀνάγειν *	..	..	xiii. 20.
ἀναδέχεσθαι	..	..	xi. 17.

* Excluding the sense "put to sea," which is peculiar to St. Luke.

TABLE III.

THE LATER PAULINE AND CATHOLIC EPISTLES.

St. Luke	Pastoral Epp.	Eph. and Col.	Other N.T. Books.
-εῖν Ev. vi. 9, 33, 35 (Acts xiv. 17 T. R.)	..	..	-εῖν Mark iii. 4 (not quite certain), Joh. Ep. III. 11.
(contr.) A. xiv. 17.	(uncontr.) 1 Tim. vi. 18.	..	..
Ev. i. 14, 44; A. ii. 46.	..	..	..
..	1 Tim. ii. 15.	..	7 times in St. Paul's other Epp.
A. xxvii. 29, 30, 40.	..	..	..
A. xxi. 24, xxiv. 18.	..	..	Joh. xi. 55; Ep. I. iii. 3.
A. iii. 17, xvii. 30.	..	E. iv. 18.	..
..	..	E .v. 19; C. iii. 16.	Apoc. ter.
A. x. 28.	..	..	..
..	-εῖν 2 Tim. ii. 5.	..	..
..	1 Tim. ii. 9.	..	..
..	1 Tim. iii. (3 T. R.) 8; Tit. i. 7.	..	..
..	Tit. iii. 14.	E. v. 11.	Matt. xiii. 22, = Mark iv. 19; 1 Cor. xiv. 14.
A. xxv. 27.	..	..	..
..	1 Tim. iv. 14.	..	Matt. xxii. 5.
..	..	..	..
..	..	E. i. 4, v. 27; C. i. 22.	Phil. ii. 15 (?); Apoc. xiv. 5. v. l. ἀμώμητα.
Ev. ii. 22, iv. 5; A. vii. 41, ix. 39, xii. 4, xvi. 34.	..	..	Matt. iv. 1; Rom. x. 7.
A. xxviii. 7.	..	..	.

Word or Phrase.	SS. JAMES AND JUDE.	ST. PETER.	HEBREWS.
ἀναθεωρεῖν			xiii. 7.
ἀναιρεῖν			x. 9.
ἀνακάμπτειν			xi. 15.
ἀναλαμβάνειν			
-λημψις			
ἀνάμνησις			x. 3.
ἀνάπτειν	Jac. iii. 5.		
ἀναστρέφεσθαι,* -στροφή, -φή	Jac. iii. 13.	I. i. 17; i. 15, 18, ii. 12, iii. 1, 2, 16, II. ii. 7, 18, iii. 11.	x. 33, xiii. 18; xiii. 7.
ἀναφέρειν †	Jac. ii. 21.	I. ii. 5, 24.	vii. 27 (bis), ix. 28, xiii. 15.
ἄνοια			
ἀνορθοῦν			xii. 12.
ἀντιλαμβάνεσθαι			
ἀντιλέγειν			
ἀντιλογία	Jud. 11.		vi. 16, vii. 7, xii. 3.
ἀντίτυπον		I. iii. 21.	ix. 24.
ἄνυδρος	Jud. 12.	II. ii. 17.	
ἀνυπότακτος			ii. 8.
ἀνώτερον			x. 8.
ἀνωφελής			vii. 18.
ἀπαλλάσσειν, -εσθαι			ii. 15.
[ἀπαλλοτριοῦσθαι]			
ἅπαξ	Jud. 3, 5.	I. iii. 18 (20 T. R.).	vi. 4, ix. 7, 26, 27, 28, x. 2, xii. 26, 27.

* In the sense correlative to the noun.
† Excluding the physical sense "to carry up." We do not draw a line between the

APPENDIX I. TABLE III.

St. Luke.	Pastoral Epp.	Eph. and Col.	Other N.T. Books.
A. xvii. 23.	..	..	..
Ev. xxii. 2, xxiii. 32; A. saepius.	..	..	Matt. ii. 16; 2 Thess. ii. 8 (prob.).
Ev. x. 6; A. xviii. 21.	..	..	Matt. ii. 12.
A. 8 times.	1 Tim. iii. 16; 2 Tim. iv. 11.	E. vi. 13, 16.	Mark xvi. 19.
Ev. ix. 51.	..	..	..
Ev. xxii. 19.	..	..	1 Cor. xi. 24-5 (‖ to Luke l. c.).
Ev. xii. 49 (A. xxviii. 2 T. R.)	..	..	..
..	1 Tim. iii. 15; iv. 12.	E. ii. 3; iv. 22.	2 Cor. i. 12; Gal i. 13.
..	..	..	..
Ev. vi. 11.	2 Tim. iii. 9.	..	..
Ev. xiii. 13; A. xv. 16 (quotn.).	..	..	..
Ev. i. 54, A. xx. 35.	1 Tim. vi. 2.	..	..
Ev. ii. 34; xx. 27 (si vera l.); A. xiii. 45, xxviii. 19, 22.	Tit. i. 9, ii. 9.	..	Joh. xix. 12 Rom. x. 21 (fr. LXX.).
..	..	..	..
Ev. xi. 24.	..	..	Matt. xii. 43 (‖ to Luke).
..	1 Tim. i. 9; Tit. i. 6, 10.	..	..
Ev. xiv. 10.	..	..	..
..	Tit. iii. 9.	..	..
Ev. xii. 58; A. xix. 12.	..	..	..
..	..	E. ii. 12, iv. 18; C. i. 21.	..
..	..	..	..

senses of "*bearing*" sins and "*offering*" sacrifice.

Word or Phrase.	SS. JAMES AND JUDE.	ST. PETER.	HEBREWS.
ἀπειλεῖν, -ή	..	-εῖν I. ii. 23.	..
ἀπέχεσθαι, c. gen.	..	I. ii. 11,	..
ἀπογράφεσθαι	..	..	xii. 23.
ἀποδέχεσθαι, -κτος, -δοχή	..	..	..
ἀποθνήσκειν, "to be dying"	..	..	xi. 21 (cf. viii. 8).
ἀπόκεισθαι	..	..	ix. 27.
ἀπόλαυσις	..	..	xi. 25.
ἀπολείπειν	Jud. 6.	..	iv. 6, 9, x. 26 (in sense different from the rest).
ἀποτίθεσθαι	Jac. i. 21.	I. ii. 1 (ἀπόθεσις I. iii. 21, II. i. 14.)	xii. 1.
ἀργὸς	Jac. ii. 20, but νεκρὰ T. R.	II. i. 8.	..
ἀρετή	..	I. ii. 9, II. i. 3, 5 bis.	..
ἀρχηγὸς	..	..	ii. 10, xii. 2.
ἀσάλευτος	..	..	xii. 28.
ἀσεβής, -βεια, -βεῖν	Jud. 4, 15 bis; -ῆς 15,18; -εῖν 15 (quotn.).	-ῆς I. iv. 18, II. ii. 5, iii. 7; -εῖν II. ii. 6.	..
ἄσπιλος	Jac. i. 27.	I. i. 19, II. iii. 14.	..
ἀστεῖος	..	..	xi. 23.
ἀσώτως, -τία	..	I. iv. 4.	..
ἀτμὶς	Jac. iv. 14.	..	..
αὐθάδης	..	II. ii. 10.	..
ἀφαιρεῖν	..	..	x. 4.

St. Luke.	Pastoral Epp.	Eph. and Col.	Other N.T. Books.
A. iv. 17, 29; ix. 1. A. xv. 29.	.. 1 Tim. iv. 3.	-η E. vi. 9. ..	.. Acts. xv. 20; 1 Thess. iv. 3, v. 22 c. ἀπό.
Ev. ii. 1, 3, 5, -φή ii. 2, A. v. 37.	..	..	..
-δέχεσθαι Ev. viii. 40, ix. 11; A. ii. 41 (xv. 4 T. R.), xviii. 27, xxi. 17, xxiv. 3, xxviii. 30.	-κτος 1 Tim. ii. 3, v. 4; -δοχή i. 15, iv. 9.	..	..
Ev. viii. 42. Ev. xix. 20.	.. 2 Tim. iv. 8. 1 Tim. vi. 17. 2 Tim. iv. 13, 20; Tit. i. 5.	.. C. i. 5.	.. ..
A. vii. 58.	..	E. iv. 22, 25; C. iii. 8.	Rom. xiii. 12.
..	1 Tim. v. 13 bis (Tit. i. 12, quotn.).	..	3 or 4 times in Matt.
..	..	..	Phil. iv. 8.
A. iii. 15. v. 31. A. xxvii. 41. ..	.. .. -ης 1 Tim. i. 9; -εια 2 Tim. ii. 16; Tit. ii. 12. 1 Tim. vi. 14.	.. ..	.. .. Rom. i. 18, iv. 5, v. 6 (xi. 26 LXX.). ..
A. vii. 20. -ως Ev. xv. 13. (A. ii. 19 LXX.). .. Ev. i. 25, x. 42, xvi. 3, xxii. 50 (∥ to Mt. Mk.)	.. Tit. i. 6. .. Tit. i. 7. ..	.. Eph. v. 18.	.. .. Matt. xxvi. 51 = Mark xiv. 47; Apoc. xxii. 19 bis (Rom. xi. 27, LXX.).

122　LANGUAGE OF THE NEW TESTAMENT.

Word or Phrase.	SS. James and Jude.	St. Peter.	Hebrews.
ἄφεσις *	..	..	ix. 22, x. 18.
[ἀφή]	..	..	..
ἀφιλάργυρος	..	..	xiii. 5.
ἀφιστάναι, -σθαι	..	..	iii. 12.
ἀχάριστος	..	..	..
[βαπτισμὸς]	..	..	vi. 2, ix. 10.
βέβηλος	..	..	xii. 16.
βίος	..	I. iv. 3; βιοῦν ib. 2.	..
βλάσφημος	..	II. ii. 11.	..
βοήθεια	..	..	iv. 16.
βουλή	..	..	vi. 17.
βραδὺς, -υτὴς, -ύνω	-ὺς Jac. i. 19 bis.	-ύνω, -υτὴς II. iii. 9.	..
βραχὺς	..	..	ii. 7 (fr. LXX.), 9, xiii. 22.
βοέφος	..	I. ii. 2.	..
βυθίζειν, -ζεσθαι	..	..	..
γενεαλογία, -γεῖσθαι	..	..	-εῖσθαι vii. 6.
γυμνάζειν, -εσθαι	..	II. ii. 14.	v. 14, xii. 11.
δελεάζω	Jac. i. 14.	II. ii. 14, 18.	..

* ἀφιέναι in the sense of "forgive" is not found in St. Paul, except Rom. iv. 7 from

St. Luke.	Pastoral Epp.	Eph. and Col.	Other N.T. Books.
Ev. i. 77, iii. 3 (|| to Mark), iv. 18 bis (LXX.), xxiv. 47; A. ii. 38, v. 31, x. 43, xiii. 38, xxvi. 18.	..	E. i. 7; C. i. 14.	Matt. xxvi. 28; Mark i. 4, iii. 29.
..	..	E. iv. 16; C. ii. 19.	..
..	1 Tim. iii. 3.	..	..
Ev. ii. 37, iv. 13, viii. 13, xiii. 27; A. v. 37-8, xii. 10, xv. 38, xix. 9, xxii. 29 : ἀποστασία xxi. 21.	1 Tim. iv. 1, vi. 5(?); 2 Tim. ii. 19 (quotn. ?).	..	2 Cor. xii. 8, ἀποστασία 2 Thess. ii. 3.
Ev. vi. 35.	2 Tim. iii. 2.	..	..
..	..	..	Mark vii. 4, 8.
βεβηλῶσαι A. xxiv. 6.	1 Tim. i. 9, iv. 7, vi. 20; 2 Tim. ii. 16.	..	βεβηλοῦσιν Matt. xii. 5.
Ev. viii. 14, 43, xv. 12, 30, xxi. 4; βίωσις A. xxvi. 4.	1 Tim. ii. 2; 2 Tim. ii. 4.	..	Mark xii. 44; Joh. Ep. I. ii. 16, iii. 17. βιωτικός Luc. xxi. 34; 1 Cor. vi. 3, 4.
A. vi. 11 (13 T. R.)	1 Tim. i. 13; 2 Tim. iii. 2.	..	Apoc. xiii. 5 ? (v. l.)
A. xxvii. 17.	..	..	..
Ev. vii. 30, xxiii. 51; A. ii. 23, iv. 28, v. 38, xiii. 36, xx. 27, xxvii. 12, 42.	..	E. i. 11.	1 Cor. iv. 5.
Ev. xxiv. 25 -ὺς (A. xxvii. 7 βραδυπλοεῖν.)	-ύνω 1 Tim. iii. 15.	..	..
Ev. xxii. 58; A. v. 34, xxvii. 28.	..	..	Joh. vi. 7.
Ev. i. 41, 44, ii. 12, 16, xviii. 15; A. vii. 19.	2 Tim. iii. 15.	..	..
Ev. v. 7.	1 Tim. vi. 9.	..	..
..	-ία 1 Tim. i. 4; Tit. iii. 9.	..	..
..	1 Tim. iv. 7.	..	..
..	..	..	..

LXX.

124 LANGUAGE OF THE NEW TESTAMENT.

Word or Phrase.	SS. JAMES AND JUDE.	ST. PETER.	HEBREWS.
δέον ἐστιν		I. i. 6.	
δεσπότης	Jud. 4.*	I. ii. 18, II. ii. 1*	
διαβῆναι (only used in aor.)			xi. 29.
διαλέγεσθαι	Jud. 9.		xii. 5.
διαμαρτύρεσθαι			ii. 6.
διάνοια		I. i. 13, II. iii. 1.	viii. 10, x. 16 (both fr. LXX.).
διασώζειν		I. iii. 20.	
διατίθεσθαι			(viii. 10, x. 16 fr. LXX.), ix. 16, 17.
δι' ἣν αἰτίαν			ii. 11.†
δόγμα			xi. 23 (v. l.).
δοκίμιον (τὸ δ. ὑμῶν τῆς πίστευς)	Jac. i. 3.	I. i. 7.	
δόξαι	Jud. 8.	I. i. 11, II. ii. 10.	
δρόμος			
δυνάστης			
ἔθος			x. 25.
εἰρηνικὸς	Jac. iii. 17.		xii. 11.
εἰσάγειν, -εσθαι			i. 6.
εἰσιέναι §			ix. 6.
εἰσφέρειν, -ενεγκεῖν			xiii. 11.

* Of God or Christ.   † ="For which cause.'   ‡ ="For what cause.

St. Luke.	Pastoral Epp.	Eph. and Col.	Other N.T. Books.
A. xix. 36.			
Ev. ii. 29,* A. iv. 24.*	1 Tim. vi. 1, 2; 2 Tim. ii. 21; Tit. ii. 9.		Apoc. vi. 10. *
Ev. xvi. 26; A. xvi. 9.			
A. decies.			Mark. ix. 34.
Ev. xvi. 28; A. ii. 40, viii. 25, x. 42, xviii. 5, xx. 21, 23, 24, xxiii. 11, xxviii. 23.	1 Tim. v. 21; 2 Tim. ii. 14, iv. 1.		1 Thess. iv. 6.
Ev. i. 51 (x. 27 fr. LXX.).		E. i. 18 (T. R.), ii. 3, iv. 18; C. i. 21.	Joh. Ep. I. v. 20 (Matt. xxii. 37; Mark xii. 30 fr. LXX.).
Ev. vii. 3; A. xxiii. 24, xxvii. 43, 44, xxviii. 1, 4.			
Ev. xxii. 29 bis; A. iii. 25.			
Ev. viii. 47; ‡ A. xxii. 24; ‡ cf. x. 21, xxiii. 28, xxviii. 20.	2 Tim. i. 6,† 12;† Tit. i. 13.†		
Ev. ii. 1; A. xvi. 4, xvii. 7.		E. ii. 15; C. ii. 14, 20 (δογματίζεσθε)	
A. xiii. 25, xx. 24.	2 Tim. iv. 7.		
Ev. i. 52; A. viii. 27.	1 Tim. vi. 15.		
Ev. i. 9, ii. 42, xxii. 39; A. vi. 14, xv. 1, xvi. 21, xxi, 21, xxv. 16, xxvi. 3, xxviii. 17.			Joh. xix. 40.
Ev. ii. 27, xiv. 21, xxii. 54; A. vii. 45, ix. 8, xxi 28, 29, 37, xxii. 24.			Joh. xviii. 16.
A. iii. 3, xxi. 18, 26.			
Ev. v. 18, 19, xi. 4 (|| to Matt.), xii. 11 (best text); A. xvii. 20.	1 Tim. vi. 7.		Matt. vi. 13

§ Other compounds of εἶμι (ἀπ- and ἐξιέναι) are peculiar to Acts (xvii. 10; xiii. 42, xvii. 15, xx. 7, xxvii. 43).

126　LANGUAGE OF THE NEW TESTAMENT.

Word or Phrase.	SS. JAMES AND JUDE.	ST. PETER.	HEBREWS.
ἐκζητεῖν . . .	. .	I. i. 10.	xi. 6, xii. 17.
ἐκλείπω . . .	. .	. .	i. 12 (fr. LXX.).
ἑκουσίως . . .	. .	I. v. 2.	x. 26.
ἐκτενής, -ῶς, -έστερον	. .	I. i. 22, iv. 8.	. .
ἐκτρέπεσθαι . .	. .	. .	xii. 13.
ἐκφέρειν,　ἐξοίσειν, ἐξενεγκεῖν . .	. .	. .	vi. 8.
ἔλεγχος . . .	. .	. .	xi. 1.
ἐμπίπτειν . .	. .	. .	x. 31.
ἐμπλέκεσθαι . .	. .	II. ii. 20 (ἐμπλοκὴ I. iii. 3.)	. .
ἔννοια . . .	. .	I. iv. 1.	iv. 12.
ἐνοχλεῖν . . .	. .	. .	xii. 15 (f. l. fr. LXX?).
ἔντρομος . . .	. .	. .	xii. 21.
ἐξάγειν . . .	. .	. .	. .
ἐξαρτίζειν * . .	. .	. .	. .
ἔξοδος . . .	. .	II. i. 15.	xi. 22.
ἐπάγειν . . .	. .	II. ii. 1, 5.	. .
ἐπακολουθεῖν . .	. .	I. ii. 21.	. .
ἐπέρχεσθαι, -ελθεῖν .	Jac. v. 1.	. .	. .
ἐπέχειν, "to attend to" . . .	. .	. .	. .
ἐπίγνωσις [τῆς] ἀληθείας . .	. .	(ἐπίγνωσις II. i. 2, 3, 8, ii. 20.)	x. 26.
ἐπιεικής . . .	Jac. iii. 17.	I. ii. 18.	. .

* Here the sense is literal (or consciously parabolic).

APPENDIX I. TABLE III.

St. Luke.	Pastoral Epp.	Eph. and Col.	Other N.T. Books.
Ev. xi. 50-1; A. xv. 17 (fr. LXX.).	..	..	Rom. iii. 11 (fr. LXX.).
Ev. xvi. 9, xxii. 32 (xxiii. 45 v. l.).	..	..	..
..	..	..	..
Ev. xxii. 44; A. xii. 5; ἐκτένεια A. xxvi. 7.	..	..	..
..	1 Tim. i. 6, v. 15, vi. 20; 2 Tim. iv. 4.	..	..
Ev. xv. 22; A. v. 6, 9, 10, 15.	1 Tim. vi. 7.	..	..
..	2 Tim. iii. 16 (T. R.).	..	..
Ev. vi. 39 * (best text: ‖ to Matt.), x. 36, xiv. 5 † (T. R.).	1 Tim. iii. 6, 7, vi. 9.	..	Matt. xii. 11.‡
..	2 Tim. ii. 4.	..	..
..	..	..	..
Ev. vi. 18 (v.l.).	..	..	..
A. vii. 32, xvi. 29.	..	..	..
Ev. xxiv. 50; A. octies.	..	..	Mar. viii. 23 (T. R.), Joh. x. 3.
A. xxi. 5.†	2 Tim. iii. 17.†	..	..
Ev. ix. 31.	..	..	..
A. v. 28.	..	..	..
..	1 Tim. v. 10, 24.	..	Mark xvi. 20.
Ev. i. 35, xi. 22, xxi. 26, 35 (T. R.); A. i. 8, viii. 24, xiii. 40, xiv. 19.	..	E. ii. 7.	..
Ev. xiv. 7; A. iii. 5.	1 Tim. iv. 16.	.	..
..	1 Tim. ii. 4; 2 Tim. ii. 25, iii. 7; Tit. i. 1.	ἐπίγνωσις E. i. 17, iv. 13; C. i. 9, 10, ii. 2, iii. 10.	Also Rom. i. 28, iii. 20, x. 2; Phil. i. 9; Philem. 6.
..	1 Tim. iii. 3; Tit. iii. 2.	..	Phil. iv. 5.

† These passages are only cited as an example of what is *not* counted.
‡ Here the sense is literal (or consciously parabolic).

Word or Phrase.	SS. JAMES AND JUDE.	ST. PETER.	HEBREWS.
ἐπίθεσις (χειρῶν) .	..	..	vi. 2.
ἐπιλαμβάνεσθαι .	..	..	ii. 16 bis, viii. 9 (fr. LXX.).
ἐπιμελεῖσθαι, -λεια, -λῶς . . .	..	..	..
ἐπίσκοπος, -πή, -πεῖν	..	-ος I. ii. 25; -ῆ ii. 12; -εῖν v. 2	-εῖν xii. 15.
ἐπίσταμαι . .	Jac. iv. 14; Jud. 10.	..	xi. 8.
ἐπιστέλλειν . .	..	..	xiii. 22.
ἐπιστρέφειν, "to convert" . .	Jac. v. 19, 20.	..	..
ἐπιφαίνειν, -φάνεια .	..	..	..
ἐπόπτης, -πτεύειν .	..	II. i. 16; I. ii. 12, iii. 2.	..
ἐπ' τῶν ἐσχάτ. ἡμερῶν, χρόνων, τοῦ χρόνου . .	Jud. 18 (ἐν ἐσχάτῳ χρ. ἡμέραις, Jac. v. 3).	I. i. 20, II. iii. 3.	i. 2.
ἐργασία . . .	..	..	..
Ἐρυθρὰ Θάλασσα *	..	..	xi. 29.
ἐσθής . . .	Jac. ii. 2 bis, 3.	..	..
ἐσώτερος . .	..	..	vi. 19.
ἑτοίμως ἔχειν . .	..	I. iv. 5.	..

* As a general rule pr. n. are not included in this list. But see p. 2; and what is 11, ix. 4.

APPENDIX I. TABLE III.

St. Luke.	Pastoral Epp.	Eph. and Col.	Other N.T. Books.
A. viii. 18.	1 Tim. iv. 14; 2 Tim. i. 6.	..	..
Ev. ix. 47, xiv. 4, xx. 20, 26, xxiii. 26; A. ix. 27, xvi. 19, xvii. 19, xviii. 17, xxi. 30, 33, xxiii. 19.	1 Tim. vi. 12, 19.	..·	Matt. xiv. 31, Mark viii. 23.
Ev. x. 34, 35; -λεια A. xxvii. 3; -ῶς E v. xv. 8.	1 Tim. iii. 5.	..	..
-ος A. xx. 28; -ἡ i. 20 (fr. LXX.); Ev. xix. 44.	-ος 1 Tim. iii. 2; Tit. i. 7; -ἡ 1 Tim. iii. 1.	..	-ος Phil. i. 1.
A. x. 28, xv. 7, xviii. 25, xix. 15, 25, xx. 18, 19, xxiv. 10, xxvi. 26 (cf. 3).	1 Tim. vi. 4.	..	Mark xiv. 68.
A. xv. 20, xxi. 25 (T. R.; may be right).	..	..	..
Ev. i. 16, 17 (not from LXX.); A. xxvi. 18 (prob.).	..	..	..
Ev. i. 79; A. xxvii. 20.	Tit. ii. 11, iii. 4; ii. 13; 1 Tim. vi. 14; 2 Tim. i. 10, iv. 1, 8.	(ἐπιφαύσκειν E. v. 14.)	-νεια 2 Thess. ii. 8; -νῆς A. ii. 20 (fr. LXX.).
..	..	..	..
..	ἐν ἐσχάταις ἡμέραις 2 Tim. iii. 1.	..	ἐσχάτη ὥρα Joh. Ep. I. ii. 18 bis.
Ev. xii. 58; A. xvi. 16, 19, xix. 24, 25.	..	E. iv. 19.	..
A. vii. 36.	..	..	..
Ev. xxiii. 11, xxiv. 4; A. i. 10, x. 30, xii. 21.	..	..	..
A. xvi. 24.	..	..	..
A. xxi. 13.	..	..	2 Cor. xii. 14; ἐν ἑτοίμῳ ἔχειν *ib.* x. 6.

said there would apply to the mention of 'Ἀαρὼν in Luke i. 5; Acts vii. 40; Heb. v. 4, vii.

130 LANGUAGE OF THE NEW TESTAMENT.

Word or Phrase.	SS. JAMES AND JUDE.	ST. PETER.	HEBREWS.
εὐαγγελιστής εὐεργέτης, -τεῖν, -σία	.. ..	.. ..	.. ..
εὔθετος εὔθυμος, -μως, -μεῖν .	.. Jac. v. 13.	.. ..	vi. 7 ..
εὐλαβής, -εια, -εῖσθαι	..	..	-εια v. 7, xii. 28; -εῖσθαι xi. 7.
εὐσεβής, -ῶς, -εια, -εῖν	..	-ής II. ii. 9 ; -εια i. 3, 6, 7, iii. 11.	...
εὔσπλαγχνος ἐφίστασθαι, ἐπιστῆ-ναι	.. ..	I. iii. 8. ..	.. ..
ἔχειν, inf. = δύνασθαι	..	II. i. 15.	vi. 13, xiii. 10 (v. l.).
ζήτησις	..	..	..
ζόφος ζωγρεῖν ζωογονεῖν	Jud. 6, 13.	II. ii. 4, 17.	xii. 18. .. ..
ζῷον ἡγούμενος	Jud. 10. ..	II. ii. 12. ..	xiii. 11. xiii. 7, 17, 24.
ἡδονή ἡλικία	Jac. iv. 1, 3. ..	II. ii. 13. ..	.. xi. 11.
ἡλίκος ἡσύχιος, -ία, -άζειν .	Jac. iii. 5 bis. ..	.. -ιος I. iii. 4.	.. ..

APPENDIX I. TABLE III.

St. Luke.	Pastoral Epp.	Eph. and Col.	Other N.T. Books.
A. xxi. 8.	2 Tim. iv. 5.	E. iv. 11.	..
Ev. xxii. 25 ; A. x. 38 ; iv. 9.	-σία 1 Tim. vi. 2.	..	..
Ev. ix. 62, xiv. 35.	..	..	..
A. xxvii. 36 ; xxiv. 10 (-στερον); xxvii. 22, 25.	..	..	..
-ῆς Ev. ii. 25 ; A. ii. 5, viii. 2, xxii. 12 (prob.); -εῖσθαι xxiii. 10 T. R.	..	..	..
A. x. 2, 7, xxii. 12 (T. R.) ; iii. 12 ; xvii. 23.	-ῶς 2 Tim. iii. 12; Tit. ii. 12; -εια 1 Tim. vi. 3 ; 2 Tim. iii. 5 ; Tit. i. 1; -εῖν 1 Tim. v. 4.	..	..
..	..	E. iv. 32.	..
Ev. septies, A. undecies.	2 Tim. iv. 2, 6.	..	1 Thess. v. 3 (not quite certain).
Ev. vii. 42, xii. 4, xiv. 14 ; A. iv. 14, xxv. 26 (bis T. R.).	Tit. ii. 8.	..	..
A. xv. 2 (?), xxv. 20 (ζήτημα quinquies).	1 Tim. i. 4, vi. 4 ; 2 Tim. ii. 23; Tit. iii. 9.	..	Joh. iii. 25.
Ev. v. 10.	2 Tim. ii. 26.	..	..
Ev. xvii. 33 ; A. vii. 19.	1 Tim. vi. 13 (best text.)	..	..
..	..	..	Apoc. passim.
Ev. xxii. 26, A. vii. 10 (xiv. 12 ?), xv. 22.	..	..	Matt. ii. 6 (quotn. not LXX.).
Ev. viii. 14.	Tit. iii. 3.	..	..
Ev. ii. 52, xii. 25 (∥ to Matt.), xix. 3.	..	E. iv. 13.	Matt. vi. 27, Joh. ix. 21, 23.
..	..	C. ii. 1.	..
-ία A. xxii. 2 ; -άζειν Ev. xiv. 4, xxiii. 56 ; A. xi. 18, xxi. 14.	..	..	-ία 2 Thess. iii. 12 ; -άζειν 1 Thess. iv. 11.

132   LANGUAGE OF THE NEW TESTAMENT.

Word or Phrase.	SS. JAMES AND JUDE.	ST. PETER.	HEBREWS.
ἦχος } vid. p. 52 n.	..	..	xii. 19.
θεμελιοῦν	..	I. v. 10.	i. 10 (fr. LXX.).
τοῦ [μεγάλου] Θεοῦ καὶ σωτῆρος * [ἡμῶν] Ἰη. Χρ.	..	II. i. 1 (cf. ii. 20; iii. 2, 18).	..
θηρίον . . .	Jac. iii. 7.	..	xii. 20 (quotn. not LXX.).
θιγεῖν . . .	..	..	xi. 28, xii. 20.
θρῆσκος, -εία .	Jac. i. 26 bis, 27.	..	..
θυμιᾶν, -αμα, -ατήριον	..	..	ix. 4.
ἰᾶσθαι, ἴασις . .	Jac. v. 16.	I. ii. 24.	xii. 13.
ἱερατεία . . .	..	..	vii. 5.
ἱερατεύειν, -ευμα .	..	-μα I. ii. 5, 9 (fr. LXX.).	..
ἱλάσκεσθαι . .	..	..	ii. 17.
ἴστε, ἴσασι . .	Jac. i. 19 (W.H.)	..	xii. 17.
καθ' ἡμέραν . .	..	..	vii. 27, x. 11 (cf. iii. 13).
καίπερ . . .	..	II. i. 12.	v. 8, vii. 5, xii. 17.
καίτοι . . .	..	..	iv. 3.
κακοποιός, -εῖν .	..	I. ii. 12, 14, iii. 16, iv. 15; -εῖν iii. 17.	..

* Σωτήρ in fact is always a predicate not a title, except in the passages cited and in

APPENDIX I. TABLE III.

St. Luke.	Pastoral Epp.	Eph. and Col.	Other N.T. Books.
Ev. iv. 37, xxi. 25 (v.l.) (declined differently); A. ii. 2.	..	..	..
Ev. vi. 48? (∥ to Matt.)	..	E. iii. 17; C. i. 23.	Matt. vii. 25.
..	Tit. ii. 13 (Χρ. Ιη. best text).	..	..
A. x. 12 (T. R.), xi. 6, xxviii. 4, 5.	Tit. i. 12 (quotn.).	..	Mark i. 13; Apoc. passim.
..	..	C. ii. 21.	..
A. xxvi. 5.	..	C. ii. 18.	..
Ev. i. 9, 10, 11. ἰᾶσθαι Ev. undecies praeter iv. 18 (LXX.); A. ter praeter iii. 11 (T.R.) et xxviii. 27 (ex. LXX.); ἴασις Ev. xiii. 32; A. iv. 22, 30.	.. ..	.. ..	Apoc. quater. Matt. viii. 8, 13, xiii. 15 (fr. LXX.), xv. 28; Mark v. 29; Joh. iv. 47, v. 13, xii. 40 (∥ to Matt.) (ἰάματα 1 Cor. xii. 9, 28, 30).
Ev. i. 9.	..	..	..
-ειν Ev. i. 8.	..	..	..
Ev. xviii. 13.	..	..	ἱλαστήριον Rom. Heb., ἱλασμὸς Joh. Ep. bis.
A. xxvi. 4.	..	E. v. 5 (v.l.).	..
Ev. ix. 23 (si. v. l.), xi. 3, xvi. 19, xix. 47, xxii. 53; A. ii. 46, 47, iii. 2, xvi. 5, xvii. 11 (cf. 17), xix. 9.	..	..	Mark xiv. 49; 1 Cor. xv. 31; 2 Cor. xi. 28.
..	..	..	Phil. iii. 4.
A. xiv. 17 (prob.), xvii. 27 (v. l.)	..	..	καίτοιγε Joh. iv. 2, v. 1; Acts ll. cc.
-εῖν Ev. vi. 9.	..	..	(Joh. xviii. 30, T. R.); Mar. iii. 4; Joh. Ep. III. 11.

Jude 25. Luke i. 47 is the nearest approach to an exception—Phil. iii. 20 is none.

134   LANGUAGE OF THE NEW TESTAMENT.

Word or Phrase.	SS. JAMES AND JUDE.	ST. PETER.	HEBREWS.
κακοῦν	..	I. iii. 13.	..
κακοῦργος	..	..	..
καλὸς, of persons	..	I. iv. 10.	..
κάμνειν	Jac. v. 15	..	xii. 3.
καταδυναστεύειν	Jac. ii. 6.	..	..
καταλαλεῖν	Jac. iv. 11 ter.	I. ii. 12, iii. 16 (-λιὰ ii. 1).	..
κατανοεῖν	Jac. i. 23, 24.	..	iii. 1, x. 24.
καταπαύειν, -σις	..	..	iv. 4, 8, 10 ; iii. 11 (fr. LXX.), 18, iv. passim.
καταπονεῖσθαι	..	II. ii. 7.	..
καταστέλλειν, -στολή	..	..	..
καταστροφὴ	..	II. ii. 6 (?)	..
καταφεύγειν	..	..	vi. 18.
καταφθείρειν	..	II. ii. 12 (T. R.).	..
κατέρχεσθαι, -ελθεῖν	Jac. iii. 15.	..	..
κεφάλαιον	..	..	viii. 1.
κῆρυξ	..	II. ii. 5.	..
κλύδων	Jac. i. 6.	..	..
κοινὸς (not in sense "unclean")	Jud. 3.	..	..
κολάζειν, -ζεσθαι	..	II. ii. 4 (v. l.), 9.	..
κοσμικὸς	..	..	ix. 1.
κράτος	Jud. 25.*	I. iv. 11,* v. 11*.	ii. 14.
κρείσσων, -ττων	..	I. iii. 17, II. ii. 21.	Ter et decies.
κρῖναι ζῶντας καὶ νεκροὺς	..	I. iv. 5.	..

* In doxologies.

APPENDIX I. TABLE III.

St. Luke.	Pastoral Epp.	Eph. and Col.	Other N.T. Books.
A. vii. 6 (fr. LXX.), 19, xii. 1, xiv. 2, xviii. 10.	..	..	..
Ev. xxiii. 32, 33, 39.	2 Tim. ii. 9.	..	..
..	1 Tim. iv. 6; 2 Tim. ii. 3.	..	Joh. x. 11 bis, 14.
A. x. 38.	..	..	..
..	..	..	κατάλαλος Rom. 30, λιὰ 2 Cor. xii. 20.
Ev. vi. 41 (‖ to Matt.), xii. 24, 27, xx. 23; A. vii. 31, 32, xi. 6, xxvii. 39.	..	..	Matt. vii. 3; Rom. iv. 19.
A. xiv. 18; vii. 49 (fr. LXX.).	..	..	..
A. vii. 24.	..	..	..
A. xix. 35, 36.	1 Tim. ii. 9.	..	..
..	2 Tim. ii. 14.	..	..
A. xiv. 6.	..	..	..
..	2 Tim. iii. 8.	..	..
Ev. iv. 31, ix. 37; A. saepius.	..	..	..
A. xxii. 28.	..	..	..
..	1 Tim. ii. 7; 2 Tim. i. 11.	..	..
Ev. viii. 24.	..	κλυδωνίζεσθαι E. iv. 14.	..
A. ii. 44, iv. 32.	Tit. i. 4.	..	..
A. iv. 21.	..	..	κόλασις Matt. xxv. 46; Joh. Ep. I. iv. 18.
..	Tit. ii. 12 (κόσμιος, -ως 1 Tim. ii. 9, iii. 2.	..	..
Ev. i. 51; A. xix. 20.	1 Tim. vi. 16.*	E. i. 19, vi. 10; C. i. 11.	Apoc. i. 6,* v. 13.*
..	..	..	Apud Paulum quator vel quinquies.
Cf. A. x. 42.	2 Tim. iv. 1.	..	..

136 LANGUAGE OF THE NEW TESTAMENT.

Word or Phrase.	SS. JAMES AND JUDE.	ST. PETER.	HEBREWS.
κριτής, de Deo et Christo	Jac. iv. 12, v. 9.	..	xii. 25.
κτίσις (of human work)	..	I. ii. 13 (?).	ix. 11 (?)
κυκλοῦσθαι (of cities)	..	..	xi. 30.
κυριότης	Jud. 8.	II. ii. 10	..
λαγχάνειν	..	II. i. 1.	..
λαμβάνειν (of "receiving" office)	..	..	v. 4 (?), vii. 5.
λαμβάνειν (with abstract object)	..	λήθην II. i. 9.	..
λανθάνειν	..	II. iii. 5, 8.	xiii. 2.
λείπειν (of defect)	λείπεσθαι, Jac. i. 4, 5, ii. 15.	..	..
λέων	..	I. v. 8.	xi. 33.
λόγια	..	I. iv. 11.	v. 12.
λοιδορία	..	I. iii. 9.	..
λούειν, -εσθαι	..	II. ii. 22.	x. 22.
λουτρὸν	..	..	..
λυτροῦν, -ωσις, -ωτής	..	I. i. 18.	ix. 12.
μακαρίζειν	Jac. v. 11.	..	..
μάστιξ (*literally*, of "scourges")	..	..	xi. 36.
μάχεσθαι	Jac. iv. 2.	..	..
μεγαλειότης	..	II. i. 16.	..
μεγαλωσύνη	Jud. 25.	..	i. 3, viii. 1.
μεσίτης	..	..	viii. 6, ix. 15, xii. 24.

* Literally of lots.

APPENDIX I. TABLE III.

St. Luke.	Pastoral Epp.	Eph. and Col.	Other N.T. Books.
A. x. 42.	2 Tim. iv. 8.	..	De hominibus bis terve apud Matt., bis apud Jacobum, novies apud Lucam.
..	..	..	..
Ev. xxi. 20.	..	..	κυκλοῦν of persons, Joh. x. 24; A. xiv. 20.
..	..	E. i. 21; C. i. 16.	..
Ev. i. 9; * A. i. 17.	..	..	Joh. xix. 24.*
Ev. xix. 12, 15; A. i. 20 (fr. LXX.), xx. 24.	..	..	..
θάρσος A. xxviii. 15.	ὑπόμνησιν 2 Tim. i. 5.	..	..
Ev. viii. 47; A. xxvi. 26.	..	..	Mar. vii. 24.
Ev. xviii. 22.	Tit. i. 5, iii. 13.	..	..
..	2 Tim. iv. 17.	..	Apoc. sexies.
A. vii. 38.	..	..	Rom. iii. 2.
..	1 Tim. v. 14.	..	..
A. ix. 37, xvi. 33.	..	..	Joh. xiii. 10; Apoc. i. 5 (T. R.).
..	Tit. iii. 5.	E. v. 26.	..
Ev. xxiv. 21; -ωσις i. 68, ii. 38; -ωτὴς A. vii. 35.	Tit. ii. 14.	..	λύτρον Matt. xx. 28 = Mar. x. 45.
Ev. i. 48.	..	..	..
A. xxii. 24.	..	..	..
A. vii. 26.	2 Tim. ii. 24.	..	Joh. vi. 52.
Ev. ix. 43; A. xix. 27.	..	..	..
..	..	..	..
..	1 Tim. ii. 5.	..	Gal. iii. 19, 20— *not* of Christ, as the rest are.

138 LANGUAGE OF THE NEW TESTAMENT.

Word or Phrase.	SS. JAMES AND JUDE.	ST. PETER.	HEBREWS.
μετ' εἰρήνης	..	..	xi. 31.
μεταλαμβάνειν	..	..	vi. 7, xii. 10.
μετατιθέναι, -σθαι	Jud. 4.	..	vii. 12, xi. 5 bis (fr. LXX.).
μέτοχος	..	..	i. 9 (fr. LXX.), iii. 1, 14, vi. 4, xii. 8.
μιαίνω, μίασμα, -σμὸς	Jud. 8.	II. ii. 10 -μὸς; 20 -σμα.	xii. 15.
μισθὸς [τῆς] ἀδικίας	..	II. ii. 13, 15.	..
μόσχος	..	..	ix. 12, 19.
μῦθος	..	II. i. 16.	..
μυριὰς	Jud. 14.	..	xii. 22.
νεώτεροι	..	I. v. 5.	..
νομικὸς	..	..	..
νομοδιδάσκαλος	..	..	..
νοσφίζεσθαι	..	..	..
ξενίζειν, -ζεσθαι	..	I. iv. 4 * 12.*	xiii. 2.†
ὅδε	Jac. iv. 13.	..	..
ὅθεν, "wherefore"	..	..	sexies.
οἰκέτης	..	I. ii. 18.	.
οἶκος τοῦ Θεοῦ, in spiritual sense	..	I. iv. 17 (cf. ii. 5).	x. 21 (cf. iii, 2-6).
οἰκτίρμων	Jac. v. 11.	..	..
ὁμοιοπαθὴς	Jac. v 17.	..	..
ὀνειδισμὸς	..	..	x. 33, xi. 26, xiii. 13.

* Of unfamiliarity. † Of hospitality.

St. Luke.	Pastoral Epp.	Eph. and Col.	Other N.T. Books.
A. xv. 33.	..	..	..
A. ii. 46, xxiv. 25, xxvii. 33, 34 (?).	2 Tim. ii. 6, μετάλημψις 1 Tim. iv. 3.	..	..
A. vii. 16.	..	..	..
Ev. v. 7.	..	..	μετέχειν Heb. ter.; 2 Cor. ix. x. quinquies; μετοχή 2 Cor. vi. 14.
..	Tit. i. 15 bis.	..	Joh. xviii. 28.
A. i. 18.	..	..	..
Ev. xv. 23, 27, 30.	..	..	Apoc. iv. 7.
..	1 Tim. i. 4, iv. 7; 2 Tim. iv. 4; Tit. i. 14.	..	..
Ev. xii. 1; A. xix. 19, xxi. 20.	..	..	Apoc. v. 11, ix. 16.
A. v. 6; νεώτερος Ev. xv. 12, 13, xxii. 26.	1 Tim. v. 1, 2, 11, 14; Tit. ii. 6: νεωτερικὸς 2 Tim. ii. 22.	..	νεώτερος Joh. xxi. 18.
Ev. vii. 30, x. 25, xi. 45, 46, 52, xiv. 3.	Tit. iii. (9), 13.	..	Matt. xxii. 35.
Ev. v. 17; A. v. 34.	1 Tim. i. 7.	..	..
A. v. 2, 3.	Tit. ii. 10.	..	..
A. x. 6. 18, 23, 32; † xvii. 20;* xxi. 16, xxviii. 7.†	..	..	..
Ev. x. 39, xvi. 25 (T. R.); A. xv. 23 (T.R.), xxi. 11.	..	..	Apoc. ii. iii. septies (τάδε λέγει).
A. xxvi. 19.	..	..	Matt. xiv. 7; Joh. Ep. I. ii. 18.
Ev. xvi. 13; A. x. 7.	..	...	Rom. xiv. 4.
..	1 Tim. iii. 15.	..	..
Ev. vi. 36.	..	..	..
A. xiv. 15.	..	..	..
(ὄνειδος Ev. i. 25, -δίζω vi. 22, sed hoc alibi).	1 Tim. iii. 7.	.	Rom. xv. 3 (fr. LXX.).

140 LANGUAGE OF THE NEW TESTAMENT.

Word or Phrase.	SS. JAMES AND JUDE.	ST. PETER.	HEBREWS.
ὀρέγεσθαι	..	..	xi. 16.
ὀρίζω	..	..	iv. 7.
ὁρμή	Jac. iii. 4.	..	..
ὅσιος	..	..	vii. 26.
παγίς	..	..	..
παθήματα (de πάσχω vid. p. 49) .	..	I. i. 11, iv. 13, v. 1, 9.	ii. 9, 10, x. 32.
παιδεία	..	..	xii. 5, 7, 8, 11.
-εύω, -ευτής	..	..	xii. 6 (fr. LXX.), 7, 10; -ευτής 9.
παλαιοῦν, -οῦσθαι	..	..	i. 11 (fr. LXX.), viii. 13 bis.
πανοπλία	..	..	..
(εἰς τὸ) παντελές	..	..	vii. 25.
πάντοθεν	..	..	ix. 4.
παρά (in comparisons)	..	..	i. 4, 9 (fr. LXX.), ii. 7 (do.), 9, iii. 3, ix. 23, xii. 24.
παραγίνεσθαι	..	..	ix. 11.
παραδέχομαι	..	..	xii. 6 (fr. LXX.).
παραιτεῖσθαι	..	..	xii. 19, 25 bis.
παρακολουθεῖν	..	..	.

APPENDIX I. TABLE III.

St. Luke.	Pastoral Epp.	Eph. and Col.	Other N.T. Books.
..	1 Tim. iii. 1, vi. 10.	..	ὄρεξις Rom. i. 27.
Ev. xxii. 22; A. ii. 23, x. 42, xi. 29, xvii. 26, 31.	..	..	Rom. i. 4.
A. xiv. 5.	..	..	..
A. ii. 27, xiii. 34, 35 (all fr. LXX.): ὁσιότης Ev. i. 75.	1 Tim. ii. 8; Tit. i. 8.	ὁσιότης E. iv. 24.	Apoc. xv. 4, xvi. 5; -ως 1 Thess. ii. 10.
Ev. xxi. 35.	1 Tim. iii. 7, vi. 9; 2 Tim. ii. 26.	..	Rom. xi. 9 (fr. LXX.).
..	2 Tim. iii. 11.	C. i. 24.	2 Cor. i. 5, 6, 7; Phil. iii. 10; contr. Rom. vii. 5, viii. 18; Gal. v. 24.
..	2 Tim. iii. 16.	E. vi. 4.	..
Ev. xxiii. 16, 22; A. vii. 22, xxii. 3.	1 Tim. i. 20; 2 Tim. ii. 25; Tit. ii. 12.	..	1 Cor. xi. 32; 2 Cor. vi. 9; Apoc. iii. 19; -ευτὴς Rom. ii. 20.
Ev. xii. 33.	..	..	..
Ev. xi. 22.	..	E. vi. 11, 13.	..
Ev. xiii. 11.	..	..	..
Ev. xix. 43.	..	..	Mar. i. 45 (prob.); Joh. xviii. 20 (Elz.).
Ev. iii. 13, xiii. 2, 4.	..	..	Rom. xii. 3.
Ev. octies, A. vicies praeter x. 32.	2 Tim. iv. 16 (prob. vid. sub συμπαραγ).	..	1 Cor. xvi. 3, Matt. ter, Mar. semel, Joh. semel, praeter viii. 2.
A. xv. 4 (v.l.), xvi. 21, xxii. 18.	1 Tim. v. 19.	..	Mar. iv. 20.
Ev. xiv. 18 bis, 19; A. xxv. 11.	1 Tim. iv. 7, v. 11; 2 Tim. ii. 23; Tit. iii. 10.	..	..
Ev. i. 3.	1 Tim. iv. 6; 2 Tim. iii. 10.	..	Mar. xvi. 17.

142   LANGUAGE OF THE NEW TESTAMENT.

Word or Phrase.	SS. JAMES AND JUDE.	ST. PETER.	HEBREWS.
παραλογίζεσθαι	Jac. i. 22.	..	..
παραλελυμένος	..	..	xii. 12 (fr. LXX.).
παρεμβολή	..	..	xi. 34, xiii. 11, 13.
παρεπίδημος	..	I. i. 1, ii. 11.	xi. 13 (LXX.).
παρέχειν, -εσθαι	..	..	..
πάροικος, -κεῖν, -κία	..	I. ii. 11; i. 17.	xi. 9.
παροξυσμός	..	..	x. 24.
παροργίζειν, -σμός	..	..	..
ἐν παντί, ἐν πᾶσιν, κατὰ πάντα	..	ἐν πᾶσιν I. iv. 11.	Vid. p. 37 n.
πάσχειν	..	Vid. p. 49.	..
πατριά	..	..	..
πατριάρχης	..	..	vii. 4.
πειθαρχεῖν	..	..	..
περίεργος	..	..	..
περιέρχεσθαι, -ελθεῖν	..	..	xi. 37.
περιέχειν	..	I. ii. 6.	..
περιπίπτειν	Jac. i. 2.	..	..
περιποιεῖσθαι, -ησις	..	-ησις I. ii. 9.	-ησις x. 39.
ἐπὶ πλεῖον	..	..	..
πλῆθος	Jac. v. 20.	I. iv. 8.	xi. 12.
		in abstract sense.	

APPENDIX I. TABLE III.

St. Luke.	Pastoral Epp.	Eph. and Col.	Other N.T. Books.
		C. ii. 4.	
Ev. v. 18, 24 (not quite certain); A. viii. 7, ix. 33.			
A. xxi.—xxiii. sexies.			Apoc. xx. 9.
Ev. vi. 29, vii. 4, xi. 7, xviii. 5; A. xvi. 16, xvii. 31, xix. 24, xxii. 2, xxviii. 2.	1 Tim. i. 4, vi. 17; Tit. ii. 7.	C. iv. 1.	Matt. xxiv. 10. = Mar. xiv. 6; Gal. vi. 17 all κόπους π., cf. Luc. xi. 7, xviii. 5.
A. vii. 6 (fr. LXX.), 29; -κεῖν Ev. xxiv. 18; -κία A. xiii. 17.		E. ii. 19.	
A. xv. 39.			παροξύνεσθαι, A. xvii. 16; 1 Cor. xiii. 5.
		E. vi. 4; C. iii. 21 (v. l.); E. iv. 26.	Rom. x. 19 fr. LXX.
Ev. ii. 4; A. iii. 25 (quotn.).		E. iii. 15.	
A. ii. 29, vii. 8, 9.			
A. v. 29, 32, xxvii. 21.	Tit. iii. 1.		
A. xix. 19.	1 Tim. v. 13.		περιεργάζεσθαι 2 Thess. iii. 11.
A. xix. 13, xxviii. 13.	1 Tim. v. 13.		
(Ev. v. 9, a different sense) A. xxiii. 25 (T. R.); -οχή viii. 32.			
Ev. x. 30; A. xxvii. 41.			
-εῖσθαι A. xx. 28.	-εῖσθαι 1 Tim. iii. 13.	-ησις E. i. 14.	-ησις 1 Thess. v. 9; 2 Thess. ii. 14.
A. iv. 17, xx. 9, xxiv. 4.	2 Tim. ii. 16, iii. 9.		
Ev. 8 times, A. 17 times in concrete sense, "the multitude," "the multitudes."			Mar. iii. 7, 8; Joh. v. 3, xxi. 6.

Word or Phrase.	SS. James and Jude.	St. Peter.	Hebrews.
πλουσίως	..	II. i. 11.	..
ποικίλος	Jac. i. 2.	I. i. 6, iii. 7 (v. l.), iv. 10.	ii. 4, xiii. 9.
ποίμνιον	..	I. v. 2, 3.	..
πολίτης, -εία, εύεσθαι, -ευμα	..	..	viii. 11 (fr. LXX.).
πόρρωθεν	..	..	xi. 13.
ποῦ ἐστιν (of a thing absent)		II. iii. 4.	..
πρεσβυτέριον	..	..	..
προγινώσκειν	..	I. i. 20, II. iii. 17.	..
πρόγνωσις	..	I. i. 2.	..
πρόδηλος	..	..	vii. 14 (the prep. having less force).
προδότης	..	..	..
προπετής	..	..	..
προσάγειν	..	I. iii. 18.	..
προσδοκᾶν, -κία	..	II. iii. 12, 13, 14.	..
προσέρχομαι (of approaching God or divine things)	..	c. πρὸς I. ii. 4.	c. dat, iv. 16, vii. 25, x. l. 22, xi. 6 ; (of places, xii. 18, 22).

APPENDIX I. TABLE III.

St. Luke.	Pastoral Epp.	Eph. and Col.	Other N.T. Books.
..	1 Tim. vi. 17; Tit. iii. 6,	C. iii. 16.	..
Ev. iv. 40.	2 Tim. iii. 6; Tit. iii. 3.	..	Matt. iv. 24; Mar i. 34; Luk. iv. 40.
Ev. xii. 32; A. xx. 28, 29.	..	..	..
Ev. xv. 15, xix. 14 ; A. xxi. 39; -εία xxii. 28; -εσθαι xxiii. 1.	..	-είας E. ii. 12.	-εσθαι Phil. i. 27; -ευμα iii. 20.
Ev. xvii. 12.	..	..	..
Ev. viii. 25.	..	..	τοῦ without ἐστιν Rom. iii. 27; 1 Cor. i. 20; ter. xii. 17 bis, 19, xv. 55 bis (fr. LXX.); Gal. iv. 15.
Ev. xxii. 66; A. xxii. 5. xxvi. 5; A. ii. 23.	1 Tim. iv. 14.	..	Rom. viii. 29 xi. 2.
..	..	..	..
..	1 Tim. v. 24-5.	..	..
Ev. vi. 16; A. vii. 52. A. xix. 36.	2 Tim. iii. 4.	..	..
	2 Tim. iii. 4.	..	..
Ev. ix. 41; A. xvi. 20; xxvii. 27 (intr.).	..	προσαγωγὴ E. ii. 18, iii. 12.	προσαγωγὴ Rom v. 2.
Ev. i. 21, iii. 15, vii. 19, 20, viii. 40, xii. 46; A. iii. 5, x. 24, xxvii. 33, xxviii. 6 bis; -κία Ev. xxi. 26; A. xii. 11.	..	..	Matt. xi. 3 (∥ to Luke vii. 19), xxiv. 50.
..	(1 Tim. vi. 3 ? v. l. προσέχ.).	..	Verbum usurpat Matt. saepissime, Mar. quinquies vel sexies, Joh. semel, Paulus nusquam praeter l. 1.

10

Word or Phrase.	SS. JAMES AND JUDE.	ST. PETER.	HEBREWS.
προσέχειν	..	II. i. 19.	ii. 1, vii. 13.
προσμένειν	..	..	..
πρόσφατος, -ως	..	..	-ον x. 20.
προσφέρειν	..	..	Saepissime.
προσφορὰ	..	..	x. 5, 8 (fr. LXX.), 10, 14, 18.
πτοεῖσθαι, -ησις	..	-ησις I. iii. 6.	..
πυκνὸς, -ότερον	..	..	..
ῥαντίζειν, -σμὸς	..	-σμὸς I. i. 2.	ix. 13, 19, 21, x. 22; xii. 24.
ῥῆμα	Jud. 17.	I. i. 25 bis (semel ex LXX.), II. iii. 2.	i. 3, vi. 5, xi. 3, xii. 19.
σκήνωμα	..	II. i. 13, 14.	..
σκιὰ	..	..	viii. 5, x. 1.
σπαταλᾶν	Jac. v. 5.	..	..
σπεύδειν	..	II. iii. 12 (trans.)	..
σπίλος, -λοῦν	Jac. iii. 6; Jud. 23.	II. ii. 13 (cf. Jud. 12.)	..

APPENDIX I. TABLE III.

St. Luke.	Pastoral Epp.	Eph. and Col.	Other N.T. Books.
Ev. xii. 1, xvii. 3, xx. 46, xxi. 34; A. v. 35, viii. 6, 10, 11, xvi. 14, xx. 28.	1 Tim. i. 4, iii. 8, iv. 1, 13; Tit. i. 14.	..	Matt. quinquies προσέχετε ἀπὸ (ut Luc. xii. 1, xx. 46) and προσέχετε μὴ (ut Luc. xxi. 34).
A. xi. 23, xiii. 43 (v.l.), xviii. 18.	1 Tim. i. 3, v. 5.	..	Matt. xv. 32 = Mar. viii. 2.
-ως A. xviii. 2.	..	..	..
Ev. v. 14, xii. 11 (T. R.), xviii. 15, xxiii. 14, 36; A. vii. 42, viii. 18, xxi. 26.	..	..	Saepe apud Matt., bis terve apud Marc., bis apud Joh., nusquam apud Paulum; sed
A. xxi. 26, xxiv. 17.	..	E. v. 2.	Rom. xv. 16.
-εἶσθαι Ev. xxi. 9, xxiv. 37.	..	..	..
Ev. v. 33; A. xxiv. 26.	1 Tim. v. 23.	..	..
..	..	..	..
Ev. undevicies, A. quater et decies.	..	E. v. 26, vi. 17.	Paulus praeter haec sexies (sed bis ex LXX.), Matt. quater praeter iv. 4 (LXX.), v. 11 (?), Marcus bis, Joh. duodecies.
A. vii. 46.	..	..	σκῆνος 2 Cor. v. 1, 4.
Ev. i. 79; A. v. 15.	..	C. ii. 17.	Matt. iv. 16 (ex LXX.), Mar. iv. 32.
..	1 Tim. v. 6.	..	..
Ev. ii. 16, xix. 5, 6; A. xx. 16, xxii. 18.	..	..	..
..	..	E. v. 27.	..

148   LANGUAGE OF THE NEW TESTAMENT.

Word or Phrase.	SS. JAMES AND JUDE.	ST. PETER.	HEBREWS.
στερεὸς		I. v. 9.	v. 12, 14.
στεφανοῦν			ii. 7 (fr. LXX.), 9.
συμπαθής, -θεῖν		I. iii. 8.	iv. 15, x. 34.
συμπαραγίνεσθαι			
συναντᾶν			vii. 1, 10.
σύνδεσμος			
συνείδησις ἀγαθὴ		I. iii. 16, 21.	σ. πονηρὰ x. 22 σ. καλὴ xiii. 18.
συνεστάναι, -στηκέναι		II. iii. 5.	
σχεδὸν			ix. 22.
σωματικὸς			
Θεὸς σωτὴρ	Jud. 25.		
σωτήριον (neut.)			
σωφρονεῖν (in ethical sense) *		I. iv. 7.	
σωφροσύνη			
ταπεινόφρων, -οσύνη		I. iii. 8; v. 5.	
τε †			
τελειότης			vi. 1.
τελείωσις			vii. 11.
τεχνίτης			xi. 10.
τηρεῖν εἰς	Jud. 6, (13?).	I. i. 4 (?), II. ii. 4, 9, (17 ?), iii. 7.	

* In Mark v. 15=Luke viii. 35 ; 2 Cor. v. 13, it is opposed to ἐκστῆναι.
† τε is about as frequent in Heb. as in the whole of St. Paul, eight times in St. Luke's Gospel (as many as in the other three), and in Acts about three times as often as in the whole N. T. without Luke and Heb.

St. Luke.	Pastoral Epp.	Eph. and Col.	Other N.T. Books.
-εοῦν, -εοῦσθαι A. iii. 7, 16, xvi. 5.	2 Tim. ii. 19.	-έωμα C. ii. 5.	..
	2 Tim. ii. 5.	..	..
..	..	..	..
Ev. xxiii. 48.	2 Tim. iv. 16 T. R.; vid. sub παραγίν.	..	..
Ev. ix. 37, xxii. 10; A. x. 25, xx. 22.	..	..	συνάντησις Matt. viii. 34 (T. R.).
A. viii. 23.	..	E. iv. 3; C. ii. 19, iii. 14.	..
A. xxiii. 1 (cf. xxiv. 16.)	1 Tim. i. 5, 19 (σ. καθαρὰ 1 Tim. iii. 9; 2 Tim. i. 3).	..	..
(Ev. ix. 32—hardly the same sense).	..	Col. i. 17.	..
A. xiii. 44, xix. 26.	..	..	..
Ev. iii. 22.	1 Tim. iv. 8.	-κῶς C. ii. 9.	..
Ev. i. 47.	1 Tim. i. 1, ii. 3, iv. 10; Tit. i. 3, ii. 11, iii. 4.	..	..
Ev. ii. 30, iii. 6; A. xxviii. 28.	(σωτήριος Tit. ii. 11).	E. vi. 17.	..
..	Tit. ii. 6.	..	Rom. xii. 3.
A. xxvi. 25.	1 Tim. ii. 9, 15 (σώφρων, -όνως, -ονίζειν, -ονισ- μὸς in his tan- tum).	..	..
A. xx. 19.	..	E. iv. 2; C. ii. 18, 23, iii. 12.	Phil. ii. 3.
..	..	..	..
..	..	C. iii. 14.	..
Ev. i. 45.	..	..	..
A. xix. 24, 38.	..	..	Apoc. xviii. 22.
A. xxv. (4 ?), 21.	..	..	Joh. xii. 7.

Word or Phrase.	SS. JAMES AND JUDE.	ST. PETER.	HEBREWS.
τίμιος . . .	Jac. v. 7.	I. i. 7 (T. R.), 19, II. i. 4.	xiii. 4.
τιμωρεῖν, -ρία . .	..	..	-ία x. 29.
τροφή . . .	Jac. ii. 15.	..	v. 12, 14.
τρυφή, -φᾶν . .	ᾶν Jac. v. 5.	-ή II. ii. 13.	..
τυγχάνειν . .	..	..	viii. 6, xi. 35.
ὑγιαίνειν . . .	..	..	..
ὑετός . . .	Jac. v. 7 (T. R.), 18.	..	vi. 7.
ὕπαρξις . . .	..	..	x. 34.
τὰ ὑπάρχοντα . .	..	..	x. 34.
ὑπεναντίος . .	..	..	x. 27.
ὑπέρ (with comp. adj.) . . .	..	..	iv. 12.
ὑπεράνω . . .	..	..	ix. 5.
ὑπερήφανος . .	Jac. iv. 6 (fr. LXX.) = 1 Pet. v. 5.	..	..
ὑπόδειγμα . .	Jac. v. 10.	II. ii. 6.	iv. 11, viii. 5, ix. 23.
ὑποδέχεσθαι . .	Jac. ii. 25.	..	..
ὑπομιμνήσκειν, -μνησις . . .	Jud. 5.	II. i. 12; i. 13, iii. 1.	..

APPENDIX I. TABLE III.

St. Luke.	Pastoral Epp.	Eph. and Col.	Other N.T. Books.
A. v. 34, xx. 24.	..	..	λίθος τ. 1 Cor. iii. 12, Apoc. quinquies, ξύλον τιμιωτάτον Apoc. semel.
-είν A. xxii. 5, xxvi. 11.	..	..	..
Ev. xii. 23, A. septies.	..	..	Matt. iii. 4, vi. 25 (∥ to Luke), x. 10, xxiv. 45; Joh. iv. 8.
-ή Ev. vii. 25.	..	..	..
Ev. (x. 30, T. R.), xx. 35, A. xxiv. 3, xxvi. 22, xxvii. 3; (xix. 11, xxviii. 2).	2 Tim. ii. 10.	..	εἰ τύχοι 1 Cor. xiv. 10, xv. 37, τυχὸν xvi. 6.
Ev. v. 31, vii. 10, xv. 27.	1 Tim. i. 10, vi. 3; 2 Tim. i. 13. iv. 3; Tit. i. 9. 13, ii. 1, 2.	..	Joh. Ep. III. 2.
A. xiv. 17, xxviii. 2.	..	..	Apoc. xi. 6.
A. ii. 45.	..	..	..
Ev. octies, A. iv. 32.	..	..	Matt. xix. 21, xxiv. 47, xxv. 14; 1 Cor. xiii. 3.
..	..	C. ii. 14.	..
Ev. xvi. 8.	..	..	..
..	..	E. i. 21, iv. 10.	..
Ev. i. 51.	2 Tim. iii. 2.	..	Rom. i. 30.
..	..	..	Joh. xiii. 15.
Ev. x. 38, xix. 6; A. xvii. 7.	..	..	..
Ev. xxii. 61.	2 Tim. ii. 14; Tit. iii. 1; 2 Tim. i. 5.	..	Joh. xiv. 26; Ep. III. 10.

152   LANGUAGE OF THE NEW TESTAMENT.

Word or Phrase.	SS. James and Jude.	St. Peter.	Hebrews.
ὑποστρέφειν	. .	II. ii. 21 (prob.)	vii. 1.
ὑποφέρειν, ὑπενεγκεῖν	. .	φέρειν I. ii. 19.	. .
(ὁ Θεὸς ὁ) ὕψιστος	. .	. .	vii. 1 *(fr. O. T.).
φέρεσθαι (of rushing motion)	. .	I. i. 13? II. i. (17, 18?) 21.	vi. 1.
φθέγγεσθαι	. .	II. ii. 16, 18.	. .
φιλάδελφος, -ία	. .	I. iii. 8; i. 22, II. i. 7 bis.	-ία xiii. 1.
φιλανθρώπως, -ία	. .	. .	. .
φιλάργυρος, -ία	. .	. .	. .
φιλόξενος, -ία	. .	-ος I. iv. 9.	-ία xiii. 2.
φρόνησις	. .	. .	. .
φύειν, -ῆναι	. .	. .	xii. 15 (fr. LXX.).
χάρις ("what thank have ye?")	. .	I. ii. 19, 20.	. .
χάριν (prep.)	Jud. 16.	. .	. .
χείρ (χεῖρες) ΘΥ or ΚΥ	. .	I. v. 6.	i. 10 (fr. LXX.), ii. 7 (fr. LXX. si. v. l.), x. 31.
χειροποίητος	. .	. .	ix. 11, 24.
χρυσοῦς	. .	. .	ix. 4, bis.
ψηλαφᾶν	. .	. .	xii. 18.

* With ὁ Θεὸς (or rather always τοῦ Θεοῦ) expressed.

St. Luke.	Pastoral Epp.	Eph. and Col.	Other N.T. Books.
Ev. saepius, A. undecies.	..	..	Mar. xiv. 40 (si vera l.), Gal. i. 17.
..	-ενεγκεῖν 2 Tim. iii. 11.	..	-ενεγκεῖν 1 Cor. x. 13.
Ev. i. 32, 35, 76, vi. 35, viii. 28 ; A. vii. 48, xvi.* 17.	..	..	Mar v. 7 * (∥ to Luke viii. 28).
A ii. 2, xxvii. 15, 17.	..	..	..
A. iv. 18.	..	..	..
..	..	..	-ία Rom. xii. 10; 1 Thess. iv. 9.
A. xxvii. 3; xxviii. 2.	-ία Tit. iii. 4.	..	..
-ος Ev. xvi. 14.	2 Tim. iii. 2 ; -ία 1 Tim. vi. 10.	.	..
..	-ος 1 Tim. iii. 2 ; Tit. i. 8.	..	-ία Rom. xii. 13.
Ev. i. 17.	..	E. i. 8.	..
Ev. viii. 6, 8.	..	..	..
Ev. vi. 32-3-4.	..	..	..
Ev. vii. 47.	1 Tim. v. 14; Tit. i. 5, 11.	E. iii. 1, 14.	Gal. iii. 19.
Ev. i. 66; A. iv. 28, 30, vii. 50 (quotn.), xi. 21, xiii. 11.	..	..	..
A. vii. 48, xvii. 24.	..	E. ii. 11.	Mar. xiv. 58.
..	2 Tim. ii. 20.	..	Apoc. passim.
Ev. xxiv. 39; A. xvii 27.	..	..	Joh. Ep. I. i. 1.

APPENDIX II.

SPECIMENS OF HELLENIC AND HELLENISTIC COMPOSITION.

An intelligent reader will be able to learn far more of the nature of Hellenistic Greek, and the difference between it and the "Hellenic" or literary Greek of the post-Alexandrine period, and again between both these and the language of classical Attic prose, by familiarity with the practice of writers of each sort than by any description of individual grammatical features. Of course, it takes time to acquire such familiarity, and time for study cannot be dispensed with; though less time may suffice for a trained "scholar," if he has the sense and humility to recognise that scholarship is a means, not an end.

But while real insight into peculiarities of style can only be gained by long habitual study, salient features may be illustrated, and guidance for study obtained, by the comparison of passages similar enough in subject to throw the differences of style into relief. A few such passages are therefore offered below to the student. First, we take two passages from the LXX., and compare them with the way they were re-written, in as classical a style as they could master, by men honestly meaning to give a faithful reproduction of the sense.

Philo omits the fourth and last of Balaam's prophecies: we notice that he expands the first, and to a less extent the third, with glosses, not very relevant; while otherwise he abridges throughout, by not preserving the parallel clauses of the original versification. In the second, he seems to correct the translation of the LXX., by the substitution of μετανοεῖ for ἀπειληθῆναι, as well as the style by substituting διαψευσθῆναι for διαρτηθῆναι, which perhaps was a colloquialism. But it is certain that his version is a classicalising paraphrase from the LXX., not an independent version from the Hebrew ; he retains its vocabulary as far as he thinks consistent with purity of language, and is not very often led to obscure it by pedantry of thought.

With Josepus it is less certain that he depended entirely on the LXX ; if the reading Σούνη in one and Σωνὰμ in the other for "Shunem" were certain, we might think that he was rather writing from his knowledge of the narrative in Hebrew. But the passage being a simpler one, the translator ran less risk of missing the sense and the paraphrast had less temptation to pervert it ; and so, though the paraphrase is looser, it is even more instructive as to the natural qualities of Hellenistic and Hellenic style.

Philo and Josepus, however, were themselves Jews, and their classicalism of style was more or less an exotic ; while on the other hand in the language of the LXX. the Hebraistic element is far larger than in most of the N. T., and moreover in a difficult passage, like parts of the prophecy of Balaam, we have examples not of the translator's style, but merely of his ignorance, and the more or less ingenious guesses whereby he supplemented it. We have therefore thought it worth while to give extracts from purely Hellenic but post-Alexandrine authors, to which it was possible to adduce passages from the N. T. more or less parallel in subject. We give specimens of the narrative and descriptive writing of Polybius, the earliest and ablest of the post-Alexandrine historians of whom we have any considerable remains, and of Plutarch, the one most nearly contemporary with the writers of the N. T.,

APPENDIX II. 157

as well as of the canonical and apocryphal Books of the LXX. With regard to the last, it must be remembered that 1 Macc. is almost certainly a translation (the incredible δύο καὶ τριάκοντα of the passage cited is supposed to be a mis-translation for δύο ἢ τρεῖς); while 2 Macc., and probably Judith, were written in Greek. With these we compare almost the only passages in the N. T. that make any approach to dealing with subjects of the same order as those of secular history.

This parallel is, however, so very imperfect that it needs supplementing from the converse case, happily less rare, where classical writers deal seriously with thoughts common to the sacred ones. Here we have again Polybius as a sample of the starting-point of post-classical Greek, and Epictetus of the language nearly contemporary with the N. T., untouched by oriental influences ; with these we compare the two Alexandrian and the two N. T. writers who show most the influence of Hellenic thought and have most command of Hellenic language, but in whom (with the exception of Philo) the Hebraic basis shows itself not only in the thoughts but in the style.

To these passages notes are appended, pointing out the divergences of their language from the earlier or classical standard. But it seems needless to do more with the first series of passages, than to indicate such various readings as are necessary to prevent our exaggerating the divergence of Philo or Josephus from his original.

NUM. xxiii. 7-10.

Ἐκ Μεσοποταμίας μετεπέμψατό
με Βαλάκ,
βασιλεὺς Μωὰβ ἐξ ὀρέων ἐπ' ἀπ'
ἀνατολῶν, λέγων, Δεῦρο ἄρασαί
μοι τὸν Ἰακώβ, καὶ δεῦρο
ἐπικατάρασαί μοι τὸν Ἰσραήλ.
Τί ἀράσωμαι (v. 1. -σομαι) ὃν
μὴ καταρᾶται (v. 1. ἀρᾶται)
Κύριος; ἢ τί καταράσωμαι ὃν
μὴ καταρᾶται ὁ Θεός; ὅτι ἀπὸ
κορυφῆς ὀρέων ὄψομαι αὐτὸν,
καὶ ἀπὸ βουνῶν προσνοήσω
αὐτόν.

Ἰδοὺ λαὸς μόνος κατοικήσει,
καὶ ἐν ἔθνεσιν οὐ συλλογισθήσεται.

Τίς ἐξηκριβάσατο τὸ σπέρμα
Ἰακώβ,
καὶ τίς ἐξαριθμήσεται δήμους
Ἰσραήλ;

Ἀποθάνοι ἡ ψυχή μου ἐν ψυχαῖς
δικαίων,
καὶ γένοιτο τὸ σπέρμα μου ὡς τὸ
σπέρμα τούτων.

Ibid. 18-24.

Ἀνάστηθι Βαλὰκ καὶ ἄκουε,
ἐνώτισαι μάρτυς. υἱὸς Σεπφώρ.
οὐχ ὡς ἄνθρωπος ὁ Θεὸς διαρτηθῆναι,
οὐδὲ ὡς υἱὸς ἀνθρώπου ἀπειληθῆναι,
αὐτὸς εἶπας, οὐχὶ ποιήσει;
λαλήσει, καὶ οὐκ ἐμμενεῖ;

PHILO DE VIT. MOYS. I. 50.

Ἐκ Μεσοποταμίας μετεπέμψατό
με Βαλάκης μακρὰν τὴν ἀπ'
ἀνατολῶν στειλάμενον ἀποδη-
μίαν, ἵνα τίσηται τοὺς Ἑβραί-
ους ἀραῖς. ἐγὼ δὲ τίνα τρόπον
ἀράσομαι τοῖς μὴ καταράτοις
ὑπὸ Θεοῦ; Θεάσομαι μὲν
αὐτοὺς ὀφθαλμοῖς ἀφ' ὑψηλ-
οτάτων ὀρῶν, καὶ τῇ διανοίᾳ
καταλήψομαι, βλάψαι δ' οὐκ
ἂν δυναίμην λαὸν, ὃς μόνος
κατοικήσει, μὴ συναριθμούμενος
ἑτέροις ἔθνεσιν, οὐ κατὰ τόπων
ἀποκλήρωσιν καὶ γῆς ἀποτομὴν,
ἀλλὰ κατὰ τὴν τῶν ἐξαιρέτων
ἐθῶν ἰδιότητα, μὴ συναναμι-
γνυμένων ἄλλοις εἰς τὴν τῶν
πατρίων ἐκδιαίτησιν. Τίς ἐπ'
ἀκριβείας εὗρε τὴν πρώτην
καταβολὴν τῆς τούτων γεν-
έσεως; τὰ μὲν σώματα αὐτοῖς
ἐξ ἀνθρωπίνων διεπλάσθη
σπερμάτων, ἐκ δὲ θείων ἔφυσαν
αἱ ψυχαί· διὸ καὶ γεγόνασιν
ἀγχίσποροι Θεοῦ. Ἀποθάνοι
μου ἡ ψυχὴ τὸν σωματικὸν
βίον, ἵν' ἐν ψυχαῖς δικαίων
καταριθμηθῇ, οἴας εἶναι συμ-
βέβηκε τὰς τούτων.

Ibid. 51.

Ἀναστὰς ἄκουε, βασιλεῦ, τὰ ὦτα
ἐπαιωρήσας. Οὐχ ὡς ἄνθρωπος
διαψευσθῆναι δύναται, οὐδ' ὡς
υἱὸς ἀνθρώπου μετανοεῖ, καὶ
ἅπαξ εἰπὼν οὐκ ἐμμένει. φθέγ-
ξεται τὸ παράπαν οὐδὲν, ὃ μὴ
τελειωθήσεται βεβαίως, ἐπεὶ
ὁ λόγος ἔργον ἐστὶν αὐτῷ.

APPENDIX II.

Ἰδοὺ εὐλογεῖν παρείλημμαι·
εὐλογήσω, καὶ οὐ μὴ ἀποστρέψω.

Οὐκ ἔσται μόχθος ἐν Ἰακὼβ,
οὐδὲ ὀφθήσεται πόνος ἐν Ἰσραήλ.
Κύριος ὁ Θεὸς αὐτοῦ μετ' αὐτοῦ·
τὰ ἔνδοξα ἀρχόντων ἐν αὐτῷ.
[ὁ]Θεὸς ὁ ἐξαγαγὼν αὐτοὺς (v. l.
αὐτὸν) ἐξ Αἰγύπτου,
ὡς δόξα μονοκέρωτος αὐτοῦ.

οὐ γάρ ἐστιν οἰωνισμὸς ἐν Ἰακὼβ,
οὐδὲ μαντεία ἐν Ἰσραήλ.
κατὰ καιρὸν ῥηθήσεται Ἰακὼβ, καὶ
τῷ Ἰσραὴλ
τί ἐπιτελέσει ὁ Θεός.

Ἰδοὺ λαὸς ὡς σκύμνος ἀναστήσεται,
καὶ ὡς λέων γαυρ[ι]ωθήσεται.
οὐ κοιμηθήσεται ἕως φάγῃ θήραν,
καὶ αἷμα τραυματιῶν πίεται.

Παρελήφθην δ' ἐπ' εὐλογίαις, οὐ
κατάραις ἐγώ.

Οὐκ ἔσται πόνος ἢ μόχθος ἐν
Ἑβραίοις. Ὁ Θεὸς αὐτῶν
προασπίζει φανερῶς, ὃς καὶ
τὴν τῶν Αἰγυπτιακῶν ῥύμην
κακῶν ἀπεσκέδασεν, ὡς ἕνα
ἄνδρα τὰς τοσαύτας μυριάδας
ἀναγαγών.

Τοιγαροῦν οἰωνῶν ἀλογοῦσι καὶ
πάντων τῶν κατὰ μαντικὴν,
ἑνὶ τῷ τοῦ κόσμου ἡγεμόνι
πιστεύοντες.

Ὁρῶ δὲ λαὸν ὡς σκύμνον
ἀνιστάμενον, καὶ ὡς λέοντα
γαυρούμενον. Εὐωχηθήσεται
θήρας, καὶ ποτῷ χρήσεται
τραυματιῶν αἵματι, καὶ κορεσθεὶς
οὐ τρέψεται πρὸς ὕπνον,
ἀλλ' ἐγρηγορὼς τὸν ἐπινίκιον
ᾄσεται ὕμνον.

Ibid. xxiv. 3-9.

Φησὶν Βαλαὰμ υἱὸς Βεὼρ,
φησὶν ὁ ἄνθρωπος ὁ ἀληθινῶς
ὁρῶν,
φησὶν ἀκούων λόγια Θεοῦ (v. l.
ἰσχυροῦ),
ὅστις ὅρασιν Θεοῦ εἶδεν,
ἐν ὕπνῳ ἀποκεκαλυμμένοι οἱ
ὀφθαλμοὶ αὐτοῦ,
Ὡς καλοί σου οἱ οἶκοι (v. l. [οἱ]
οἶκοί σου), Ἰακὼβ,
αἱ σκηναί σου, Ἰσραήλ.
ὡσ[εὶ] νάπαι σκιάζουσαι,
καὶ ὡσεὶ παράδεισος (v. l. -σοι)
ἐπὶ ποταμῶν (v. l. μῷ),
καὶ ὡσεὶ σκηναὶ ἃς ἔπηξεν Κύριος,
[καὶ] ὡσεὶ κέδροι παρ' ὕδατα.

Ibid. 52.

Τάδε φησὶν ὁ ἄνθρωπος ὁ ἀληθινῶς
ὁρῶν ὅστις καθ' ὕπνον
ἐναργῆ φαντασίαν εἶδε Θεοῦ
τοῖς τῆς ψυχῆς ἀκοιμήτοις
ὄμμασιν.

Ὡς καλοί σου οἱ οἶκοι, στρατιὰ
Ἑβραίων, αἱ σκηναί σου
ὡς νάπαι συσκιάζουσαι, ὡς
παράδεισος ἐπὶ ποταμοῦ, ὡς
κέδρος παρ' ὕδατα.

Ἐξελεύσεται ἄνθρωπος ἐκ τοῦ
σπέρματος αὐτοῦ,
καὶ κυριεύσει ἐθνῶν πολλῶν·
καὶ ὑψωθήσεται ἡ [vel. ἢ] Γὼγ
βασιλεία [αὐτοῦ]
καὶ αὐξηθήσεται [ἡ] βασιλεία
αὐτοῦ.
[ὁ] Θεὸς ὡδήγησεν αὐτὸν ἐξ
Αἰγύπτου,
ὡς δόξα μονοκέρωτος αὐτῷ.
Ἔδεται ἔθνη ἐχθρῶν αὐτοῦ,
καὶ τὰ πάχη αὐτῶν ἐκμυελιεῖ.
καὶ ταῖς βολίσιν αὐτοῦ κατατοξ-
εύσει ἐχθρόν.
Κατακλιθεὶς ἀνεπαύσατο ὡς λέων
καὶ ὡς σκύμνος·
τίς ἀναστήσει αὐτόν ;
Οἱ εὐλογοῦντές σε εὐλόγηνται,
καὶ οἱ καταρώμενοί σε κεκατήραν-
ται.

Ἐξελεύσεταί ποτε ἄνθρωπος ἐξ
ὑμῶν, καὶ ἐπικρατήσει πολλῶν
ἐθνῶν, καὶ ἐπιβαίνουσα ἡ τοῦδε
βασιλεία καθ' ἑκάστην ἡμέραν
πρὸς ὕψος ἀρθήσεται. Ὁ λαὸς
οὗτος ἡγεμόνι τῆς ἀπ' Αἰγύπτου
πάσης ὁδοῦ κέχρηται Θεῷ καθ'
ἓν κέρας ἄγοντι τὴν πληθύν.
Τοιγαροῦν ἔδεται ἔθνη πολλὰ
ἐχθρῶν, καὶ ὅσυν ἐν αὐτοῖς πῖον
ἄχρι μυελοῦ λήψεται, καὶ ταῖς
ἐκηβολίαις ἀπολεῖ τοὺς δυσ-
μενεῖς. Ἀναπαύσεται κατα-
κλιθεὶς ὡς λέων, ἢ σκύμνος
λέοντος, μάλα καταφρονητικῶς
δεδιὼς οὐδένα, φόβον τοῖς
ἄλλοις ἐνειργασμένος. Ἄθλιος
δὲ ὃς ἂν αὐτὸν παρακινήσας
ἐγείρῃ. Οἱ μὲν εὐλογοῦντές
σε εὐφημίας ἄξιοι, κατάρας δὲ
οἱ καταρώμενοι.

1 REG. (sive SAM.) xxviii. 3-8.

JOSEPI ARCHAEOL. VI. xiv. 2.

Καὶ Σαοὺλ περιεῖλεν τοὺς ἐνγασ-
τριμύθους καὶ τοὺς γνώστας
ἀπὸ τῆς γῆς. Καὶ συναθροί-
ζονται οἱ Ἀλλόφυλοι, καὶ
ἔρχονται καὶ παρεμβάλλουσιν
εἰς Σωνάμ καὶ συναθροίζει
Σαοὺλ πάντα ἄνδρα Ἰσραὴλ,
καὶ παρεμβάλλουσιν εἰς Γελβουέ.
καὶ εἶδε Σαοὺλ τὴν παρεμβολὴν
τῶν Ἀλλοφύλων, καὶ ἐφοβήθη,
καὶ ἐξέστη ἡ καρδία αὐτοῦ
σφόδρα. καὶ ἐπηρώτησε Σαοὺλ
διὰ Κυρίου, καὶ οὐκ ἀπεκρίθη
αὐτῷ Κύριος ἐν τοῖς ἐνυπνίοις
καὶ ἐν τοῖς δήλοις καὶ ἐν τοῖς
προφηταῖς.

Ἔτυχε δὲ Σάουλος ὁ τῶν Ἑβραίων
βασιλεὺς τοὺς μὲν μάντεις καὶ
τοὺς ἐγγαστριμύθους καὶ πᾶσαν
τὴν τοιαύτην τέχνην ἐκ τῆς
χώρας ἐκβεβληκώς, ἔξω τῶν
προφητῶν, ἀκούσας δὲ τοὺς
Παλαιστίνους ἤδη παρόντας καὶ
ἔγγιστα Σούνης, πόλεως ἐν
τῷ πεδίῳ κειμένης, ἐστρατ-
οπεδευκότας, ἐξώρμησεν ἐπ'
αὐτοὺς μετὰ τῆς δυνάμεως· καὶ
παραγενόμενος πρὸς ὄρει τινὶ
Γελβουὲ καλουμένῳ βάλλεται
στρατόπεδον ἀντικρὺ τῶν πολεμίων. Ταράττει δ' αὐτὸν οὐχ
ὡς ἔτυχεν ἰδόντα ἡ τῶν ἐχθρῶν
δύναμις, πολλή τε οὖσα καὶ
τῆς οἰκείας κρείττων ὑπονοου-
μένη· καὶ τὸν Θεὸν διὰ τῶν
προφητῶν ἠρώτα περὶ τῆς
μάχης καὶ τοῦ περὶ ταύτην
ἐσομένου τέλους προειπεῖν.

Καὶ εἶπε Σαοὺλ τοῖς παισὶν αὐτοῦ·
Ζητήσατέ μοι γυναῖκα ἐγγαστρίμυθον, καὶ πορεύσομαι πρὸς
αὐτήν, καὶ ζητήσω ἐν αὐτῇ.
καὶ εἶπαν οἱ παῖδες αὐτοῦ πρὸς
αὐτόν· Ἰδοὺ γυνὴ ἐγγαστρίμυθος
ἐν Ἀενδὼρ [Ἀελδώ]. καὶ συνεκαλύψατο (v. 1. περιεκαλ.)
Σαοὺλ καὶ περιεβάλετο ἱμάτια
ἕτερα, καὶ πορεύεται αὐτὸς καὶ
δύο ἄνδρες μετ' αὐτοῦ, καὶ
ἔρχονται (v. 1. ἦλθον) πρὸς
τὴν γυναῖκα νυκτός. καὶ εἶπεν
αὐτῇ· Μάντευσαι δή μοι ἐν τῷ
ἐγγαστριμύθῳ, καὶ ἀνάγαγέ
μοι ὃν ἐὰν εἴπω σοι.

οὐκ ἀποκριναμένου δὲ τοῦ
Θεοῦ, ἔτι μᾶλλον ὁ Σάουλος
κατέδεισε καὶ τὴν ψυχὴν
κατέπεσε, τὸ κακὸν, οἷον εἰκὸς,
οὐ παρόντος αὐτῷ κατὰ χεῖρα
τοῦ Θεοῦ προορώμενος. Ζητηθῆναι δ' αὐτῷ κελεύει γύναιόν
τι τῶν ἐγγαστριμύθων καὶ τὰς
τῶν τεθνηκότων ψυχὰς ἐκκαλουμένων, ὡς οὕτω γνωσόμενος
εἰ κατὰ νοῦν χωρεῖν αὐτῷ
μέλλει τὰ πράγματα· τὸ γὰρ
τῶν ἐγγαστριμύθων γένος
ἀνάγον τὰς τῶν νεκρῶν ψυχὰς
δι' αὐτῶν προλέγει τοῖς
δεομένοις τὰ ἀποβησόμενα.
Μηνυθέντος δ' αὐτῷ παρά
τινος τῶν οἰκετῶν εἶναί τι
γύναιον τοιοῦτον ἐν πόλει
Ἐνδώρῳ, λαθὼν πάντας τοὺς
ἐν τῷ στρατοπέδῳ καὶ μετεκδὺς
τὴν βασιλικὴν ἐσθῆτα, δύο
παραλαβὼν οἰκέτας οὓς ᾔδει
πιστοτάτους ὄντας, ἧκεν εἰς
τὴν Ἔνδωρον πρὸς τὴν γυναῖκα,
καὶ παρεκάλει μαντεύεσθαι καὶ
ἀνάγειν αὐτῷ ψυχὴν οὗπερ ἂν
αὐτὸς εἴπῃ.

SPECIMENS OF HELLENIC AND HELLENISTIC NARRATIVE AND DESCRIPTIVE COMPOSITION.

I.

POLYB. HIST. X. xxvii. 3-9.

Περιοικεῖται δὲ (ἡ Μηδία) πόλεσιν Ἑλληρίσι κατὰ τὴν ὑφήγησιν τὴν Ἀλεξάνδρου, φυλακῆς ἕνεκεν[1] τῶν συγκυρούντων αὐτῇ βαρβάρων πλὴν[2] Ἐκβατάνων. αὕτη δ' ἔκτισται μὲν ἐν τοῖς πρὸς τὰς ἄρκτους μέρεσι τῆς Μηδίας, ἐπίκειται δὲ τοῖς μέρει τὴν Μαιῶτιν καὶ τὸν Εὔξεινον μέρεσι τῆς Ἀσίας, ἦν δὲ βασίλειον ἐξ ἀρχῆς Μήδων,[3] πλούτῳ δὲ καὶ τῇ τῆς κατασκευῆς πολυτελείᾳ μέγα τι παρὰ τὰς ἄλλας δοκεῖ διενηνοχέναι πόλεις· κεῖται μὲν οὖν[4] ὑπὸ τὴν παρώρειαν τὴν παρὰ τὸν Ὀρόντην, ἀτείχιστος οὖσα, ἄκραν δ' ἐν αὐτῇ[5] χειροποίητον ἔχει, θαυμασίως πρὸς ὀχυρότητα κατεσκευασμένην. ὑπὸ δὲ ταύτην ἐστὶ τὰ βασίλεια, περὶ ὧν καὶ τὸ λέγειν κατὰ μέρος καὶ τὸ παρασιωπᾶν[6] ἔχει τινὰ ἀπορίαν· τοῖς μὲν γὰρ αἱρουμένοις τὰς ἐκπληκτικὰς τῶν διηγήσεων[7] προφέρεσθαι καὶ μετ' αὐξήσεως ἕνα

II.

GEN. xiv. 5-11.

Ἐν δὲ τῷ τεσσαρεσκαιδεκάτῳ ἔτει ἦλθεν Χοδολλογόμορ καὶ οἱ βασιλεῖς οἱ[1] μετ' αὐτοῦ, καὶ κατέκοψαν τοὺς[1] Γίγαντας τοὺς[1] ἐν Ἀσταρωθ Καρναίν, καὶ ἔθνη ἰσχυρὰ[2] ἅμα αὐτοῖς,[3] καὶ τοὺς Σομμαίους[1] τοὺς[1] ἐν Σαυῆ τῇ πόλει, καὶ τοὺς Χορραίους τοὺς[1] ἐν τοῖς ὄρεσιν Σηείρ, ἕως τῆς[3] τερεμίνθου τῆς Φαράν, ἥ ἐστιν ἐν τῇ ἐρήμῳ, καὶ ἀναστρέψαντες ἤλθοσαν[u] ἐπὶ τὴν[5] πηγὴν τῆς κρίσεως, αὕτη[1] ἐστὶν Καδής, καὶ κατέκοψαν πάντες τοὺς ἄρχοντας Ἀμαλὴκ καὶ τοὺς Ἀμορραίους τοὺς κατοικοῦντας ἐν Ἀσασὰν Θαμάρ. Ἐξῆλθεν δὲ βασιλεὺς[9] Σοδόμων καὶ βασιλεὺς[9] Γομόρρας καὶ βασιλεὺς[9] Ἀδαμὰ καὶ βασιλεὺς[9] Σεβωεὶμ καὶ βασιλεὺς[9] Βάλακ, αὕτη[1] ἐστὶν Σήγωρ, καὶ παρετάξαντο αὐτοῖς[1] εἰς πόλεμον ἐν τῇ κοιλάδι τῇ ἁλυκῇ,[2] πρὸς Χοδολλογόμορ βασιλέα Αἰλὰμ καὶ

III.

JUDITH i. 1-10.

Ἔτους[1] δωδεκάτου τῆς βασιλείας Ναβουχοδονόσορ, ὃς ἐβασίλευσεν Ἀσσυρίων ἐν Νινευὴ τῇ πόλει τῇ μεγάλῃ, ἐν ταῖς ἡμέραις[1] Ἀρφαξὰδ, ὃς ἐβασίλευσε Μήδων ἐν Ἐκβατάνοις, καὶ ᾠκοδόμησεν ἐπ' Ἐκβατάνων καὶ κύκλῳ τείχη ἐκ λίθων λελαξευμένων εἰς πλάτος πηχῶν τριῶν καὶ εἰς[3] μῆκος πηχῶν ἕξ, καὶ ἐποίησε τὸ ὕψος τοῦ τείχους πηχῶν ἑβδομήκοντα, καὶ τὸ πλάτος αὐτοῦ πηχῶν πεντήκοντα· καὶ τοὺς πύργους αὐτοῦ ἔστησεν ἐπὶ ταῖς πύλαις αὐτῆς πηχῶν ἑκατὸν, καὶ τὰ πλάτη αὐτῶν ἐθεμελίωσεν εἰς πήχεις ἑξήκοντα· καὶ ἐποίησε τὰς πύλας αὐτῆς πύλας[4] διεγειρομένας[5] εἰς ὕψος πηχῶν ἑβδομήκοντα, καὶ τὸ πλάτος αὐτῶν πήχεις τεσσαράκοντα εἰς ἐξόδους δυνάμεων δυνατῶν αὐτοῦ διατάξεις τῶν πεζῶν αὐτῶν·[6] καὶ[7] ἐποίησε πόλεμον ὁ βασιλεὺς Ναβουχοδονόσορ

καὶ διαθέσεως εἰθεσμένος ἐξαγγέλλειν καλλίστην ὑπόθεσιν ἡ τρεμμένη πόλις ἔχει, τοῖς δ' εὐλαβῶς προσπορευομένοις πρὸς πᾶν [τὸ] παρὰ τὴν κοινὴν ἔννοιαν λεγόμενον ἀπορίαν παρασκευάζαι καὶ δυσχρηστίαν. πλὴν ἔστι γε τὰ βασίλεια τῷ μὲν μεγέθει σχεδὸν ἑπτὰ σταδίων ἔχοντα τὴν περιγραφήν, τῇ δὲ τῶν κατὰ μέρος κατασκευασμάτων πολυτελείᾳ μεγάλην ἐμφαίνοντα τὴν τῶν ἐξ ἀρχῆς καταβαλλομένων εὐκαιρίαν.

Θαλγὰδ βασιλέα ἐθνῶν καὶ Ἀμαρφὰλ βασιλέα Σενναὰρ καὶ Ἀριὼχ βασιλέα Ἐλλασάρ, οἱ τέσσαρες οὗτοι βασιλεῖς πρὸς τοὺς πέντε. Ἡ δὲ κοιλὰς ἡ ἁλυκὴ φρέατα ἀσφάλτου. ἔφυγεν δὲ βασιλεὺς Σοδόμων καὶ βασιλεὺς Γομόρρας, καὶ ἐνέπεσαν ἐκεῖ· οἱ δὲ καταλειφθέντες εἰς τὴν ὀρινὴν ἔφυγον. Ἔλαβον (v.l. -βεν) δὲ τὴν ἵππον πᾶσαν τὴν Σοδόμων καὶ Γομόρρας καὶ πάντα τὰ βρώματα αὐτῶν καὶ ἀπῆλθον.

πρὸς βασιλέα Ἀρφαξὰδ ἐν τῷ πεδίῳ τῷ μεγάλῳ, τοῦτό ἐστιν ἐν τοῖς ὁρίοις Ῥαγαῦ. καὶ συνήντησαν πρὸς αὐτὸν πάντες οἱ κατοικοῦντες τὴν ὀρεινήν, καὶ πάντες οἱ κατοικοῦντες τὸν Εὐφράτην καὶ τὸν Τίγρην καὶ τὸν Ὑδάσπην, καὶ ἐν τῷ πεδίῳ Ἀριὼχ ὁ βασιλεὺς Ἐλυμαίων· καὶ συνῆλθεν ἔθνη πολλὰ εἰς παράταξιν υἱῶν Χελεούδ. καὶ ἀπέστειλε Ναβουχοδονόσορ ὁ βασιλεὺς Ἀσσυρίων ἐπὶ πάντας τοὺς κατοικοῦντας τὴν Περσίδε καὶ ἐπὶ πάντας τοὺς κατοικοῦντας πρὸς δυσμαῖς, τοὺς κατοικοῦντας Κιλικίαν καὶ Δαμασκὸν, τὸν Λίβανον καὶ Ἀντιλίβανον, καὶ πάντας τοὺς κατοικοῦντας κατὰ πρόσωπον τῆς παραλίας, καὶ τοὺς ἐν τοῖς ἔθνεσι τοῦ Καρμήλου καὶ Γαλαὰδ, καὶ τὴν ἄνω Γαλιλαίαν καὶ τὸ μέγα πεδίον Ἐσδρηλὼμ, καὶ πάντας τοὺς ἐν Σαμαρείᾳ καὶ ταῖς πόλεσιν αὐτῆς, καὶ πέραν τοῦ Ἰορδάνου ἕως Ἱερουσαλήμ, καὶ Βετάνη καὶ Χελοὺς καὶ Κάδης καὶ τοῦ ποταμοῦ Αἰγύπτου, καὶ Ταφνὰς καὶ Ῥαμεσσῆ καὶ πᾶσαν γῆν Γεσέμ, ἕως τοῦ ἐλθεῖν ἐπάνω Τάνεως καὶ Μέμφεως, καὶ πάντας τοὺς κατοικοῦντας τὴν Αἴγυπτον ἕως τοῦ ἐλθεῖν ἐπὶ τὰ ὅρια τῆς Αἰθιοπίας.

IV.

POLYB. HIST. XV. xi. 1-7.

Ὁ μὲν οὖν Πόπλιος τοιαύτην ἐποιήσατο τὴν παραίνεσιν, ὁ δ' Ἀννίβας τὰ μὲν θηρία πρὸ πάσης τῆς δυνάμεως, ὄντα πλείω τῶν [1] ὀγδοήκοντα, μετὰ δὲ ταῦτα τοὺς μισθοφόρους ἐπέστησε, περὶ μυρίους ὄντας καὶ δισχιλίους τὸν ἀριθμόν. οὗτοι δ' ἦσαν Λιγυστῖνοι. Κελτοί. Βαλιαρεῖς. Μαυρούσιοι. τούτων δὲ κατόπιν παρενέβαλε τοῖς ἐγχωρίοις Λίβυας καὶ Καρχηδονίους, ἐπὶ δὲ πᾶσι τοὺς ἐξ Ἰταλίας ἥκοντας μεθ' αὑτοῦ, πλεῖον ἢ στάδιον ἀποστήσας τῶν προτεταγμένων. τὰ δὲ κέρατα διὰ τῶν ἱππέων ἠσφαλίσατο, θεὶς ἐπὶ μὲν τὸ λαιὸν [2] τοὺς συμμάχους Νομάδας, ἐπὶ δὲ τὸ δεξιὸν τοὺς τῶν Καρχηδονίων ἱππεῖς. παρήγγειλε δὲ τοὺς ἰδίους στρατιώτας [3] ἕκαστον παρακαλεῖν, ἀναφέροντας τὴν ἐλπίδα τῆς νίκης ἐφ' ἑαυτῶν καὶ τὰς μεθ' αὑτοῦ παραγεγενημένας δυνάμεις· τοὺς δὲ Καρχηδονίους ἐκέλευσε τοὺς ἡγουμένους τὰ συμβησόμενα περὶ τέκνων καὶ γυναικῶν ἐξαρ-

V.

MACCAB. I. vi. 30-40.

Καὶ ἦν ὁ ἀριθμὸς τῆς δυνάμεως αὐτοῦ ἑκατὸν χιλιάδες πεζῶν καὶ εἴκοσι χιλιάδες ἱππέων, καὶ ἐλέφαντες δύο καὶ τριάκοντα εἰδότες πόλεμον. καὶ ἦλθοσαν[1] διὰ τῆς Ἰδουμαίας καὶ παρενέβαλοσαν[1] ἐπὶ Βαιθσούραν, καὶ ἐπολέμησαν ἐπὶ ἡμέρας πολλὰς καὶ ἐποίησαν μηχανάς. καὶ ἐξῆλθον καὶ ἐνεπύρισαν αὐτὰς ἐν[2] πυρί, καὶ ἐπολέμησαν ἀνδρωδῶς. καὶ ἀπῆρεν Ἰούδας ἀπὸ τῆς ἄκρας καὶ παρενέβαλεν [3] εἰς Βαιθζαχαρία ἀπέναντι τῆς παρεμβολῆς[3] τοῦ βασιλέως. καὶ πρωί[3] καὶ ἀπῆρε ὁ βασιλεὺς τὸ πρωϊ καὶ ὥρμησεν[4] ὁ τὴν παρεμβολὴν ἐν ὁρμήματι αὐτῆς κατὰ τὴν ὁδὸν Βαιθζαχαρία, καὶ διεσκευάσθησαν αἱ δυνάμεις εἰς τὸν πόλεμον καὶ ἐσάλπισαν ταῖς σάλπιγξι. καὶ τοῖς ἐλέφασιν ἔδειξαν αἷμα σταφυλῆς[5] καὶ μόρων τοῦ παραστῆσαι αὐτοὺς εἰς τὸν πόλεμον. καὶ διεῖλον τὰ θηρία εἰς τὰς φάλαγγας, καὶ παρέστησαν ἑκάστῳ ἐλέφαντι χιλίους ἄνδρας τεθωρακισμένους ἐν

VI.

MACCAB. II. xi. 1-12.

Μετ' ὀλίγον δὲ παντελῶς χρόνον Λυσίας ἐπίτροπος τοῦ βασιλέως καὶ συγγενὴς καὶ ἐπὶ τῶν πραγμάτων,[1] λίαν βαρέως φέρων ἐπὶ[2] τοῖς γεγονόσι, συναθροίσας περὶ τὰς[3] ὀκτὼ μυριάδας καὶ τὴν ἵππον πᾶσαν παρεγένετο ἐπὶ τοὺς Ἰουδαίους, λογιζόμενος τὴν μὲν πόλιν Ἕλλησιν οἰκητήριον ποιήσειν, τὸ δὲ ἱερὸν ἀργυρολόγητον, καθὼς τὰ λοιπὰ τῶν ἐθνῶν τεμένη, πρατὴν δὲ τὴν ἀρχιερωσύνην κατ' ἔτος ποιήσειν, οὐδαμῶς ἐπιλογιζόμενος τὸ τοῦ Θεοῦ κράτος, πεφρενωμένος[5] δὲ ταῖς μυριάσι[6] τῶν πεζῶν καὶ ταῖς χιλιάσι[7] τῶν ἱππέων καὶ τοῖς ἐλέφασι τοῖς[7] ὀγδοήκοντα. εἰσελθὼν δὲ εἰς τὴν Ἰουδαίαν καὶ συνεγγίσας[8] Βαιθσούρᾳ, ὄντι μὲν ἐρυμνῷ χωρίῳ, ἀπὸ δὲ Ἱεροσολύμων ἀπέχοντι ὡσεὶ[9] σταδίους πέντε τοῦτο ἔθλιβεν.[1] ὡς δὲ μετέλαβον οἱ περὶ τὸν Μακκαβαῖον πολιορκοῦντα αὐτὸν τὰ ὀχυρώματα, μετ' ὀδυρμῶν καὶ δακρύων ἱκέτευον σὺν τοῖς ὄχλοις

θμεῖσθαι καὶ τιθέναι πρὸ ὀφθαλμῶν. ἐὰν ἄλλως πως[4] ἐκβῇ τὰ τῆς μάχης. οὗτοι μὲν οὖν οὕτως ἐποίουν τὸ παραγγελθέν· Ἀννίβας δὲ τοὺς μεθ᾽ αὑτοῦ παραγεγονότας ἐπιπορευόμενος ἠξίου παρεκάλει διὰ πλειόνων μνησθῆναι μὲν τῆς πρὸς ἀλλήλους ἑπτακαιδεκάτους συνηθείας, μνησθῆναι δὲ τῶν πλήθους τῶν προγεγονότων αὐτοῖς πρὸς Ῥωμαίους[5] ἀγώνων, ἐν οἷς ἀηττήτους γεγονότας οὐδ᾽ ἐλπίδα τοῦ νικᾶν οὐδέποτ᾽ ἔφη Ῥωμαίοις[5] αὐτοὺς ἀπολελοιπέναι.

ἀλυσιδωτοῖς, καὶ περικεφαλαίαι χαλκαῖ[7] ἐπὶ τῶν κεφαλῶν αὐτῶν, καὶ πεντακοσία ἵππος διατεταγμένη ἑκάστῳ θηρίῳ ἐκλελεγμένη. οὗτοι πρὸ καιροῦ οὗ ἐὰν ἦν[18] τὸ θηρίον ἦσαν, καὶ οὗ ἐὰν ἐπορεύετο[8] ἐπορεύοντο ἅμα, καὶ οὐκ ἀφίσταντο[9] ἀπ᾽ αὐτοῦ. καὶ πύργοι ξύλινα ἐπ᾽ αὐτοὺς ὀχυροὶ σκεπαζόμενοι ἐφ᾽ ἑκάστου θηρίου ἐξωσμένοι ἐπ᾽ αὐτοῦ μηχαναῖς, καὶ ἐφ᾽ ἑκάστου ἄνδρες δυνάμεως[1] δύο καὶ τριάκοντα[2] οἱ πολεμοῦντες ἐπ᾽ αὐτοῖς καὶ ὁ Ἰνδὸς αὐτοῦ. καὶ τὴν ἐπίλοιπον ἵππον ἔνθεν καὶ ἔνθεν[3] ἔστησαν ἐπὶ τὰ δύο μέρη τῆς παρεμβολῆς καταπείοντες καὶ καταφρασσόμενοι ἐν ταῖς φάλαγξιν. ὡς δὲ ἔστιλβεν ὁ ἥλιος ἐπὶ τὰς χρυσᾶς καὶ χαλκᾶς ἀσπίδας, ἔστιλβε τὰ ὄρη ἀπ᾽ αὐτῶν καὶ κατηύγαζεν ὡς λαμπάδες πυρός.[4]

τὸν Κύριον, ἀγαθὸν ἄγγελον ἀποστεῖλαι πρὸς σωτηρίαν τῷ Ἰσραήλ. αὐτὸς δὲ πρῶτος ὁ Μακκαβαῖος ἀναλαβὼν τὰ ὅπλα προετρέψατο τοὺς ἄλλους, ἅμα αὐτῷ διακινδωνεύειν· τὰς ἐπιβοηθεῖν τοῖς ἀδελφοῖς[2] αὐτῶν. ὁμοῦ δὲ καὶ προθύμως ἐξώρμησαν. αὐτόθι δὲ καὶ πρὸς τοῖς Ἱεροσολύμοις ὄντων, ἐφάνη προηγούμενος αὐτῶν ἔφιππος ἐν λευκῇ ἐσθῆτι, πανοπλίαν χρυσῆν κραδαίνων,[3] ὁμοῦ δὲ πάντες εὐλόγησαν τὸν ἐλεήμονα Θεόν, καὶ ἐπερρώσθησαν ταῖς ψυχαῖς· οὐ μόνον ἀνθρώπους, ἀλλὰ καὶ θῆρας τοὺς ἀγριωτάτους καὶ σιδηρᾶ τείχη τιτρώσκειν[4] ὄντες ἕτοιμοι, προσῆγον ἐν διασκευῇ[5] τὸν ἀπ᾽ οὐρανοῦ σύμμαχον ἔχοντες, ἐλεήσαντος αὐτοὺς τοῦ Κυρίου. λεοντηδὸν δὲ ἐπιτινάξαντες[6] εἰς τοὺς πολεμίους, κατέστρωσαν αὐτῶν χιλίους πρὸς τοῖς μυρίοις, ἱππεῖς δὲ ἑξακοσίους πρὸς τοῖς χιλίοις· τοὺς δὲ πάντας ἠνάγκασαν φυγεῖν. οἱ πλείονες δὲ αὐτῶν τραυματίαι γυμνοὶ διεσώθησαν, καὶ αὐτὸς δὲ ὁ Λυσίας αἰσχρῶς φεύγων διεσώθη.

VII.

MATT. xxvii. 62-66.

Τῇ δὲ ἐπαύριον,¹ ἥτις ἐστὶν μετὰ τὴν παρασκευήν,² συνήχθησαν ³ οἱ ἀρχιερεῖς καὶ οἱ Φαρισαῖοι πρὸς Πειλᾶτον λέγοντες, Κύριε,⁴ ἐμνήσθημεν ὅτι ἐκεῖνος ὁ πλάνος εἶπεν ἔτι ζῶν, Μετὰ τρεῖς ἡμέρας ἐγείρομαι·⁵ κέλευσον οὖν ἀσφαλισθῆναι.⁶ τὸν τάφον ἕως τῆς τρίτης ἡμέρας, μήποτε ἐλθόντες οἱ μαθηταὶ [αὐτοῦ] κλέψωσιν αὐτὸν καὶ εἴπωσιν τῷ λαῷ, Ἠγέρθη⁷ ἀπὸ τῶν νεκρῶν,⁸ καὶ ἔσται⁹ ἡ ἐσχάτη πλάνη χείρων τῆς πρώτης. ἔφη [δὲ] αὐτοῖς ὁ Πειλᾶτος, Ἔχετε κουστωδίαν· ὑπάγετε ἀσφαλίσασθε⁶ ὡς οἴδατε. οἱ δὲ πορευθέντες ἠσφαλίσαντο¹ τὸν τάφον σφραγίσαντες τὸν λίθον μετὰ τῆς κουστωδίας.

VIII.

ACT. APOST. xxiii. 31-35.

Οἱ μὲν οὖν στρατιῶται κατὰ τὸ διατεταγμένον¹ αὐτοῖς ἀναλαβόντες¹ τὸν Παῦλον, ἤγαγον διὰ νυκτὸς εἰς τὴν Ἀντιπατρίδα· τῇ δὲ ἐπαύριον ¹ ἐάσαντες τοὺς ἱππεῖς ἀπέρχεσθαι σὺν αὐτῷ ὑπέστρεψαν εἰς τὴν παρεμβολήν· οἵτινες εἰσελθόντες εἰς τὴν Καισαρίαν καὶ ἀναδόντες ¹ τὴν ἐπιστολὴν τῷ ἡγεμόνι παρέστησαν καὶ τὸν Παῦλον αὐτῷ. ἀναγνοὺς δὲ καὶ ἐπερωτήσας ἐκ² ποίας ἐπαρχείας ἐστὶν καὶ πυθόμενος ὅτι ἀπὸ ² Κιλικίας Διακούσομαί¹ σου, ἔφη, ὅταν καὶ οἱ κατήγοροί σου παραγένωνται· κελεύσας ἐν τῷ πραιτωρίῳ [τοῦ] Ἡρῴδου φυλάσσεσθαι αὐτόν.

IX.

DIONYS. HALIC. ANT. ROM., V, iii, iv.

Ταῦτα μαθὼν ὁ Ποστούμιος ἐξεβοήθει διὰ ταχέων, πρὶν ἢ συνελθεῖν τοὺς πολεμίους ἅπαντας· ἀναγὼν δ' ἐν νυκτὶ τὴν σὺν αὐτῷ στρατιὰν πορείᾳ συντόνῳ,¹ πλησίον γίνεται τῶν Λατίνων ἐστρατοπεδευκότων παρὰ λίμνῃ Ῥηγίλλῃ ² καλουμένῃ ἐν ἐχυρῷ χωρίῳ· καὶ τίθεται τὸν χάρακα² κατὰ κεφαλῆς⁴ τῶν πολεμίων ἐν ὑψηλῷ λόφῳ καὶ δυσβάτῳ, ἐν ᾧ ὑπομένων πολλὰ πλεονεκτήσειν ἔμελλεν. Οἱ δὲ τῶν Λατίνων ἡγεμόνες, Ὀκτάουός τε ὁ Τουσκλανὸς, Ταρκύνιον τοῦ βασιλέως γαμβρός, ὡς δέ τινες γράφουσιν υἱὸς τοῦ γαμβροῦ, καὶ Σέξτος Ταρκύνιος· ἐπύγχανον γὰρ ἤδη τηρικαῦτα χωρὶς ἀλλήλως ἐστρατοπεδευκότες· εἰς ἓν συνάγουσι τὰς δυνάμεις χωρίον· καὶ παραλαβόντες τοὺς χιλιάρχους, καὶ λοχαγοὺς, ἐσκόπουν ὅστις ἔσται τρόπος τοῦ πολέμου· καὶ πολλαὶ γνῶμαι ἐλέχθησαν. οἱ

μὲν γὰρ ἐξ ἐφόδου χωρεῖν ἤξίουν
ἐπὶ τοὺς ἅμα τῷ δικτάτωρι καταλα-
βομένους τὸ ὄρος, ἕως τινὲς ἦσαν
αὐτοῖς φοβεροί· οὐκ ἀσφαλείας
σημεῖον εἶναι νομίζοντες τὴν τῶν
ἐχυρῶν κατάληψιν, ἀλλὰ δειλίας· οἱ
δὲ τοὺς μὲν ἀποταφρεύσαντας ὀλίγῃ
τινὶ καθείργνυν φυλακῇ· τὴν δ' ἄλλην
δύναμιν ἀναλαβόντας, ἐπὶ τὴν Ῥώμην
ἄγειν ὡς ῥᾳδίαν ἁλῶναι, τῆς κρα-
τίστης νεότητος ἐξεληλυθυίας.

NOTES ON THE HISTORICAL EXTRACTS.

I. POLYBIUS (cir. 140 B.C.)

[1] ἕνεκεν] A form rare in prose, but quite classical as a poetical one.

[2] πλὴν] This is excepted as on a different footing from the Greek cities founded according to Alexander's scheme. The lax or rather pregnant use of the word may be considered classical, but should be noticed; it is however rather as an adv. than as a prep. that its use was extended in late Greek.

[3] Μήδων] "Of Media"—of the Medes as a nationality or as a kingdom. Τῶν Μήδων would be "of the Medians that we have been speaking of"—who might, according to circumstances, be the whole nation, or only certain individuals of it.

[4] μὲν οὖν] Μὲν really belongs, not so much to the main clause in which it is inserted, as to the secondary ἀτείχ. οὖσα; still perhaps there is the sense "The city is neither placed on (but under) the mountains, nor fortified, *but* it has a strong citadel." Οὖν can hardly be thought to coalesce in meaning with μὲν; it is probably the *resumptive* use of the word, as the historian returns to the description of the site, after the mention of its former political greatness.

[5] αὐτῇ] For the question of the breathing see *Language of the New Testament*, pp. 64-5.

παρασιωπᾶν] "To pass by in silence"—the prep. cannot here be considered meaningless. Yet Polybius himself (who is the first known author who uses the compound) has it in the constr. παρασιωπᾶν περὶ (XX. xi. 1); where, though the choice of the word is intelligible, it adds hardly anything to what would be expressed by the simple σιωπᾶν.

7 τὰς ἐκπλ. τῶν δ.] "Such stories as are astonishing," much as we might say "the *most* astonishing of the stories told." The constr. is quite good Greek, but perhaps a more spontaneous writer would have been less disposed to use it here than a self-conscious man of letters.

8· μετ' αὐξ . . . καὶ διαθ.] "With exaggeration and arrangement"—i.e. artificial arrangement for effect. Both the sense of this word, and the fact that the same group of words occur in another passage of the same writer (II. lxi. 1), are suggestively *modern*.

9 εὐκαιρίαν]. "Prosperity"—a sense of the word first found in Polybius.

II. SEPTUAGINT VERSION OF THE PENTATEUCH
(cir. 280 B.C. ?).

1 οἱ . . . τοὺς . . . τοὺς]. These articles are used idiomatically by the translator, according to what he thinks to be the sense, the analogous Hebrew use of the art. having no place here. Οἱ represents the Hebrew relative, and the double τοὺς is inserted without any corresponding words.

² ἔθνη ἰσχυρὰ]. It is idle to speculate why the name of "the Zuzim" (or whatever was read in place of it) was translated, when those following were not. It has the art. in the Heb., while "the Rephaim" have not; "the Emim" and "the Horim" below have. And in ver. 7 the double art., τοὺς Ἀμ· τοὺς κατοικ. is literal.

170 *LANGUAGE OF THE NEW TESTAMENT.*

[3] ἅμα αὐτοῖς]. The Hebrew letters with a different pronunciation might be read "among them" instead of "in Ham."

[4] Σομαίους] Probably the Σ is a διττογραφία, though found in the oldest MSS. Τῇ πόλει stands, of course, for Kiriathaim, "[of] the Two Cities."

[5] τῆς ... τὴν]. Here again the art. is not expressed in the Heb.; but though the significant words are treated as pr. nn., they are not written as compounds.

[6] ἤλθοσαν]. On this form see *Language of the New Testament,* p. 36.

[7] αὕτη ἐστίν] The pron. introduced abruptly and parenthetically is a literal reproduction of the Heb.; but the insertion of the copula is a concession to Greek idiom.

[8] ἄρχοντας]. This must represent a different reading from the Hebrew text.

[9] βασιλεὺς]. Anarthrous as in Heb., though hardly natural Greek.

[1] αὐτοῖς] This use of the dat. is found in classical Greek. The most literal translation of the Heb. would be παρέταξαν μετ' αὐτῶν πόλεμον.

[2] τῇ ἁλυκῇ.] Either a different reading or a mistranslation of the Heb.; see ver. 3, where the LXX. has the same translation of "the Vale of Siddim," "the Salt Sea" being ἡ θάλασσα τῶν ἁλῶν. The double art. is again according to Greek idiom, the Heb. being different.

[3] οἱ τέσσ. οὗτοι]. The Heb. use and non-use of the art. would be represented by τέσσ. βασ. πρὸς τοὺς (or more exactly μετὰ τῶν) πέντε.

[4] φρέατα]. As we should say in rather colloquial modern English, "was *all* pits of bitumen." In Hebrew the word for "pits" is twice repeated.

[5] ἔφυγεν]. The Heb. has the verb in the pl. here as in the following clauses.

NOTES ON HISTORICAL EXTRACTS. 171

⁶ ἐνέπεσαν]. This form is held to be post-classical, though sometimes found in MSS. of Attic writers.
⁷ ἵππον]. A different pronunciation of the Heb. for "goods" would give the sense of "a horse."

III. BOOK OF JUDITH (Date unknown; prob. translated from the Aramaic; first cited A.D. 97).

¹ Ἔτους δωδ.]. The gen. is not ordinarily used in Greek in giving a date in this form, but the use of ἔτους ἑκάστου "every year," and the Thucydidean τοῦ αὐτοῦ θέρους and the like, may be held to justify it.
² ἐν ταῖς ἡμέραις]. The common Hebraic mode of marking a date, from Gen. xiv. 1 (Heb., not LXX.) to Luke i. 5.
³ εἰς] The prep. would hardly have been repeated in pure Greek : see *Language of the New Testament*, p. 158.
⁴ πύλας]. The repetition of the subst. is obviously un-Hellenic. It is no doubt a predicate, "he made the gates of it gates rising," etc.
⁵ διεγ. εἰς ὕψος]. One can see no possible meaning for these words but "rising" or "raised to the height. . . ." But they certainly are not good Greek in that sense ; διεγείρω is a rather late word anyhow, and its only meaning is "to awake," not "to erect." But the simple ἐγείρω is in late Greek used of "erecting" a building—according to a grammarian, as early as Thucyd. also. The tendency to give it the latter meaning has some interest, as illustrating the equivalence in the N. T. of ἐγείρειν and ἀνιστάναι (*e.g.* Acts iii. 15, 26).
⁶ αὐτοῦ]. The repetition of the pron. again is Hellenistic ; see *Language of the New Testament*, p. 57.
⁷ καί]. Here virtually begins the apodosis to the date in ver. 1, and the long relative clauses about Arphaxad. Perhaps it is as likely that the writer or translator

lost his way among these as that he introduced what he felt as an apodosis by a Hebraistic καί. No doubt, the general plan of the passage is imitated from Gen. xiv., but there are no detailed resemblances in language—least of all to distinctive idioms of the LXX.

[8] κατὰ πρόσωπον]. Used more or less as a Hebraic equivalent to a prep.; it is not found in the N. T. in that use, but is pure Greek in itself, see *Language of the New Testament*, pp. 149, 155.

IV. POLYBIUS.

[1] Τῶν]. Apparently an incorrect extension of a use of the art. found in good Greek, where, if a larger number is divided into two smaller ones, the art. is used with either or both of these. We in English should only use it with the second. See Thuc. I. cxvi. 1.

[2] λαιὸν]. Exclusively poetical in earlier Greek—*i.e.* not Attic nor Herodotean Ionic, but taken into the "common dialect" from some other.

[3] στρατιώτας]. Apparently in the sense of "mercenaries" as in Demosthenes, since these seem to be distinguished both from the Carthaginian citizens and from Hannibal's veterans. Yet the last were at least equally professional "soldiers."

[4] ἄλλως πως]. The combination of these two adverbs is classical; but though ἄλλως in good Attic often means "at random," "vainly," or the like, it seems hardly to have got so far as here towards a mere euphemism for "wrongly."

[5] 'Ρωμαίοις]. The second use of the anarthrous pr. n., at least, is to be explained as in I. note 3. It may be a question whether the first has the same force, or means, "You have fought with *Romans*, and know how to deal with them."

NOTES ON HISTORICAL EXTRACTS. 173

V. I MACCABEES (translated from a Hebrew work—
written cir. 105 B.C. ?).

[1] See *Language of the New Testament*, p. 36.
[2] The Hebraistic instrumental use of ἐν.
[3] The absolute use of this cognate verb and subst., as technical military terms, is not found before Polybius. The use of εἰς, "came to B. and encamped there," does not go beyond pure Greek use.
[4] Ὀρθρίζω is an exclusively biblical word, recognised however by a grammarian as non-Attic "Hellenic." But the redundant use with τὸ πρωΐ, and still more the constr. ὤρθρισεν καὶ ἀπῆρε for "removed early," are manifest Hebraisms.
[5] A Hebraism still more manifest. In Gen. xlix. 11, Deut. xxxii. 14, Ecclus. xxxix. 26, l. 15, the phrase is more or less poetical; but here it seems to be used with no consciousness of such a tone, only because mulberry juice would hardly be called wine.
[6] A constr. more frequent in Hellenistic than in pure Greek.
[7] Notice the way that a nom., with the verb subst. understood, so forming a sort of parenthetic sentence, is put co-ordinately with the main sentence, where we should in pure Greek have had an acc., co-ordinate with that forming the obj. of the main sentence.
[8] For the use of the past indic. in a rel. clause with ἄν see *Language of the New Testament*, p. 11.
[9] The asyndeton, and the whole phrase, are Hebraistic in tone, though there is nothing in it that we can say is bad Greek.
[1] "Men of might" for "mighty men" is a very decided Hebraism.
[2] As this number is incredible, it is guessed to be a misreading of the Hebrew original, which may have been "two or three."

174 *LANGUAGE OF THE NEW TESTAMENT.*

³ ἔνθεν καὶ ἔνθεν . . . ἐπὶ τὰ δύο μέρη]. The combination of the two clauses, perhaps the form of the second even if it stood alone, is Hellenistic.

⁴ πυρός]. Hebraistic in constr., besides being almost poetically redundant.

VI. II MACCABEES (First century B.C. ?).

¹ Ἐπὶ τῶν πραγμάτων]. So Dem. de Cor. § 307 (247). But phrases of this type approached nearer in later Greek than in good Attic to the character of technical titles, as this seems to be here ; see *e.g.* the spurious decrees in that speech, §§ 47, 147-8 (38, 115-6).

² βαρέως φέρων ἐπὶ τοῖς]. A classical constr., though rarer than that with the simple acc.

³ τὰς]. Cf. IV. note 1.

⁴ ἐθνῶν]. Used of course in its religious sense of non-Israelites ; and here apparently distinguished from Ἑλλήνων. "The nations" had each their own religion, which could be identified or combined with that of the ruling race, as that of Israel refused to be.

⁵ πεφρενωμένος]. Quite a late sense of the word, the classical meaning of which is "instructed."

⁶ μυριάσι . . . χιλιάσι]. It is a Hebraism of thought if not exactly of idiom to use the words thus absolutely.

⁷ τοῖς ὀγδ.] A pure Greek writer could hardly have used a numeral thus like an epithet, though he meant something distinctive by the unusual place he gives to it, " his elephants, of which there were eighty," or rather " his elephants in all their number of eighty."

⁸ συνεγγίσας]. A late word, first in Polybius. Even the simple ἐγγίζειν is not much older.

⁹ ὡσεί]. Occasionally found in this sense in good writers, but much oftener in Hellenistic Greek.

¹ ἔθλιβεν]. A late sense of the word altogether ; and a

pure Greek writer of any age would hardly have used it here.

² ἀδελφοῖς]. The extended sense of this word is not found in pure Greek.

³ κραδαίνων]. Made its way comparatively late from the language of poetry into that of prose. Here its use is incorrect; one can "brandish" a weapon, but hardly a suit of armour.

⁴ τιτρώσκειν]. Again a scarcely admissible sense of the word; it is used of "piercing" a ship, or even an egg-shell, but not in the general sense of "assailing," which seems to be meant here.

⁵ διασκευῇ]. A late word, and in pure Greek meaning "equipment" rather than "order," which seems to be the sense here.

⁶ λεοντηδὸν . . . ἐπιτινάξαντες]. Both ἅπαξ λεγόμενα, of poetical tone, and the latter incorrectly formed; for the simple τινάσσω is never intr.

VII. ST. MATTHEW (cir. 60 A.D. ?).

¹ ἐπαύριον]. The compound, not differing in sense from the simple αὔριον, is exclusively biblical.

² παρασκευήν]. Used in all the Gospels in the technical sense, which St. Mark only thinks it necessary to explain.

³ συνήχθησαν]. Though συνάγειν, "to assemble" people, is quite classical, this use of the middle and pass. of peoples "assembling together" is, to say the least, much more frequent and distinctive in Hellenistic than in pure Greek.

⁴ Κύριε]. We hardly have examples before the N. T. period of the merely complimentary use of this word, but it no doubt came easier to orientals than to Europeans. Very scrupulous Jews—at least the Zealots of Galilee—would have refused it to any man,

as Christians afterwards did; and perhaps here it has the same significance as John xix. 15. But this may be building too much upon a mere word. Though Domitian was the first emperor who officially claimed the title *dominus*, we can quite believe that it was given to Nero (Acts xxv. 26) even by Romans, when they were speaking Greek.

5 ἐγείρομαι]. For the force of the pres. see *Language of the New Testament*, pp. 99, 100.

6 ἀσφαλισ.] Both the act. and pass. and the med. are common from Polybius onwards; but purists continued to maintain that the word was not good Greek.

7 ἠγέρθη]. One hardly knows whether to say that the aor. is virtually equivalent to a perf. (see *Language of the New Testament*, p. 101), or that the matter is conceived dramatically; that the people ask what became of Him, or argue that His claims are refuted by His accursed death, and the disciples say "He rose from the dead," as a sufficient answer to either.

8 ἀπὸ τῶν νεκρῶν]. Not the concrete way of putting it; in pure Greek we should rather have had ἐκ τοῦ θανάτου.

9 καὶ ἔσται]. Prob. the sense is that of the A.V.; but it is possible that the fut. is co-ordinate with the two aorists subj., and depends on μήποτε.

1 κουστωδίαν]. See *Language of the New Testament*, p. 18.

VIII. St. Luke (A.D. 63, or later).

1 The chief point to notice here is the large number of compound verbs, and the small significance of the prepositions in most of them. Ἀναλαβεῖν indeed has a distinctive sense (cf. xx. 14, where indeed this is clearer, but also II Tim. iv. 11, where it is less so); and ἀναδοῦναι of delivering a letter is appropriate, though the word has not that sense before Polybius. But διατάσσειν in classical Greek has always more of

NOTES ON HISTORICAL EXTRACTS. 177

the sense of *dis*posing complicated arrangements ; and ἀπέρχεσθαι does not seem appropriate—it hardly can have the sense "to go on to their destination ; " Διακονεῖν is first used, so far as we know, of judicial hearing in the LXX. of Deut. i. 16 ; but the sense of the prep. is a legitimate one, and the use, though late, is not confined to biblical Greek. The constr., however, with a gen. of the person is not classical.

² ἐκ . . . ἀπό]. For the interchangeable use of these, see pp. 138, 145, Part I.).

IX. DIONYSIUS (cir. B.C. 7).

¹ π. συντόνῳ]. As a technical phrase for a "forced march" not found before Polybius, but the sense of σύντονος is classical.

² 'Ρηγίλλῃ]. A correction, the name being corrupt in the MSS. ; but it seems plain that it has a fem. form given to it to agree with λίμνη, as the Latin masc. does with *lacus*.

³ χάρακα]. Not exactly a classical sense of the word, but used of the distinctively Roman institution of the palisaded camp. It may be a question whether there is sufficient reason for the use of the med. τίθεται.

⁴ κατὰ κεφαλῆς]. Perhaps the most questionable phrase in the whole of this passage, from an author who means to write in pure literary Attic. Κατὰ κ. is good Greek for "over the head" in the sense of pouring a thing down upon it—hardly of a position held at some distance above.

⁵ καταλαβομένους]. The med. is used in a sense much like this, of "securing, taking possession of" a thing ; but the act. is usual of military occupation. Perhaps this use of the med. was a point in which an elaborately classicising writer was apt to overdo refinement of idiom.

SPECIMENS OF HELLENIC AND HELLENISTIC COMPOSITION UPON QUESTIONS OF RELIGIOUS PHILOSOPHY.

I.

POLYBIUS HIST. VI. LVI. 9-12.

Καί μοι δοκεῖ τὸ παρὰ τοῖς ἄλλοις ἀνθρώποις ὀνειδιζόμενον, τοῦτο συνέχειν τὰ Ῥωμαίων[1] πράγματα, λέγω δὲ τὴν δεισιδαιμονίαν. ἐπὶ τοσοῦτον γὰρ ἐκτετραγῴδηται[2] καὶ παρεισῆκται τοῦτο τὸ μέρος παρ᾽ αὐτοῖς εἴς τε τοὺς κατ᾽ ἰδίαν βίους καὶ τὰ[3] κατὰ τῆς πόλεως ὥστε μὴ καταλιπεῖν ὑπερβολήν. ὃ καὶ δόξειεν ἂν πολλοῖς εἶναι θαυμάσιον. ἐμοί γε μὴν δοκοῦσι τοῦ πλήθους χάριν τοῦτο πεποιηκέναι. εἰ μὲν γὰρ ἦν σοφῶν ἀνδρῶν πολίτευμα συναγαγεῖν, ἴσως οὐδὲν [ἂν][4] ἀναγκαῖος ὁ τοιοῦτος τρόπος· ἐπεὶ δὲ πᾶν πλῆθός ἐστιν ἐλαφρὸν καὶ πλῆρες ἐπιθυμιῶν παρανόμων, ὀργῆς ἀλόγου, θυμοῦ βιαίου,[3] λείπεται τοῖς ἀδήλοις φόβοις καὶ τῇ τοιαύτῃ τραγῳδίᾳ[2] τὰ πλήθη συνέχειν. διόπερ οἱ παλαιοὶ δοκοῦσί μοι τὰς περὶ θεῶν ἐννοίας

II.

SAPIENTIA SALOMONIS, XIII. 1-9.

Μάταιοι μὲν γὰρ πάντες ἄνθρωποι φύσει, οἷς παρῆν Θεοῦ ἀγνωσία, καὶ ἐκ τῶν ὁρωμένων ἀγαθῶν οὐκ ἴσχυσαν εἰδέναι τὸν ὄντα, οὔτε Ν[1] τοῖς ἔργοις προσέχοντες ἐπέγνωσαν τὸν τεχνίτην. ἀλλ᾽ ἢ πῦρ, ἢ πνεῦμα, ἢ ταχινὸν ἀέρα, ἢ κύκλον ἄστρων, ἢ βίαιον ὕδωρ, ἢ φωστῆρας οὐρανοῦ πρυτάνεις[3] κόσμου θεοὺς ἐνόμισαν. ὧν εἰ μὲν τῇ καλλονῇ[4] τερπόμενοι ταῦτα θεοὺς ὑπελάμβανον, γνώτωσαν πόσῳ τούτων ὁ Δεσπότης ἐστὶ βελτίων[5] ὁ γὰρ τοῦ κάλλους γενεσιάρχης ἔκτισεν αὐτά· εἰ δὲ δύναμιν καὶ ἐνέργειαν ἐκπλαγέντες, νοησάτωσαν ἀπ᾽ αὐτῶν πόσῳ ὁ κατασκευάσας αὐτὰ δυνατώτερός ἐστιν· ἐκ γὰρ μεγέθους καὶ καλλονῆς[4] κτισμάτων ἀναλόγως ὁ γενεσιουργὸς[5] αὐτῶν

III.

PHILO. QUOD DEUS IMMUT. 2 (p. 273-4).

Τίνι γὰρ εὐχαριστήσεων ἄλλῳ πλὴν Θεῷ,[1] διὰ τίνων δέ, ὅτι μὴ διὰ τῶν ὑπ᾽ αὐτοῦ δοθέντων; οὐδὲ γὰρ ἄλλων εὐπορῆσαι δυνατόν. Χρεῖος[2] δὲ οὐδενὸς ὢν κελεύει προσφέρειν αὐτῷ τὰ ἑαυτοῦ δι᾽ ὑπερβολὴν τῆς πρὸς τὸ γένος ἡμῶν εὐεργεσίας. Μελετήσαντες γὰρ εὐχαριστικῶς[3] ἔχειν καὶ τιμητικῶς[4] αὐτοῦ, καθαρευόντων ἀδικημάτων, ἐκνιψάμενοι τὰ καταβρυπαίνοντα τὸν βίον ἔν τε λόγοις καὶ εἴδεσι[5] καὶ ἔργοις. Καὶ γὰρ εὔηθες, εἰς μὲν τὰ ἱερὰ μὴ ἐξεῖναι βαδίζειν, ὃς ἂν μὴ πρότερον λουσάμενος φαιδρύνηται τὸ σῶμα, εὔχεσθαι δὲ καὶ θύειν ἐπιχειρεῖν ἔτι κεκηλιδωμένῃ καὶ πεφυρμένῃ διανοίᾳ.[6] Καίτοι τὰ μὲν ἱερὰ λίθων καὶ ξύλων ἀψύχου τῆς[6] ὕλης πεποίηνται,[7] καθ᾽ αὐτὸ δὲ καὶ

καὶ τὰς ὑπὲρ τῶν ἐν ᾅδου διαλήψεις οὐκ εἰκῇ καὶ ὡς ἔτυχεν εἰς τὰ πλήθη παρεισαγαγεῖν, πολὺ δὲ μᾶλλον οἱ νῦν εἰκῇ καὶ ἀλόγως ἐκβάλλειν αὐτά.

θεωρεῖται. ἀλλ' ὅμως ἐπὶ τούτοις ἐστὶ μέμψις ὀλίγη, καὶ γὰρ αὐτοὶ τάχα πλανῶνται Θεὸν ζητοῦντες καὶ θέλοντες εὑρεῖν· ἐν γὰρ τοῖς ἔργοις αὐτοῦ ἀναστρεφόμενοι διερευνῶσι, καὶ πείθονται τῇ ὄψει ὅτι καλὰ τὰ βλεπόμενα. πάλιν δὲ οὐδ' αὐτοὶ συγγνωστοί· εἰ γὰρ τοσοῦτον ἴσχυσαν εἰδέναι ἵνα δύνωνται στοχάσασθαι τὸν αἰῶνα, τὸν τούτων Δεσπότην πῶς τάχιον οὐχ εὗρον;

τὸ σῶμα ἄψυχον ἄψυχον οὐ προσάψεται, μὴ περιβραντηρίοις καὶ καθαρσίοις ἁγνευτικοῖς χρησάμενον, ὑπομενεῖ δέ τις τῷ Θεῷ προσελθεῖν, ἀκάθαρτος ὢν ψυχὴν τὴν ἑαυτοῦ τῷ καθαρωτάτῳ, καὶ ταῦτα μὴ μέλλων μετανοήσειν; ὁ μὲν γὰρ πρὸς τῷ μηδὲν ἐπεξεργάσασθαι δικαιώσας γεγηθὼς προσίτω· ὁ δ' ἄνευ τούτων δυσκάθαρτος ὤν, ἀφιστάσθω. λήσεται γὰρ οὐδέποτε τὸν τὰ ἐν μυχοῖς τῆς διανοίας ὁρῶντα, καὶ τοῖς ἀδύτοις αὐτῆς ἐμπεριπατοῦντα.

IV.

LUCAE ACT. APOST. XVII. 22-28.

Ἄνδρες Ἀθηναῖοι, κατὰ πάντα ὡς δεισιδαιμονεστέρους¹ ὑμᾶς θεωρῶ.² διερχόμενος γὰρ καὶ ἀναθεωρῶν³ τὰ σεβάσματα ὑμῶν εὗρον καὶ βωμὸν ἐν ᾧ ἐπεγέγραπτο ΑΓΝΩΣΤΩ ΘΕΩ. ὃ οὖν ἀγνοοῦντες εὐσεβεῖτε, τοῦτο ἐγὼ καταγγέλλω⁴ ὑμῖν. Ὁ θεὸς ὁ ποιήσας τὸν κόσμον καὶ πάντα τὰ ἐν αὐτῷ, οὗτος οὐρανοῦ καὶ γῆς ὑπάρχων⁵ κύριος οὐκ ἐν χειροποιήτοις ναοῖς κατοικεῖ, οὐδὲ ὑπὸ χειρῶν ἀνθρωπίνων θεραπεύεται προσδεόμενός⁶ τινος, αὐτὸς διδοὺς πᾶσι ζωὴν καὶ πνοὴν καὶ τὰ πάντα· ἐποίησέν⁷ τε ἐξ ἑνὸς πᾶν ἔθνος ἀνθρώπων κατοικεῖν⁷ ἐπὶ παντὸς προσώπου⁸ τῆς γῆς, ὁρίσας προστεταγμένους καιροὺς καὶ τὰς ὁροθεσίας τῆς κατοικίας αὐτῶν, ζητεῖν τὸν θεὸν εἰ ἄρα γε ψηλαφήσειαν αὐτὸν καὶ εὕροιεν, καί γε⁹ οὐ μακρὰν ἀπὸ¹⁰ ἑνὸς ἑκάστου ἡμῶν ὑπάρχοντα.⁵ ἐν αὐτῷ γὰρ ζῶμεν καὶ κινούμεθα καὶ

V.

PAULI EP. AD ROM. I. 18-25.

Ἀποκαλύπτεται γὰρ ὀργὴ Θεοῦ ἀπ᾽ οὐρανοῦ ἐπὶ πᾶσαν ἀσέβειαν καὶ ἀδικίαν ἀνθρώπων τῶν τὴν ἀλήθειαν ἐν ἀδικίᾳ κατεχόντων, διότι τὸ γνωστὸν τοῦ Θεοῦ φανερόν ἐστιν ἐν αὐτοῖς, ὁ Θεὸς γὰρ αὐτοῖς ἐφανέρωσεν. τὰ γὰρ ἀόρατα αὐτοῦ ἀπὸ κτίσεως κόσμου τοῖς ποιήμασιν νοούμενα καθορᾶται, ἥ τε ἀΐδιος αὐτοῦ δύναμις καὶ θειότης, εἰς τὸ³ εἶναι αὐτοὺς ἀναπολογήτους, διότι γνόντες τὸν Θεὸν οὐχ ὡς Θεὸν ἐδόξασαν ἢ ηὐχαρίστησαν,⁴ ἀλλὰ ἐματαιώθησαν⁵ ἐν τοῖς διαλογισμοῖς αὐτῶν, καὶ ἐσκοτίσθη ἡ ἀσύνετος αὐτῶν καρδία·⁶ φάσκοντες εἶναι σοφοὶ ἐμωράνθησαν, καὶ ἤλλαξαν τὴν δόξαν τοῦ ἀφθάρτου Θεοῦ ἐν⁷ ὁμοιώματι εἰκόνος φθαρτοῦ ἀνθρώπου καὶ πετεινῶν καὶ τετραπόδων καὶ ἑρπετῶν. Διὸ παρέδωκεν αὐτοὺς ὁ Θεὸς ἐν ταῖς ἐπιθυμίαις τῶν καρδιῶν αὐτῶν εἰς ἀκαθαρσίαν, τοῦ⁸ ἀτιμάζεσθαι τὰ σώματα αὐτῶν ἐν αὐτοῖς, οἵτινες

VI.

EPICT. DISS. I. XIV. 5-10.

Ἀλλὰ τὰ φυτὰ μέν,¹ καὶ τὰ ἡμέτερα σώματα οὕτως ἐνδέδεται τοῖς ὅλοις καὶ συμπέπονθεν· αἱ ψυχαὶ δὲ αἱ ἡμέτεραι οὐ (v.l. πολλῷ) πολὺ πλέω; ἀλλ᾽ αἱ ψυχαὶ μὲν¹ οὕτως εἰσὶν ἐνδεδεμέναι καὶ συναφεῖς τῷ Θεῷ, ὅ, τε αὐτοῦ μόρια οὖσαι καὶ ἀποσπάσματα· οὐ παντὸς δ᾽ αὐτῶν κινήματος, ἅτε οἰκείου καὶ συμφυοῦς, ὁ Θεὸς αἰσθάνεται; Ἀλλὰ σὺ μὲν¹ περὶ τῆς θείας διοικήσεως καὶ περὶ ἑκάστου τῶν θείων, ὁμοῦ δὲ καὶ περὶ ἀνθρωπίνων πραγμάτων ἐνθυμεῖσθαι δύνασαι, καὶ ἅμα μὲν αἰσθητικῶς² ἀπὸ³ μυρίων πραγμάτων κινεῖσθαι, ἅμα δὲ διανοητικῶς² ἅμα δὲ [τοῖς μὲν] συγκαταθετικῶς, τοῖς δ᾽ ἀνανευστικῶς ἢ ἐφεκτικῶς·² τοσούτους δὲ τοσούτων ἀφ᾽ οὕτω πολλῶν καὶ ποικίλων πραγμάτων ἐν τῇ σαυτοῦ ψυχῇ φυλάττεις, καὶ ἀπ᾽³ αὐτῶν κινούμενος εἰς ἐπινοίας ὁμοειδεῖς ἐμπίπτεις τοῖς πρώτοις⁴ τετυπωκόσι, τέχνας τ᾽ ἄλλας ἐπ᾽ ἄλλας καὶ

ἐσμέν, ὡς καί τινες τῶν καθ' ὑμᾶς ποιητῶν εἰρήκασιν..¹
Τοῦ γὰρ καὶ γένος ἐσμέν.

μετήλλαξαν τὴν ἀλήθειαν τοῦ Θεοῦ ἐν τῷ ψεύδει, καὶ ἐσεβάσθησαν καὶ ἐλάτρευσαν τῇ κτίσει παρὰ⁹ τὸν κτίσαντα, ὅς ἐστιν εὐλογητὸς εἰς τοὺς αἰῶνας.¹⁰ ἀμήν.

μνήμας ἀπὸ μυρίων πραγμάτων διασώζεις· ὁ δὲ Θεὸς οὐχ οἷός τ' ἐστὶ πάντα ἐφορᾶν, καὶ πᾶσι συμπαρεῖναι,⁵ καὶ ἀπὸ πάντων τινὰ ἰσχύειν διάδοσιν ; Ἀλλὰ φωτίζειν μὲν ¹ οἷός τε ἐστὶν ὁ ἥλιος τηλικοῦτον μέρος τοῦ παντός, ὀλίγου δὲ τὸ ἀφώτιστον ἀπολιπεῖν, ὅσον ὥν τ' ἐπέχεσθαι ὑπὸ σκιᾶς ἣν ἡ γῆ ποιεῖ· ὁ δὲ καὶ τὸν ἥλιον αὐτὸν πεποιηκὼς καὶ περάγων, μέρος ὤν αὐτοῦ μικρὸν ὡς πρὸς τὸ ὅλον, οὗτος δ'⁶ οὐ δύναται πάντων αἰσθάνεσθαι.

NOTES ON THE PHILOSOPHICAL EXTRACTS.

I. POLYBIUS (cir. B.C. 140).

[1] Ῥωμαίων]. "Of the Romans" as a community; almost as we might say "of Rome." The omission of the article with a national name in this sense is quite classical.

[2] ἐκτετραγ . . . τραγῳδίᾳ]. The earliest instance extant of the substantive τραγῳδία in this sense of "solemn story." But the verb τραγῳδεῖν is found as early as Plato, and the Attic orators, and the compound ἐκτραγ. in Theophrastus; always however with more irony than there seems to be, at least in the former of these two places.

[3] For perfect symmetry, the εἴς τε τοὺς should have been followed by καὶ εἰς τὰ. . . . It can, however, hardly be said that this slight irregularity is characteristic of late date. In less classical Greek, τε becomes increasingly rare.

[4] For the omission of ἄν, if it be rightly omitted, cf. Eur. Hec. 1113, Plat. Symp. 198 c. The omission becomes more frequent in later Greek (see a rather extreme case in Philo de Joseph, § 5, εἰ ἐπὶ γῆς ἐτάφης, τῆς σῆς, παρηγορούμην· ἐθεράπευσε, κ.τ.λ. an impf. and of aorists standing all without ἄν in apodosis); and is found several times in the N. T. (e.g. Gal. iv. 15, true text). In modern Greek it is the rule with past indic. tenses.

NOTES ON PHILOSOPHICAL EXTRACTS. 183

5 The asyndeton would scarcely have occurred in a non-rhetorical passage in an Attic writer; but by Polybius' time a writer was always self-conscious, and never free from rhetorical influences. We are reminded of the longer asyndeta (mostly, like this, catalogues of vices) in St. Paul, Rom. i. 29, *sqq.*, etc.; but the difference in style is as marked as the likeness; St. Paul has never the balanced epithet with his substantives.

6 εἰκῇ καὶ ὡς ἔτυχεν . . . εἰκῇ καὶ ἀλόγως]. Possibly Polybius was influenced in the use of these double, nearly synonymous terms by the Latin phrases *forte temere, temere ne casu* and the like. But perhaps such phrases are characteristic of late rhetoric generally; it is in Cicero, rather than in any *extant* Greek writer, that analogies to them are commonest.

II. WISDOM OF SOLOMON (first century B.C. ?).

1 Θεοῦ]. Used absolutely by Jewish and Christian writers in a monotheistic sense, the art. being prefixed or omitted under much the same conditions as with a pr. n. In pagan writers, instances occur of the same use; but as a rule "God" as the author or providential ruler of the world is ὁ Θεός, θεός by itself being used of "a god."

2 οὔτε]. Very often, as here, MS. evidence fluctuates between οὔτε and οὐδέ; here the latter has as high authority. But it seems plain that the rule, nearly universal in classical Greek, that οὔτε is now used *singly* is now and then disregarded in the later language—less often, it seems, however, in the true text of the N. T. than at a still later date.

3 πρυτάνεις]. In this sense of "rulers," the word is almost exclusively poetical. In prose it is a technical term

184 *LANGUAGE OF THE NEW TESTAMENT.*

for the "president," whether of an assembly or of a state. [Is the writer quoting something current under the name of Heraclitus?]

⁴ καλλονῇ]. Rare and mostly poetical, and therefore probably preferred by the writer to the common κάλλει.

⁵ γενεσιάρχης]. ἅπαξ λεγόμενον; γενεσιουργός is also late, but not so uncommon.

⁶ συγγνωστοί]. Part-alexandrine in this construction. In classical Greek it is used of the fault to be excused, not of the person needing excuse.

⁷ αἰῶνα]. Perhaps an extreme instance of the approximation of αἰών in sense to κόσμος; in the same book xiv. 6, xviii. 4 are not quite such strong cases, though we should have to translate "world" in both. Cf. Hebr. i. 2; and contrast Philo de Plant. Noe. 12 (p. 336-7), where with βασιλεύων τῶν αἰώνων (from Ex. xv. 17) before him, he refuses himself to use the word except in the sense of duration.

III. PHILO (cir. A.D. 39).

¹ C. II., Note 1.

² Χρεῖος]. Rare and only poetical in older Greek; rather a favourite word with Philo.

³ εὐχαριστιεῶς]. ἅπαξ λεγόμενον. The adj. εὐχάριστος began in rather late Attic to bear the sense "thankful" among others, and the subst. εὐχαριστία and verb εὐχαριστεῖν were afterwards formed from it. But these and kindred forms are much commoner in Jewish and Christian than in secular writings.

⁴ τιμητικῶς ἔχειν]. Here again the adv. seems to be ἅπαξ λεγόμενον, and the adj. τιμητικός, though found in this sense, has more commonly a different one. A really classical writer, even of Philo's age, would hardly have written these four words; the idiom of an adv. with ἔχειν is of course quite classical, but it

NOTES ON PHILOSOPHICAL EXTRACTS. 185

is something of a classicalising affectation to use it here.

[5] εἴδεοι]. Apparently "looks"—we are to avoid seeing, as well as saying or doing anything that may defile. This sense of the word is not classical.

[6] Here it seems as though the later scholar failed to feel the instinct which guided Greek writers of the best age in the use of the art. Plato would probably have written κεκ. καὶ πεφ. τῇ διανοίᾳ "with the understanding stained and polluted." And still more surely, the art. would not have been placed where it is, in ἀψύχου τῆς ὕλης. Probably the sense which Philo wants, "stones and timber, matter that is without life," would have seemed sufficiently expressed to an Athenian by ὕλης ἀψύχου· and probably in the next clause he would have written τὸ ἄψυχον σῶμα, or τὸ σῶμα ἄψυχον ὄν. But he would have understood Philo's desire to accentuate the concurrence ἄψυχον ἀψύχων, and it would be rash to deny that a good Attic writer could, for a special purpose, have arranged words in this order. Cf. Aesch. Ag. 1225-6, Soph. Aj. 573, in the former of which the reason for the order is stronger (ἐμῷ being an afterthought), in the latter perhaps weaker. But it is more certain that the Athenian had a distinctive reason for deviating from the regular order than that the Alexandrian had.

[7] πεποίηνται]. An Attic writer would almost certainly have used the sing.

[8] μὴ . . . χρησάμενον]. Here μή has its proper force, "*unless* he used." Still we see the transition to the habit of later Greek, using μή almost always with participles.

[9] καθαρσίοις ἁγν.]. καθάρσιον is used substantivally in quite classical Greek in the sense of "a purifying offering.' But it may be doubted if it was in the best age ever

felt to be enough of a subst. to carry another adj. as its epithet.

IV. St. Luke (a.d. 63, or later).

[1] δεισιδαιμονεστέρους]. The use of the comp. may be considered classical (so καινότερον in v. 21; but see on p. 94, Part I.) whatsoever we understand to be the precise shade of meaning in the adj. Probably the R. V. "somewhat superstitious" is more in accordance with the usage of contemporary Greek than either the severer "*too* superstitious" of the A. V., or the complimentary "[very] religious" of the R.V. margin; though the last may commend itself on rhetorical grounds.

[2] ὡς δ. ὑμᾶς θεωρῶ]. θεωρεῖν is quite classical, though not very early, in the sense of "observing" critically or philosophically; and like "observe" in English, it passes, from denoting the process, to denote the result arrived at, the fact "observed." In v. 16 just above, there is nothing in the least surprising in the use of the word; and here the mere fact of its use is not very peculiar. But the constr. with ὡς seems to be unique; the nearest approach is Lycurg. c. Leocr. p. 151 § 28, καὶ ταῦτα δέ, ὦ ἄνδρες, ἐμοῦ θεωρήσατε, ὡς δικαίαν τὴν ἐξέτασιν ποιουμένου; and there the particle is not placed with the direct object of the verb. Perhaps as, in v. 16, the writer inserted the partp., as though feeling θεωροῦντος κατείδωλον τὴν πόλιν to be harsh, so here he thought he must introduce the predicate in another way.

[3] ἀναθεωρῶν]. The compound, though late (first in Theophrastus) is hardly post-classical or meaningless; it implies *thorough* contemplation.

[4] καταγγέλλω]. Peculiar, in the N. T., to the Acts and St. Paul; and not apparently used by other writers

NOTES ON PHILOSOPHICAL EXTRACTS. 187

in exactly the same sense. Here the sense is simply "give official notice;" that is part of the meaning, no doubt, in most Greek; but it is generally used *in malam partem*, καταγγέλλειν πόλεμον, ῥύσια, etc., as we say "to *denounce* war, reprisals"—besides the somewhat earlier use, of *denouncing* a person or an offence.

⁵ ὑπάρχων . . . ὑπάρχοντα]. Here has its proper force, "being from the first," *i.e.*, in the former place, "being eternally," in the latter, "being there before we find him." But in the N. T. the word is oftener used than in earlier Greek, and sometimes comes to be little more than a verb subst. more fully declinable than εἰμί; Luke viii. 41, I Cor. vii. 26, are perhaps the places where its proper force is weakest.

⁶ προσδεόμενος] Quite classical; the act., though on the analogy of the simple verb, it should be used in this sense, is in fact hardly found except in the impers. προσδεῖ.

⁷ ἐποίησέν τε . . . κατοικεῖν]. The constr. seems a pregnant one, "He made out of one every race of men," combined with "He made every race of men dwell."

⁸ προσώπου]. A real Hebraism, perhaps the only one in this speech. In Hebrew לִפְנֵי is virtually a prep., and so in Acts xiii. 24, πρὸ προσώπου τῆς εἰσόδου αὐτοῦ; and we get the same use as here from Gen. ii. 6 onward.

⁹ καί γε]. So all critical texts for καίτοιγε. καίτοι would be quite classical, though less usual than καίπερ. No other instance of καί γε with a part. is alleged; Luke xix. 42 (*si vera l.*) is similar in constr., but different in sense.

¹⁰ ἀπό]. Notice the non-elision of the vowel, though it is one of the few liable to elision in N. T. usage. The *sense* of the word, "at a distance from" without notion of motion, is of course quite classical.

188　LANGUAGE OF THE NEW TESTAMENT.

[11] καθ' ὑμᾶς]. "Who belonged to you," "who lived among you." An extension of the use οἱ καθ' ἡμᾶς "the men of our time ; " real parallels to this do not seem to be found before Polybius. Note the v. l. καθ' ἡμᾶς, which however will not affect the force of the constr. ; the question is only whether St. Paul considered Aratus to belong to himself as a Cilician, or to his audience as a Greek man of letters.

V. ST. PAUL (A.D. 58).

[1] Cf. II., Note 1.
[2] καθορῖται]. "Are descried, discerned ; " we have an exactly similar use (apparently ; but otherwise explained by L. and Sc. *s. v.*) in III. Macc. iii. 11, οὐ καθορῶν τὸ τοῦ μεγίστου Θεοῦ κράτος. In classical Greek the word is used first of physical discernment, *e.g.*, Thuc. III. xx. 3, cxii. 4) ; thence it comes to be used of mental perception, but hardly of so purely abstract a discernment as here.
[3] εἰς τὸ εἶναι]. An instance of the Hellenistic tendency to construct final clauses with the inflected inf. ; see p. 119, Part I.).
[4] ηὐχαρίστησαν]. See III., Note 3.
[5] ἐματαιώθησαν]. An exclusively Biblical word ; see LXX. in 2 Chr. xxi. 8 (the parallel 2 Sam. xxiv. 10, has ἐμωράνθην), and 2 Kings xvii. 15, Jer. ii. 5.
[6] καρδία]. The heart is regarded in classical Greek as the seat of the *emotions* (notice Hom. *Od.* xx. 17, 18, as suggesting how easily this arises from the physical sense) ; but not as in Hebrew or Latin as the seat of the intellect, and hardly as in Hebrew or modern languages as the seat of the character.
[7] ἤλλαξαν . . . ἐν]. A phrase consciously reproduced from the LXX. of Ps. cv. (cvi.) 20, being the literal representation of the Hebrew idiom. The use of an

instrumental dative with verbs of exchanging, instead of the usual gen., is found in classical Greek, and is common in the LXX. (Ex. xiii. 13, etc.); and as ἐν is used often in an instrumental sense in Hebraistic Greek, no difficulty is felt in its use here; see p. 144, Part I. But in ver. 24 it seems needless to take ἐν ταῖς ἐπιθ. as having any but the simplest use of the prep.

[8] τοῦ ἀτιμ.]. Most simply taken in a final sense, "that they should . . . ," but can be understood as directly dependent on ἀκαθ., "the uncleanness of dishonouring." This is at any rate near enough to the truth to illustrate how the verbal gen. gets its final force.

[9] παρά]. "More than," rather than simply "besides." This sense of the prep., naturally arising out of the local sense "beyond," is classical, but proportionately commoner in late and especially Hellenistic Greek.

[10] εὐλογητὸς εἰς τοὺς αἰῶνας]. Of course such devotional— we may almost say liturgical—phrases are the most Hebraic of all.

VI. EPICTETUS (cir. A.D. 118).

[1] μέν]. As often in pure Greek, but hardly ever in the N. T., the really emphatic clause is that with δέ, that with μὲν being not so much stated as taken for granted. "*If it be true that* plants and human bodies are organically united to the Universe, are not human souls more? If human souls are conscious, *as they are*, of their union with the Divine Soul, is not that Soul still more surely conscious?"

[2] αἰσθητικῶς . . . διανοητικῶς, κ. τ. λ. κινεῖσθαι]. Rather a piece of Stoical technicality of language than a peculiarity of style, but see III., Note 3. We should say, "To have your senses or your intellect *acting*, and that in assent to some things, denial to others,

suspense of judgment on others:" but the Greek, at least the Stoic, considers these κινήσεις as passive, or perhaps rather middle.

[3] ἀπό]. Approximating in sense to ὑπό, see p. 138, Part I.

[4] πρώτως]. A somewhat late form, first in Aristotle.

[5] συμπαρεῖναι] In classical Greek always means more than the simple παρεῖναι, and here it may be "present *to help*." But in less classical writers than Epictetus such double compounds certainly tended to lose their distinctive force.

[6] ὁ δὲ . . . . πεποιηκὼς . . . . οὗτος δέ]. This double δέ, both in protasis and apodosis, is quite classical, but perhaps commoner in Herodotus than in any Attic writer.

www.ingramcontent.com/pod-product-compliance
Lightning Source LLC
Chambersburg PA
CBHW072129160426
43197CB00012B/2047